THE AMERICAN IDEA OF HOME

ROGER FULLINGTON SERIES IN ARCHITECTURE

The American Idea of Home

Conversations about Architecture and Design

BERNARD FRIEDMAN

FOREWORD BY MEGHAN DAUM

UNIVERSITY OF TEXAS PRESS

AUSTIN

Publication of this book was made possible in part by support from Roger Fullington and a challenge grant from the National Endowment for the Humanities.

Requests for permission to reproduce material from this work should be sent to:
    Permissions
    University of Texas Press
    P.O. Box 7819
    Austin, TX 78713-7819
    http://utpress.utexas.edu/index.php/rp-form

The paper used in this book meets the minimum requirements of ANSI/NISO Z39.48-1992 (R1997) (Permanence of Paper). ∞

Design by Lindsay Starr

Library of Congress Cataloging-in-Publication Data

Names: Friedman, Bernard, author. | Daum, Meghan, 1970– writer of supplementary textual content.
Title: The American idea of home : conversations about architecture and design / Bernard Friedman; foreword by Meghan Daum.
Description: First edition. | Austin : University of Texas Press, 2017. | Includes index.
Identifiers: LCCN 2016037108
    ISBN 978-1-4773-1286-5 (cloth : alk. paper)
    ISBN 978-1-4773-1287-2 (pbk. : alk. paper)
    ISBN 978-1-4773-1288-9 (library e-book)
    ISBN 978-1-4773-1289-6 (non-library e-book)
Subjects: LCSH: Architecture—United States. | Architects—Interviews. | Architectural design.
Classification: LCC NA705 .F75 2017 | DDC 720.973—dc23
LC record available at https://lccn.loc.gov/2016037108

doi:10.7560/312865

To my parents, Judy and Abel Friedman,
who understood so well how a home worked.

CONTENTS

PART 4
Cities, Suburbs, Regions

PART 5
Technology, Innovation, Materials

FOREWORD

No Place Like It

MEGHAN DAUM

In the canon of common dreams, it's a classic among classics: the dream in which we discover an unfamiliar room in a familiar house. The way it usually goes is that we're in some kind of living space, maybe our own, maybe a space that's inexplicably taken some other form ("It was my grandmother's house, but somehow the prime minister of France lived there!"), and suddenly there's more of it. Suddenly the place has grown a new appendage. But it's not exactly new. There's a sense that it's been there all along yet has managed to escape our notice. Sometimes there's just one new room, sometimes there are several. Sometimes there's an entire wing, a greenhouse, a vast expanse of land where we'd once only known a small backyard.

We are amazed, enchanted, even chastened by our failure to have seen this space before now. We are also, according to psychologists and dream experts, working through the prospect of change, the burgeoning of new possibilities. The standard interpretation of the extra-room dream is that it's a portent, or just a friendly reminder, of shifting tides. The room represents parts of ourselves that have lain dormant but will soon emerge, hopefully in a good way, but then again, who knows? *Look harder*, says the extra-room dream, *the geometry of your life is not what it seems. There are more sides than you thought. The angles are wider, the dimensions far greater than you'd given them credit for.*

Not that we can hear much on that frequency. The human mind can be tragically literal. Chances are we exit the dream thinking only that our property value

has increased. But upon fully waking up, the extra room is gone. There's a brief moment of disappointment, then we enter our day and return to our life. We organize our movements in relation to the architecture that is physically before us. That is to say, we live our lives in the spaces we've chosen to call home.

Let's get one thing straight. A house is not the same as a home. Home is an idea, a social construct, a story we tell ourselves about who we are and who and what we want closest in our midst. There is no place like home because home is not actually a place. A house on the other hand (or an apartment, a trailer, a cabin, a castle, a loft, a yurt) is a physical entity. It may be the flesh and bones of a home, but it can't capture the soul of that home. The soul is made of cooking smells and scuffmarks on the stairs and pencil lines on a wall recording the heights of growing children. The soul evolves over time. The old saying might go, "You buy a house but you make a home," but, really, you grow a home. You let it unfold on its own terms. You wait for it. Home is rarely in the mix the day we move into a new house. Sometimes it's not even there the day we move out. It's possible we should consider ourselves lucky if we get one real home in a lifetime, the same way we're supposedly lucky if we get one great love.

"All architecture is shelter," said the postmodernist Philip Johnson. "All great architecture is the design of space that contains, cuddles, exalts, or stimulates the persons in that space."

If all architecture, no matter its purpose, is shelter, then architecture *intended* as shelter must be the ultimate haven. If an airport or a library can cuddle, exalt, and stimulate, a house's embrace must be at once profoundly intimate and ecstatically transportive, erotic even.

I guess this is where I come clean. I write this as a person for whom houses can have an almost aphrodisiacal quality. I say "almost" because the other charge I get from a beautiful house feels like something close to the divine. A perfect house—and by that I mean a respected house, one that was honorably designed and solidly built and allowed to keep its integrity henceforth—is a tiny cathedral. But a perfect house is also lust made manifest. It can make its visitors delirious with longing. It can send butterflies into their bellies in ways a living, breathing human being rarely can. A house that's an object of lust says, *You want me, but you'll never have me.* It says, *You couldn't have me even if you could afford me. You couldn't have me even if I didn't already belong to someone else.* And that is because houses, like most objects of lust, lose their perfection the moment we're granted access. To take possession of a house is to skim the top off of its magic the minute you sign the deed. It is to concede that the house you live in will never be the house you desired so ravenously. It is to accept that the American dream of homeownership is contingent upon letting go of other dreams—for instance, the kind where the rooms appear where there were none before.

Maybe that's why architects are such sources of fascination, even aspiration. If they want an extra room, they just draw it. If they want a bigger window, a wider archway, a whole new everything, the pencil will make it so. At least that's the layperson's fantasy. It's not surprising that so many fictional heroes in literature and film are architects. The profession, especially when practiced by men, seems to lend itself to a particularly satisfying montage of dreamboat moments. Here he is, artistic and sensitive at his drafting table. Here he is, perched on the steel framework of a construction site high above the earth, hard hat on his head, building plans tucked under his arm in a scroll. Here he is, gazing skyward at his final creation, his face lit by the sun's refraction off his glass and steel, awestruck by the majesty of it all and awesome in his own right.

Nearly always, these are men on a mission. Theirs is not a vocation but a passion that both guides them and threatens to ruin them. In Ayn Rand's novel *The Fountainhead* (perhaps the ne plus ultra of architect fetishization), the grindingly uncompromising Howard Roark winds up laboring at a quarry because he won't betray his aesthetic principles. In Graham Greene's *A Burnt-Out Case*, the internationally renowned but existentially bereft architect hero flees to a leper colony for solace. Hollywood, too, seems to prefer its architects miserable and brooding, not just in the form of adorably widowed dads like Tom Hanks's character in *Sleepless in Seattle* and Liam Neeson's in *Love Actually* (and wasn't the distinctly nonbrooding architect patriarch of *The Brady Bunch* technically a widowed dad?) but also adorably commitment-phobic boyfriends and jealous, cuckolded husbands. More often than not, the intensity of their vision has contributed mightily to their demise. Why did Woody Harrelson's character, a struggling architect, let Robert Redford's character sleep with his wife for a million dollars in *Indecent Proposal*? Because he was deeply in debt from trying to build his dream house.

Well, what better way to go down?

The interviews in these pages range far but also plunge deep. They venture into the realms not just of the technical and the aesthetic but also of the political, the historic, the anthropological, the economic, the environmental, and the climatologic. The list goes on, of course. The list is infinite because home, as a concept, as a *feeling*, has infinite permutations. The question "Where is home for you?" is considered a form of small talk, a conversational nicety. But I've always found it not only unanswerable but strangely threatening. To my ear, it's tantamount to "Who do you think you are?," which are often fighting words for which there is absolutely no good response. Who we think we are changes on a moment-to-moment basis. It pushes constantly against the colliding forces of who we used to be, who we wish we were, and who we fear we've become.

I think part of my problem with "Where is home?" (and the arguably worse "Where are you from?") is that it denies people their complications. We all have one definitive birthplace (unless we were born at sea or in flight, I suppose), but after that it's a matter of interpretation. The dwellings in which we are raised do not necessarily constitute "home." The towns where we grow up do not always feel like hometowns, nor do the places we wind up settling down in as adults. Census data tell us that the average American moves eleven times over a lifetime. For my part, I'm sorry to say I have lived in at least thirty different houses or apartments over the course of my years. Actually, I'm not sorry; each one thrilled me in its own way. But despite those thrills, only a handful felt anything like "home," and even then, the feeling was the kind that visits you for a moment and then flutters away. As with "happiness," another abstraction Americans are forever trying to isolate and define, "home" has always felt to me so ephemeral as to almost not be worth talking about. As with happiness, it's great when you happen upon it, but it can't be chased.

A house, on the other hand, is eminently chaseable. There's a reason shopping for a house or an apartment is called hunting. Real estate turns us into predators. We can stalk a house online or from the street. We can obsess over it, fight over it, mentally move into it and start knocking down walls before we've even been inside. We can spend Sundays going to open houses as though going to church. We can watch home design programs on television twenty-four hours a day. We can become addicted to Internet real estate listing sites as though the photos and descriptions were a form of pornography—which of course they totally are.

"I wish I had never seen your building," says Patricia Neal as Dominique Francon, the austere and tortured lover-then-wife of Howard Roark in the film version of *The Fountainhead*. "It's the things we admire or want that enslave us."

It's pretty clear that houses, despite being among our greatest sources of protection, are also among our greatest enslavers. You might say that's because we go into too much debt for them and make them too large and fill them with too much junk. You might say it's because they're forever demanding our attention, always threatening to leak or crack and be in the way of a tornado. They are sanctuaries, but they are also impending disasters. And most tyrannically of all, they are mirrors. They are tireless, merciless reflections of our best and worst impulses. Unlike the chaos and unsightliness of the outside world, which can easily be construed as hardly our responsibility, the scene under our roofs is of our own making. The careless sides of ourselves—the clutter, the dust, that kitchen drawer jammed with uncategorizable detritus that plagues every household—are as much a part of us as the curated side. Our houses are not just showplaces but hiding places.

Our homes, on the other hand, are glorious, maddening no-places. They are what we spend our lives searching for or running away from or both. They are the stuff of dreams, the extra rooms that vanish upon waking, the invisible possibilities we tamp down without even knowing it. They are the architecture of the unconscious mind—which is a physically uninhabitable space. Thank goodness there are people out there building houses.

INTRODUCTION

BERNARD FRIEDMAN

Creating a home is one of the most meaningful things people do. Before we walk into that home, a designer has set the stage to enable us to make a house a home. The stage-setting craft implicit in that design takes us halfway to homemaking. That craft enables us to live our lives in that building freely and joyfully, and most of us haven't a clue that the stage-setting has preceded our own steps toward making a house just as we'd like it.

Everyone needs a place to live in. To many, the ideal is to have their own house. But what we all want is a home: a space that warms and comforts us, that harbors our loved ones, protects us from the storms of life, and expresses our true selves—an intangible set of desires that can only be met with a concrete structure. What does it take to make a house a home? That depends on whom you ask, of course. But one thing everyone agrees on is that it takes passion and vision.

When we employ an architect in the process, it can become a work of art—and a home that we truly love. But only a fraction of the homes built every year in America are designed by architects, and very few of us are privy to the intense thought process and myriad decisions that go into their sketches, plans, and elevations. I thought that I'd talk to a few architects about their craft, their stage-setting, to raise an awareness of just how much thought precedes our own homemaking.

My own passion for homemaking began a dozen years ago, when my wife and I bought a midcentury house in the Hollywood Hills. It was an elegant post-and-beam structure—a simple, open plan with generous outdoor views in every direction.

It took time for the "home" to emerge, however; we couldn't recognize it at first.

Our realtor's first words were: "You can't see it, but there's a great house here." We knew he was right, took the leap of faith, and made our offer. The structure had had a number of different owners since its initial construction in 1955. Each occupant had left a mark, every family had added an overlay—a partition, a bit of siding, new built-in shelves, and countless coats of paint—their attempts to turn the house into a home, I surmised. But all the additions had compounded into a ramshackle mishmash of forms that largely obfuscated the architect's original intention.

Then began the odyssey of finding that original, architect-inspired house. The more we stripped away, the more we wanted to uncover. There was a different hue of paint for every decade since 1955—layer upon layer on the walls, siding, even the brickwork; paint was everywhere. The sandblasting alone took days. The original cork flooring—meant to be warm and pliable underfoot—had been supplanted by a layer of cold, hard marble. You could almost feel the structure breathe a sigh of relief when we stripped it back.

As the house began to reveal itself, I gained new appreciation for the architect's vision and original design. To supervise the remodel, I had brought in the Los Angeles architects Peter and Hadley Arnold, a forward-thinking couple that *Dwell* magazine called "environmentally attuned," and who had recently redesigned my workplace. I was inspired by their contribution of maintaining and enhancing the integrity of the original home design while modernizing materials in order to reduce the home's environmental impact.

Later, for a small addition to the home, we engaged another visionary team from Los Angeles: Frank Escher and Ravi GuneWardena. They helped integrate a brand-new concept into the Mid-Century Modern design: a "home office" was not exactly a mainstream idea in 1959. Now, it's my favorite room.

Perhaps the biggest reward of this whole process was my deepening appreciation of residential architects. Good design can create a home that is cherished for generations. It's a complex art that combines myriad sensory experiences: texture; luminosity; feelings of expansion, contraction, coziness, and grandeur. A beautiful home produces feelings of pleasure, peace, and serenity, and this emotional need for a true home appears to be hardwired into our DNA.

Our primal response to the place we live predates civilization, according to the archaeologist Margaret Conkey, whose trailblazing work in the 1990s proved that cave dwellers did not actually live in caves—at least not exclusively. And why would they? Caves are dark, uninviting, cramped, damp, and not terribly comfortable.

According to Conkey, a professor emerita at Berkeley, "Home is a place where you reconnect with people or memories." It must be a place of beauty, not a dark cave.

Our ancestors certainly spent times in caves—they provide safety and reliable shelter, after all. But cave dwellers' idea of "home" was far more expansive, suggests

Conkey. Their home may have contained a cave for the brutal winter months; but it also had a stream, a wooded area, a meadow—places of beauty and pleasure. They staked out a certain area of the landscape and called that "home." The meadow was their front porch or an outdoor eating area; the woods, their backyard; the stream, their bathroom, and so on. In other words, they had "rooms" just as we did. They took pleasure in their home. They were, according to Margaret Conkey, "spatially ambitious"—just like us.

The Great Recession of 2008 has been laid at the feet of the "housing bubble," meaning we'd been building big homes we couldn't afford by the millions. Owning a home isn't just a part of the American dream—it's been the heart of the American dream. And Americans will go to any length to keep this dream alive, including making catastrophic economic decisions.

Many architects in this book believe that a financial and moral sensitivity to scale in our homes must become a new norm. A hundred years ago, residential architecture was used to convey financial success—a grand façade with Corinthian columns indicated the wealth and power of a home's inhabitants, an overt expression of materialism. But that cycle of accumulation is waning, even becoming archaic. Given the finite space on this increasingly populated planet, we could all afford to live with a more modest footprint.

There are growing environmental pressures on our homes as well, like earthquakes and extreme weather—hurricanes, coastal flooding, drought. Good design of our homes is more important than ever. A thoughtful architect must consider an array of forces—site and zoning restrictions, local vernacular, history, tradition, technology, innovation, as well as her or his own particular aesthetic. It is an admirable balancing act that produces an outcome that affects our everyday lives.

After finishing our remodel, I went on a quest to meet more architects and find out how they think. It began as a short documentary (*American Homes*, 2012) that I started working on in 2006. Fascinated and obsessed with what architects do, I intended to interview several dozen notable designers to give the audience a glimpse into the many decisions that go into designing a home—a peek under the hood, if you will, into the design process.

For the visuals, I had turned to a book: *American Homes: The Illustrated Encyclopedia of Domestic Architecture* (Black Dog & Leventhal, 1981), by the architect Lester Walker, an encyclopedic volume of hundreds of line drawings of different home styles, arranged by decade from the Pueblo period to the present day.

"If you look back to when architects first got involved, say, in the early eighteenth century, they were doing buildings that were designed to impress people," said Lester Walker when I interviewed him. "They weren't doing buildings to be beautiful and part of nature."

Then, Frank Lloyd Wright comes along and gives us the Prairie Style—with fewer, more open-planned rooms and a harmonious relationship to its site. The architects in this collection are deep admirers of Wright's work and legacy.

I was fortunate to have talked with quite a few notable designers, thirty in all, including three Pritzker Prize winners (Thom Mayne, Richard Meier, and Robert Venturi); the Pulitzer Prize–winning critic Paul Goldberger; the director of the American Institute of Architects (AIA), Robert Ivy; the legendary Denise Scott Brown, Kenneth Frampton, and Robert A. M. Stern, to name a few. I even had the pleasure of conversing with the Chicago maverick Douglas Garofalo before his untimely death.

Architects universally love to talk about architecture. My discourse with these designers was lively, opinionated, full of passion, inspiring to me, and also energizing. But I was only able to use fragments of the interviews in my short film, which is the reason I decided to create this book: to share longer conversations with these esteemed designers.

This is an important time for us to be thinking about our homes, which seem to be under increasing pressure from forces beyond our control—from extreme weather to real estate bubbles. The architects in this book have thought deeply about these issues and readily share their insights. While the interviews range widely, certain themes clearly emerge, which is why I chose to break the book into five parts. There are overlaps, of course, and readers should freely jump around and make their own way through the book.

The thirty architects, educators, and cultural visionaries in this collection all aspire to improve the quality of our lives through thoughtful design. Their varied ideas and eclectic opinions weave a tapestry of thought around the American idea of home. Many factors that go unnoticed or we take for granted go into the dwellings we inhabit, and yet they have daily impact on our lives.

In the interviews that follow, I've attempted to draw out that thought process so all of us can partake in a discussion of what goes into the design of the American home.

The Functions and Meanings of Home

If a single theme runs through the thirty interviews in this collection, it is diversity—these architects, educators, and writers present a rich and eclectic range of opinions and approaches to the "American idea of home," particularly and deliberately so in Part 1, which tackles what our homes mean to us and how we inhabit them. From the majestic work of Richard Meier to the small-is-better philosophy of Sarah Susanka, this section illustrates the many ways we can think about the subject.

Library in the William Watts Sherman House. The interior of the nineteenth-century home was designed by Stanford White. It is at 2 Shepard Avenue, Newport, Rhode Island.

RICHARD MEIER

"Stanford White's houses are
famous and influenced a whole
style of building in this country,
especially in the East in the early
part of the twentieth century."

Long before Richard Meier (b. 1934) became an architect with the star power to
command the largest institutional commissions, he had spent the better part of a
decade pondering architecture on a residential scale. Meier established his private
practice with a home designed for his parents in Essex Fells, New Jersey, in 1963.
Several years later, his white-and-glass Smith House in Darien, Connecticut, pro-
pelled him onto the national stage. And by 1969, Meier—born in Newark, New
Jersey, with a BA in architecture from Cornell in 1957—was named one of the "New
York Five," in a landmark meeting at the Museum of Modern Art.

Meier has received the Pritzker Architecture Prize and also a gold medal from
the American Institute of Architects (AIA). While an ardent admirer of Le Corbusier and Ludwig Mies van der Rohe, he feels equally indebted to Italian Renaissance
architects Donato Bramante and Francesco Borromini.

"Architecture is a tradition, a long continuum," says Meier. "Whether we break
with tradition or enhance it, we are still connected to that past."

Meier's largest and most visible commission is the $1 billion Getty Center in
Los Angeles, California. There is also the Barcelona Museum of Contemporary Art,
High Museum in Atlanta, Frankfurt Museum for Decorative Arts, and more. But
throughout, Richard Meier never stopped designing homes. His many residential
commissions, like the elegant 2013 Fire Island House, have given him the liberty
to create innovative structures using, as he puts it, "human dimensions as a unit of
measure."

Richard Meier begins our collection of conversations by addressing, among other things, the one variable that remains constant in residential architecture: "accommodating to and understanding of human scale." It is a quality he admires in the architecture of Frank Lloyd Wright, an architect who has influenced most, if not all, the designers interviewed. Wright, according to Meier, had a profound understanding of "the way in which you move through and experience space."

Which architects have influenced you the most?

Richard Meier: Probably the most influential residential architect, in terms of ideas, is Frank Lloyd Wright. Wright did more houses than any other architect I know of. And he had an enormous influence on people's understanding of what residential architecture could be. Not that they followed Wright or designed like him, but the quality of Wright's architecture is amazing, and that has to do with the quality of human scale and the way in which you move through and experience space. The spaces in Wright's architecture were very small and confined, not like the huge mansions you see being built around the country today. They were refined and well-defined spaces, and they had a wonderful quality about them. When I think of Frank Lloyd Wright and all that he contributed to American architecture, it's surprising that what we see today takes so little of his influence and uses it in a good way.

H. H. Richardson did some extraordinary residential work. Stanford White's houses are famous and influenced a whole style of building in this country, especially in the East in the early part of the twentieth century.

Each era is different, and I think today people are interested in more openness, transparency, and freedom of movement than existed fifty or a hundred years ago in residential design. So today's houses indicate a different way of living, with less maintenance. They set up a relationship between interior and exterior spaces that allows for ease of movement from inside to outside. And they are more responsive to the nature all around. Nature is ever changing—the color of the light changes throughout the day, the color of the season changes. But architecture is static, inert, and that creates a dialogue between the human made—architecture—and the organic and dynamic—the natural world.

What are your favorite styles of architecture?

Meier: My favorite style of American architecture is the style of the moment, which is contemporary architecture, modern architecture. It suits our way of living today in terms of our transparency and openness and in terms of its relationship to nature, the way in which the scale and the light are composed, experienced, and inhabited.

And pre-1900?

Meier: Pre-1900 there wasn't much architecture in America. There was architecture in Europe; architects made palaces and large-scale residential works. But architecture is really a late-nineteenth- or twentieth-century phenomenon in this country. Up until the twentieth century, American architecture borrowed heavily from European styles, but it also had its own indigenous quality in terms of the work of architects such as Stanford White.

Do you think there is an American architecture today?

Meier: I don't think there's an American architecture, no. I think that the work you see in the United States is like the work you see in Tokyo or Shanghai or any other major city in which big architecture firms are practicing. In Berlin and Frankfurt, there are as many buildings by US firms as there are in major cities in America, and maybe even more so in places like Beijing. I don't think there is an American architecture. American architecture has been exported to influence the rest of the world.

How has globalization changed architecture?

Meier: The speed of communication is such today that when a young architect in Argentina completes a work, it's not only seen reproduced in publications in Argentina, but also in publications in America, Europe, and elsewhere. What's interesting is that the quality of the workmanship and the materials used might be indigenous to Argentina, but they're not foreign. The stonework looks like one would use stone in France or Minnesota. What may be lost is a recognition of place through the architecture.

Nevertheless, I think that certain parts of the world still maintain a regional architecture. If one thinks of residential work in Switzerland, for example, especially in the mountains, all the houses have pitched roofs, because the snow load would be too heavy for a flat roof. However, in other parts of Switzerland, you will see flat-roofed houses. So I think the international influences on the architecture depend a great deal on the particularities of a place.

Do you think regional architecture will die out completely at some point in the future?

Meier: I think that it depends on what region you're talking about. Some regions of the world are very dependent on local customs, materials, and ways of building. Much of the residential architecture in the Middle East and Africa, for example, is made out of adobe—mud huts, as it were—because that's what people can afford. In poor countries, the housing is often makeshift. It's not really architecture; it's what's affordable.

Do you think the globalization of architecture is a good thing?

Meier: We live in a world culture. It's the same with everything, not just architecture. The television programs that you watch at night are the same television programs that people in Abu Dhabi and Moscow watch, so it's not as though our lives are so different. The physical and political climate we live in is different. But information travels at such a speed that regionalism and nationalism no longer exist as they once did.

In America, the kind of regionalism we saw earlier in the century is less prevalent today. A building in Michigan is not any different from a building in Louisiana or Texas. The styles of architecture have less to do with regional characteristics than they do with individual tastes and desires.

How has the relevance of the architect changed in recent years?

Meier: Culturally, there is a greater awareness of and interest in architecture and what good architecture is than there's ever been before. I think this will continue, and as a result, the quality of our built environment will improve. People appreciate quality and are willing to go out of their way to experience it. For example, when we travel, what do we do? We go and look at architecture.

But when we think of the private residences that are built across our nation, a very small percentage is actually designed by an architect. I don't know the exact figure, but the majority of homes are put up by developers as part of suburban subdivisions. One would like to think that architecture, when it's good, influences even the work that is not done by architects. But I'm not sure that's the case.

A lot of the houses designed by developers and contractors are based on older styles of American architecture.

Meier: In order to give people a choice, they'll do a pseudo-Tudor house, pseudo-colonial house, pseudo-contemporary house, and God knows what else. But it's just changing the front door appearance while keeping the same basic organization of the building.

How has technology affected residential architecture?

Meier: Architecture and technology probably have a greater relationship in larger-scale buildings—office, industrial, and commercial buildings—than they do in residential buildings. Residences are still, for the most part, built one at a time on a fairly small scale. Also, the building codes are such that houses can be built rather inexpensively when they're made out of wood, whereas an industrial method of building is by and large more expensive. So I don't think technology has been as important in residential architecture as it might have been. But it certainly has affected what goes into the house, in the mechanical systems, kitchen appliances, and sound and video systems. Technology has manifested itself in the things we use more than in the spaces we inhabit.

What things would you like to see change in architecture?

Meier: I would like to see more good architecture. There's a lot of bad architecture, but it's not something that one can change. It happens through education, appreciation, and awareness. I think New York is changing, for instance. The residential buildings are getting better because people realize they can make more money if they do a good building than if they do a mediocre building. Sometimes things change because of necessity, and sometimes things change because of economics or political interest. Cities like Shanghai change because the economy of the country has changed, creating a need for more and more work and residential space. Most cities that are viable and active undergo constant change. That's one of the things that makes New York so fascinating.

What makes a successful house, and has that changed over time?

Meier: Architecture is a captivating subject, and people have been and will continue to be fascinated by other people's homes. What happens in architecture today influences tomorrow, and people are constantly looking and thinking about how to change the way they live. But most importantly, the best residential work is that which is accommodating to and understanding of human scale. And that doesn't change.

From the north porch of the Hill-Stead House, 35 Mountain Road, Farmington, Connecticut.
The view takes in the Farmington Valley and Talcott Mountain range.

GRANT HILDEBRAND

"Well, refuge and prospect on the interior of the building is essentially a small space connected to a larger and brighter one. It gives an option between a cozy, reclusive space and a bright and expansive experience."

Grant Hildebrand (b. 1934) is an architectural theorist. His writing explores how we derive pleasure from our homes by moving, for example, from a large space to a small space or vice versa. These transitions through diverse volumes create a sense of possibility—which is a key component of feeling innate pleasure. Hildebrand posits that our instinctual need for refuge feeds our pleasure response within a home. Why does a hillside home with a bucolic view give us deep comfort and satisfaction? It's from the ancestral memory of having an entire range before us and the security of a cave behind, says Hildebrand.

Hildebrand is a professor emeritus of the Departments of Architecture and Art History at the University of Washington, where he received the university's Distinguished Teaching Award in 1975. He holds a BA and MArch from the University of Michigan. His productive scholarly career includes numerous books, such as *Origins of Architectural Pleasure* (University of California Press, 1999) and *The Wright Space: Pattern and Meaning in Frank Lloyd Wright's Houses* (University of Washington Press, 1991).

Grant Hildebrand, who likes to look at architecture through the lens of anthropology, builds on the foundation laid by Richard Meier by discussing the need for variations of scale and illumination within a home—the need for both "refuge and prospect," which triggers an emotional response in a home's inhabitants. "We build a lot of houses now that are composed of a whole bunch of big rooms with fourteen-foot ceilings and vast amounts of space . . . but the cozy nook is of value as well as the drop-dead, two-story entry."

An avid proponent of the need for us to downsize our living spaces, Hildebrand says with pride: "My wife and I live in 950 square feet . . . and we're fine."

In your book *Origins*, which proposes a theory about how human beings psychologically and physiologically relate to architecture, you use the words "prospect," "refuge," "enticement," "peril," and "complex order." Please explain these terms.

Grant Hildebrand: Well, refuge and prospect on the interior of the building essentially mean a small space connected to a larger and brighter one. They give an option between a cozy, reclusive space and a bright, expansive experience. I could describe those things more deeply as part of our genetics or our human psyche, but just on the face of it, people like alternatives in the spaces they experience. The notion of enticement is the trail that disappears around the bend or the object we don't quite see or that we want to discover. It's a very powerful thing; I think we have an insatiable lust for knowledge and we seek it out. If that is presented in architecture—for example, the corridor that instead of proceeding straight bends a bit to some lit and interesting further experience—it interests us; it makes the building much more lively and intriguing, and this seems to persist over great lengths of time. People who have houses that have this quality sometimes will say they've lived there for years and continue to discover new things.

The idea of peril is trickier. I think we build Space Needles and Eiffel Towers to get that thrill and elation of being on the edge of danger. It's a more rare thing. You don't often find that in buildings, although people who live in high-rise buildings and enjoy decks and terraces get some thrill of peril, hovering at the edge of what could be a very dangerous void.

Complex order is in a way the easiest and in a way the most difficult to define. I think it pervades all of our art forms. Music is complexly ordered sound, and dance is complexly ordered human movement. Every culture we know of that's ever walked the face of the earth has engaged in dance and music. I think it's what makes architecture, too. You think of buildings that you like—a great cathedral, the Parthenon, Frank Lloyd Wright's Fallingwater—they're complicated things. At the same time, they have an order that pervades them, and that's something we like. We had to order our surroundings to survive, and we had to have a keen eye for little differences. Is that my child? Is my child well or in danger? Is that a food source or a poison? And in this vast amount of information we take in, we have to make those judgments, and we translate them into art forms and make dance and music and architecture.

If these yearnings that draw us to certain constructs are hardwired into our psyche, what is your hope for our design future?

Hildebrand: I think these characteristics have shown themselves in vernacular buildings that have been intuitively done in the past. Eiffel doesn't talk about peril and the teasing of danger, but we all know it's there if we follow our intuitions, and we know we like that. But I think architects can benefit a lot from bringing this to a more conscious level. We build a lot of houses now that are composed of a whole bunch of big rooms with 14-foot ceilings and vast amounts of space. We don't give thought to the notion that contrast would be dramatic, and the cozy nook is of value as well as the drop-dead, two-story entry. I think the more we are conscious of these intuitions, the more we can develop them architecturally.

When you think of the next step in researching how human beings respond to architecture, do you have any inkling of what that would be?

Hildebrand: Oh, someone who is really experienced in sampling human reactions could test these ideas and discover others. It could be shown that peril is a rare and exotic desire. We already know that refuge is stronger in women and prospect in men; that's been shown by my colleague Judith Heerwagen. Someone else may come up with another half-dozen terms that are better than mine, or different. But the idea that certain reactions to certain kinds of spaces are built into us is really worth pursuing.

Your work takes in the sweep of millennia across the entire world. Is there anything specific about the American experience that you notice is different?

Hildebrand: Well, we're a young country, and a lot of these characteristics show up in other countries, sometimes in indigenous work or work that lies in the deep past. We don't do many buildings with the wonderfully complex order of Exeter, Canterbury Cathedral, or Notre Dame, Paris. And it's not a country of the Cotswold Cottages that just tell us they're a haven—the refuge and a warm spot. We've had a more brief, rough-and-tumble history, and I think that maybe we have a little growing up to do in that sense. We seem to be focused more on pretension, status, and enormous houses than the qualities that might really make people happy. A bunch of huge rooms may impress people that you're wealthy, but after that, what's the point? I hope you don't live in a large house.

No, I live in a little farmhouse.

Hildebrand: Well, there you are. I imagine that it has some of these qualities.

It does, and that's what attracted me to it.

Hildebrand: You have a little stove in the kitchen, a little place to read and snuggle, and you like it, don't you?

I do.

Hildebrand: And then you walk out onto a porch in the sun and that's part of it, too. See, way back when, we had to get away from predators, protect the little kids, and sleep in safety. We're terribly vulnerable creatures; we don't have fur or natural weapons, like sharp teeth. That was our hiding place and we had to have it. If you didn't have an intuition for it, you were a goner. But you also had to have that foraging ground where you could see. I think our liking for sunlight is because it gives us more information about sources of food and danger, and we had to like that, too, or we would have starved and our kids wouldn't have made it. So, we're heirs to that paired set of conditions.

Do you think that is the relationship between the house and the yard— the shelter and the foraging space?

Hildebrand: It's also the relationship between that corridor and the larger room where we are now. This room is a prospect space. But we're back here in a dark corner by ourselves, and there's the fire in the fireplace, creating a refuge within it.

What qualities must a home have in order to connect to our essential nature?

Hildebrand: I think that the opportunity within a home for different kinds of spaces—reclusive and expansive—is key. I think very few people would find that the presence of spaces that offer a real variety of experiences is not an amenity. I have a friend who says he wants an entirely prospect house. He built one in Bellevue; it is very open, it looks out everywhere, except to either side, where the neighbors are. But he has surrounded half of it with a dense forest, and there's the refuge. And then the rest of it looks out at the water. So he's kidding himself. He really likes the haven, too. If the front were just open to the highway, that wouldn't do it. So, I think we all like that combination of a haven and a broad meadow in which to stand upright and stride out.

I think the enormous houses that are being built now for pretension are not a happy way to achieve a good architecture. And they use up a lot of resources, including water and land. I have a friend in Scottsdale in a community of thirty miles of mega houses on 1- and 2-acre lots, 7,000 square feet each, and almost all for retired couples. That is not a good way for civilization to build. And we can't. The desert is gone. They moved there for the desert, but they've taken the desert; the whole desert floor is covered. They're borrowing water from everywhere. And every house has a huge swimming pool. No, I think that's got to change. My wife and I life in 950 square feet here and we're fine. I'm not trying to impress anybody, but I'm happy, and people who come here seem to think it's okay.

Do you think that eventually some of those mega houses will be remodeled into multiple-family dwellings?

Hildebrand: I have no idea. But it seems to me that if people in Scottsdale had been amenable to the idea—and obviously they weren't—they could have built a series of condominium towers with many wonderful high-quality spaces that were not very large. House people in a small footprint, and the desert is still theirs. But now you look out and you don't see the desert anymore, you see huge houses and people trying to impress you with false arches and stonework and drop-dead entryways. I don't know how we get it back. And there aren't an awful lot more opportunities out there. People say, well, there's a lot of land in this country. Yeah, but you can't build in the Rocky Mountains, you can't build in Death Valley. And if we build on all of the available land, then where does our food come from?

I really regret the loss of the Scottsdale desert. Frank Lloyd Wright moved there in 1937 when Scottsdale was a crossroads; there were five buildings. He built Taliesin West and that was really something exciting. But now it's like Houston or the distant reaches of Bellevue, except the plants are different, there are mountains on the horizon, and the climate is a little different. But the desert is gone. It's a shame.

Is there one thing in your work you've discovered that has surprised you?

Hildebrand: No, not really. I started out as an architect. It's not one of the proudest things, none of us were all that pleased with it when it was done, but I was on the design team of the World Trade Center back in a wasted youth. I went into teaching after, partly to think things over, and found I loved it. I seem now to be a writer. I didn't start out having anything to do with writing, and I suppose it's a surprise that I like it. I try to do a little poetry, not with a lot of success, but I enjoy working with words.

The groundwork for *Origins* was laid by others, colleagues and my hero, Jay Appleton, who really started this whole idea in terms of landscape. I took the argument into architecture, but it was started elsewhere.

Have you enjoyed the "intelligent design" debates, given your interest in evolution?

Hildebrand: No, I don't much. Talking about the totally indemonstrable does not interest me. One advocate of intelligent design told me that he thought evolution was quite a convoluted argument. It's simplicity itself compared to the convolutions of the other camp. One of the really fine people in the field is Richard Dawkins. Dawkins talks about the blind watchmaker as a sophisticated approach to an intelligent design, but the argument that it took too long has been shown to be utterly wrong. Daniel Dennett at Tufts has done computer simulations of evolutionary processes, and once the first success is made, it goes just like that. And nature does so much with interchangeable parts. Slugs have a gut and a mouth; lions and eagles have eyes; fish have two eyes; and we have spines, intestines, hearts, and lungs. Once it gets a good set of parts, nature plays games like an auto dealer making cars. The argument that it took too long is nonsense.

Is that what the argument is? That evolution took too long?

Hildebrand: One of the arguments is that the evolutionary process would have taken too long, so there must have been someone pulling the strings.

I thought it was the pure and amazing complexity of it.

Hildebrand: Well, that one has a built-in problem, too, because if you say that Chopin's music is too complicated to have just happened, so some supreme being made it happen, then presumably this supreme being is more complicated than Chopin. So you've got to have another supreme being to create that supreme being, and this goes on long into the evening hours, unless you change horses in midstream and you get to invent a complicated thing where I don't, changing the rules of the game. People try that, they argue that this couldn't have just happened, it's too complicated, but then something else complicated—God—could just happen. Well, stick to the rules or don't make any, but don't argue that with me. I hope I'm not offending you.

Oh, no, I was just being playful about that because of your interest in evolution.

Hildebrand: It bugs me because I think that evolution is in danger in our school systems, which is really worrisome. It's going to deny our children a process of thinking that they're going to need. The opponents of evolution are glad to sign on for science when it works in their favor. They get on a 747, and it flies because of Bernoulli's principle about differential air pressures. That's okay, but....

I think the world has gotten so complex that a lot of people are desperate for simple answers. A lot of my work, and the whole of evolution studies, is based on survival intuitions. For a creature who wants to survive, inventing a system that lets you live forever is great stuff. But I thought we were beyond that.

I think as long as human beings exist, we will always long for a sense of transcendence.

Hildebrand: I lost a son eleven, twelve years ago, and I would love to see him again. But that is a longing, and to transfer that to an ocean of reason is to mistake emotion for the mind. That just doesn't work.

Have you ever read Mark Twain on the subject? He has an acidic passage where he's talking about the sleeping sickness in Africa. He says this person we called "Father" subjected these thousands of people to horrible death for hundreds of years. And Twain says, now that we have discovered a cure after all these centuries, we thank this same Father. Of all the people on earth that we call "Father," there's only one for whom we use the term who would treat his children that way.

WITOLD RYBCZYNSKI

"I think private space is necessary for dreaming. . . . Private space is part of a house, but it also occurs in many other places."

Witold Rybczynski (b. 1943) is a scholar, prolific author, professor, and architect. His book *Home: A Short History of an Idea* (Penguin, 1987) takes us through five centuries of interior home design, both great and small. A gratifying explication of the very notion of "home," the book demonstrates, among other things, how wall-hung religious tapestries evolved into wall-to-wall carpeting, and how social upheavals influence social patterns of place making.

His best-known book, *A Clearing in the Distance* (Simon and Schuster, 2013), is an acclaimed biography of the Central Park designer Frederick Law Olmsted. He also wrote the loquaciously-titled *Last Harvest: How a Cornfield Became New Daleville: Real Estate Development in America from George Washington to the Builders of the Twenty-First Century, and Why We Live in Houses Anyway* (Scribner, 2007), along with books on the origin of the screwdriver, building a house by hand, the design of cities, and the urge to control new technology.

Born in Edinburgh, Scotland, of Polish parentage and raised in Surrey, England, before moving at a young age to Canada, Rybczynski received a Bachelor of Architecture (1960) and MArch (1972) from McGill University in Montreal. He lives in Philadelphia, where he works as a professor of urbanism at the University of Pennsylvania School of Design.

Facing: The reading room alcove of Evergreen, 4545 North Charles Street, Baltimore, Maryland. The house was built in the mid-1800s and remodeled several times.

In discussing the functions and meaning of home, Witold Rybczynski talks about "discovering the limits of modernism." He points out that the early modern architects, in their minimalist approach, "compensated for the lack of decoration by creating larger spaces" and dispensing with the need for comfort, which they saw as a bourgeois invention. But comfort is tied to a sense of "coziness," which is essential—Rybczynski agrees with Grant Hildebrand—for the enjoyment of our home.

How has the relationship between public and private space changed over time?

Witold Rybczynski: In America, and increasingly all over the world, the population is becoming more and more heterogeneous, and it's not clear that the members of this huge, diverse group share very much in common. I think the movement toward creating a private place—which includes your friends and family—is characteristic of our time; it reflects the need to find things that we share with people, which in the public realm we do a lot less. We also tolerate a range of behaviors in public that would never have been the case a hundred years ago. The public realm has become a place that we pass through on the way to somewhere else; it isn't the relaxing place that it may have been in the past. It's not that the private realm is destroying the public, but rather that the private realm has become a refuge from the public realm, unfortunately.

In what ways is private space not only a refuge?

Rybczynski: I think private space is necessary for dreaming. We create the sense of privacy around us; it could be walking down the street or sitting by a lake. Dreaming is by definition an individual, personal act, but it can take place almost anywhere. You could be sitting on a train or you could be alone in your house. Private space is part of a house, but it also occurs in many other places.

Do you think it's fair to say that since the postwar housing boom, Americans as a whole have become less enthusiastic about, or even hostile to, large residential developments?

Rybczynski: Yes, I think that's true. It relates to several things. One is a loss of confidence about the future and a feeling that if only things would stay the same, the world would be a better place. This attitude is very hard to maintain in the United States, where we build almost two million houses a year and where we have constant immigration and movement around the country. Many parts of the country, especially the Northeast, the Northwest, and California, have become very resistant to these kinds of developments, seeing them as—pick your adjective—scary, negative, destructive.

That's not the case in the South, the Midwest, and Texas. The country is divided, as in so many things, by two different attitudes. On the one hand, we're building all these houses. On the other hand, we're worried about change. We don't have confidence that the future is going to be better than the past. And we are, quite frankly, very selfish in wanting to keep our surroundings the way they were when we moved here, so we don't want anybody else to move here.

All of those attitudes come together and create a conundrum where you have a growing country and yet a lot of people in the country don't want it to grow. It creates serious problems because the resistance to development leads to extremely expensive housing. Housing is expensive not because construction is expensive and not really because we are running out of land. We're not Switzerland. The problem is that we've made it so difficult to build in some places, such as around Philadelphia, New York, and Los Angeles, that when you do build, you have something that is worth an enormous amount of money. Consequently, few people can afford it. It has some serious effects. It's not simply that it makes life difficult for developers, which it may, but they can take care of themselves. It also creates extremely expensive housing in large parts of the country. The difference in the cost of housing between Atlanta and Philadelphia is enormous. It's purely a question of the ease with which you can acquire and develop land.

Some people argue that the problem with modern houses is that they don't offer the traditional coziness and comfort of home.

Rybczynski: When I was writing *Home*, I made the connection between coziness and comfort. I think comfort has a lot to do with thermal qualities, such as gathering around the fire. Coziness in the tropics doesn't really make sense; it's a northern attribute. But it's true that modern architecture, when created in a very minimal, bare approach, compensated for the lack of decoration by creating larger spaces. Frank Lloyd Wright was perhaps the rare example of an architect who created small spaces, but of course he worked with decoration, and to that extent he was unusual as a modernist.

But in the way things have played out, it seems the modernists were correct. It's not so much that the builders are imposing large houses on people; people want large houses. If you try to sell a small house, you'll run into a problem. Space has become a value in its own right. People with money have always valued space in the past. Historically, tall ceilings and lots of room were characteristic of the houses of the wealthy, it's just that there were very few of them. There are a lot more millionaires in this country than there used to be, so you have a lot more houses that really rival those built here at the turn of the last century. Most people, including me, would have thought it was an anomaly that would never be repeated. But we're building hundreds of houses in excess of 20,000 to 30,000 square feet, which is roughly the size of the average big mansion in 1900.

There is an argument that modernists sought to undermine decoration because they perceived it as a feminine and bourgeois invention.

Rybczynski: Modernism wasn't so much anti-feminine, but it was very anti-bourgeois. Comfort, as I make the point in the book, is essentially a bourgeois invention and tradition. To that extent, early modernists were overtly trying to undermine this tradition, which meant getting rid of all the comfortable chairs and other trappings that had accumulated in the home. Again, I think architects like Wright were an exception to this.

I didn't write about this, but I think the Scandinavian modernists were an exception. I'm not sure exactly why, but even going back to Alvar Aalto, they had this interest in natural things, which the Germans and French never did. You can't see Le Corbusier being interested in wooden furniture, whereas the modernist Scandinavians never lost the folk tradition of woodworking and using natural materials like cane.

It's almost a cliché of modernism to like tradition but not like traditional forms. I think it's not so easy to separate the two. The tradition and the forms of tradition, if we're talking about interiors, are very much linked. A wing chair is a particular kind of chair, and it carries with it a whole range of experiences. We've seen paintings of people in wing chairs and we've seen them in old houses. So to say that it's somehow the principle of the wing chair that is important—and not the chair—is to unravel the whole thing. In some ways, the traditions are too precious to redefine in that way. For me, *Home* was a kind of coming out of the closet and discovering the limits of the modernism that I had been taught and had practiced.

Why do you think Andrea Palladio was so influential? Why do people still go back and look at his houses from the sixteenth century, and why do they touch us today?

Rybczynski: That's a difficult question. I think the reason Palladio is so important is that he is the beginning of many things. He is one of the first modern architects. He is exploring things that become key parts of the Western tradition of architecture. Generation after generation goes back to him and reinterprets him. I make this comparison to Shakespeare and the English language. It's very hard at some point to unravel the two, because William Shakespeare was so frequently quoted that the English language itself became formed by the expressions from his plays; it's all mixed up together. I think Palladio is like that. When you're looking at Palladio, you're also looking at buildings that came later. He really becomes part of the language of architecture. He enters the bigger culture. Even if you don't know who Palladio is, you know the porch in front of a house, the Greek temple fronts, and all of those things.

I stayed in one of Palladio's houses for a week, hoping that I would discover something that might explain what you just asked me: why he was so influential and why the houses touch us. In the end, I thought it was the sense of balance in his work. He was, on the one hand, very conservative in his architecture, because he didn't want to take chances. On the other hand, he wanted it to work at a practical level. He didn't ask you to make big compromises the way some architects do. Yet he had this eye for beauty and was not willing to sacrifice that.

The buildings themselves have this sense of balance about them. They're not there to shock you. He creates a kind of perfectly balanced world, yet it actually works as a house. He created these very magical interiors that are absolutely organized geometrically, and yet at the same time, you walk out of the house and essentially into a farmyard. He brings you right back down to earth, in other words. It's a dream, but it's a very real dream.

When you look at the sweep of the history of residential architecture, what are the things that you feel must endure?

Rybczynski: Tastes change. When I think of the things I was so impressed by as an adolescent, they don't impress me anymore at all. And there were things I grew up with and took for granted that I now realize are quite marvelous. I'm not a big preservationist, but I understand the impulse. In a sense, you'd love to save everything in the world of architecture because one never knows where the next lesson will come from. For example, Frank Gehry makes you look at a whole range of buildings from the past in a different way. Suddenly buildings that look like weird dead ends are not dead ends because they eventually lead to Gehry and acquire a different meaning than they had. I'm thinking of Hans Scharoun's Berlin Philharmonic concert hall. It's always had great acoustics, but it seemed like such an odd duck when it opened in 1963. Now it really isn't. It's in the mainstream, and you see it differently because of Gehry. I think there's a place for everything, even that horrible Victorian architecture that I don't particularly like. That may come back, and we'll learn something from it that we don't see in it now.

Your question makes me think of two other issues that are important to consider. One is that not everybody lives in houses. We in the West are a culture of houses. That's an important part of the story, because not all cultures are. The ancient Chinese were, and most African cultures are. There are more people who live in houses than don't, but not all people do.

The other important thing is that two of the Founding Fathers were really good architects. And the fact that both George Washington and Thomas Jefferson were essentially Palladians gives that style a resonance in the United States that it probably doesn't have elsewhere, even in Italy.

I went to Mount Vernon for the first time not too long ago, and it is extremely beautiful. That shocked me. I'd seen pictures of it, but that site over the river is just extraordinary. Once you've seen it, you can imagine how it becomes a model for people, a kind of dream. We can't all live that way, but in some ways, it's the way we'd like to live. Of course, it's highly idealized, but it brings together the notion of space and nature and the individual.

This whole idea of the house of a Founding Father as a kind of shrine is interesting because it shows you how that must have affected the way we think about houses generally. In most cases, Europeans don't celebrate the homes of their historical figures, unless they happen to be really big palaces. Something like Mount Vernon really doesn't have a parallel in most other cultures. I think it also is probably why American colonial architecture has been so durable. It's not simply about aesthetics. It's about Washington and Jefferson and the connection to that history. The English also have Georgian architecture, but it was just one historical style among many, whereas the Georgian architecture that was present at the time of the American Revolution is not just an architectural style. It's tied to the individuals. A lot of it is mythic, but it's still part of our culture.

LESTER WALKER

"I found that in the vernacular, all these
methods and materials that have been
passed down over hundreds of years
have been developed in such a way
that they're the most expedient and
direct way of solving problems."

The compendium *American Homes: The Illustrated Encyclopedia of Domestic Architecture* (first published by Black Dog & Leventhal in 1981) by Lester Walker (b. 1939) is widely recognized as an indispensable resource for residential architects and students of residential architecture. His clear and elegant line drawings distill a wide variety of styles and periods and imbue the history of American residential architecture with a collective import.

Walker is the author of eight books, including *The Tiny Book of Tiny Houses* (Overlook, 1993); *American Shelter: Housing Styles and Their Evolution in America* (Overlook, 1997); and *Carpentry for Children* (Overlook, 1985), which won an American Library Association Award. Walker's essays, often illustrated with his drawings and photographs, have been published in numerous national magazines, including *Yankee*, *House Beautiful*, *Popular Science*, and *Family Circle*. Walker has an abiding interest in the graphic arts and loves to draw.

Walker, who received his MArch from Yale University, lives in Woodstock, New York, and has been practicing architecture for nearly thirty years in the Hudson Valley. Prior to that, he was a founding member of Studio Works in New York City, which won several national awards for innovative design.

Window at the Peak House, 322 South Second Street, Manhattan, Kansas.
The house, since torn down, dated back to the turn of the twentieth century.

Lester Walker picks up the conversation from Hildebrand and Rybczynski, bemoaning the "statement" mentality held by most developers and realtors, who believe they have fifteen to twenty seconds to sell a house, and therefore create these "soaring two-story entryways that are designed purely to impress." Walker encourages us to draw inspiration for our homes from the simple, practical solutions of enduring local vernacular and the inviting challenges of environment and site.

When you look back at the past several hundred years of American residential design, what are some of the qualities that endure?

Lester Walker: That's a zinger to start with. I think my architecture is based more on the vernacular than most other architects that I admire. In writing *American Homes*, I found that in the vernacular, all these methods and materials that have been passed down over hundreds of years have been developed in such a way that they're the most expedient and direct way of solving problems. When I come up with a problem in my own work, I tend to think, how would this have been done one or two hundred years ago, before there were architects? How would they do this roof? How would they think about this window? I find it really comfortable to look at it from a builder's point of view, because builders like to do things most directly. So my architecture is fairly simple, easy to build, and related more to the vernacular styles.

If you look back to when architects first got involved, say, in the early eighteenth century, they were doing buildings that were designed to impress people. They weren't doing buildings to be beautiful and part of nature. For example, the Georgian style, which is really the first style that came along in America, was based on the English Georgian style, which was based on the Italian Renaissance. The plantation houses and the very early houses in the English settlements up and down the Atlantic coast were designed to say, "Hey, I'm wealthy, I'm better than you. I'm a big-time landowner and I'm going to have a house that's better than your house." It wasn't the kind of building that I like. I like the sweeter folk architecture better than the stylish architecture of the past.

What are some of the persistent qualities of vernacular architecture that you appreciate?

Walker: In the vernacular, I look for the quality, the general style, and the pragmatic functions, like the idea of shedding rain off the roof. The roof was designed a certain way to shed the bad weather in various climates for hundreds of years before architects got a hold of it. I could give you comparable examples of windows, siding, stairways, foundations, doors, walls, surfaces, and so forth that have been passed down through the years and are used by me and many other architects today. I think about my professors and gurus, the architects of history that I absolutely love, and say, how would they solve this problem? How did Charles Moore, one of my favorites, solve this problem? It can get you out of a rut when you can't think straight.

All of architecture relates to the various forces that are acting upon it. It always gets back to weather, site, culture, availability of material type, and so on. And if you allow the building to be a product of all of those forces, it can be beautiful and simple.

What is an example of a successful home from American history?

Walker: The Cape Cod house is built like an upside-down boat. It was built by boatbuilders, not architects, who really knew what they were doing. They built the houses on 12" × 12" sill plates, instead of on a foundation, so that when the sand washed away, they could get a team of horses to haul the house to another location on the sand. There were no roof overhangs because of the wind; they didn't want the building to get lifted. You may look at the Cape Cod house and say that it's the most boring, straightforward house that was ever built. But its engineering and design are incredible because they're a true function of the site.

Conversely, what design qualities have we got to finally, as a culture, shake off, discard, or exorcise?

Walker: I'd say we've got to shake off preconceived ideas about really excellent building materials like concrete blocks. They're one of the most beautiful building materials ever invented, and people hate them. You can do a beautiful building using nothing but concrete blocks, except for the roof, of course. They are very straightforward, simple, and inexpensive. Plywood is the same way; people hate plywood. Metal buildings. I think you have to allow the most simple, straightforward solution to a problem to happen. Usually, if you refine it down to what the program and site needs are, it can be a beautiful building no matter what the materials are. If it's a really tight budget, you might use concrete blocks and plywood. To my mind, if you keep it simple and straightforward and allow it to give a little bit toward the site constraints and the program requirements, you can design a beautiful building. So we've got to get rid of preconceived ideas.

Are there any current design philosophies or qualities that you rail against?

Walker: I just gave a course at university, and a fellow instructor was saying that realtors think they have about fifteen or twenty seconds to sell a house. So these big home companies are designing for that first fifteen seconds, rather than designing a beautiful house that functions well with the site. They have these soaring two-story entryways that are designed purely to impress. To me that is ridiculous.

The size of the average new house has gotten to be crazy. In the last ten years, we've gone from 1,900 to 2,300 square feet in house size. Houses just keep growing and growing. I like to design a house where each room is designed specifically for the people that are using the house. You can make a relatively small house that's comfortable, and then when the kids leave and go to college, you still have a relatively small house that you can grow old in. You don't have to sell your big house to another family and go and live in a nursing home.

One of the unique accomplishments of your book *American Homes* is its organization. Out of chaos, you arrived at a methodology that brought order, chronology, and delineation to this long and wildly diverse design history. Please talk about your process of organizing the material.

Walker: It was really simple. There are a hundred styles in the book. I would take each style and ask, who designed this building and why is it the shape that it is? Why are all these decisions made the way they are made? I'm not a historian. I was educated as an architect and a designer, to design furniture, stationery, all the way up through big buildings. I've had to teach myself history by reading books, traveling, and so on.

I decided to do the book around 1978, after I had researched one house that I thought was boring, the Cape Cod house, and found it to be one of the most exciting houses ever built. I said to myself, there must be hundreds of styles of houses out there that are equally exciting but that look dull from the road. I said, well, why don't I just start with the earliest style and work my way through the latest style? I'll do my own research and then figure out how to lay out the book later. So I started out with the earliest American Indian dwelling. I researched it, made drawings to fit the page, and typed up what I had written about it, basically explaining the drawings. If I had to do it again, I'd have the drawings explain the text, going back and forth a little bit.

You can see in the finished book that the writing was done using a typewriter and instant lettering. I designed every page on a piece of cardboard. I completely finished the first American Indian style, getting it so that I really liked it, put it away, and went to the next American Indian style. Pretty soon, I had six or eight early American Indian styles, and then the pilgrims landed. What did they do? The Indians helped them build little huts—wigwams—on the ground. They had landed on December 20, and half of them died that winter. When the summer came along, they started to build themselves little medieval cabins. From there on, I researched styles, basically by date. I got into the Victorian period, 1750–1820. I think I have seventeen Victorian styles, all the way up to the Queen Anne. Finally, I had researched a hundred styles of houses, and I put them all together. I went back to look at the beginning of the book, and it wasn't nearly as good as the last half because I'd learned how to render better. So I did the first half of the book all over again. It was very easy to lay it out chronologically. As you read through the book, you start out with AD 300 and you end up with AD 2006, and you get a history of the American house.

I included some houses like those made of baled hay and sod that I thought were fun because they were hippie architecture or settlers' architecture, quick architecture. I put them in just to give the book a little bit of funkiness.

How did your research for the book change your appreciation of house styles over time?

Walker: It was really exciting reading about any house style. Why is the mansard roof on the Second Empire house? Every style has interesting aspects, even shacks or shanties. During World War II, Quonset huts were developed. From the technology of war, a whole host of prefabricated buildings inspired houses.

There's a lot of culture in the book, because houses are built in response to cultural pressures. For example, my favorite is the split-level. I had experienced it firsthand, but it never hit my consciousness that the split-level house existed because television came along in the 1950s and dramatically changed American society, and the American house. All of a sudden, we were gathered around the TV, and our parents didn't want that television in the living room. My mother hated having it in the living room. You watched the TV during your dinner, and you didn't want the informality of the television all mixed up with the formal living room with the plastic slipcovers.

At the very same time, at least in the East, we wanted to import the good life from California, so we wanted to grill outside. The backdoor patio replaced the front porch. You could grill on the back patio, then walk up half a level to the kitchen and living room. You walked up another half level to the bedrooms, and the bedrooms would go over the family room. The split-level was born.

In the book, you learn that those cultural pressures, the good life from California and the television, really made the split-level house. It wouldn't have happened otherwise. And the style of it, there's a lot of California ranch and there's a lot of early colonial architecture, because people like shutters. It's almost a builder's kind of vernacular, a straightforward, non-architect-designed house. But it's a terrific house for the 1950s. Now we're putting the televisions in the living room, the great room. But then, the living room just sat there like a place where nobody ever went except when your parents had a party, and even then, they ended up in the family room. The living room was a shrine to furniture.

Were there many precursors to your book that attempted an encyclopedic or near-encyclopedic scope?

Walker: I did learn from a lot of stylebooks, but they weren't as complete. For example, I used the book *What Style Is It?: A Guide to American Architecture* (John Wiley and Sons, 2003). But none of them started with the Native Americans and went up through time. I really went all the way from beginning to end. And none of them had the geodesic dome or sod houses.

American Homes makes a great bathroom book. Each chapter is about the length of time that you spend on the toilet. You can get the complete history of American house building in about a hundred days.

In addition to your work as an architect, you're an educator. What aspects of teaching architecture are being missed, misunderstood, or approached wrongly these days?

Walker: I would say that in the colleges that I'm associated with, the design work is excellent. But when I went to college, we were more involved with vernacular architecture and the history of architecture than students are today. And that might be good or bad. I tend to think it's not good. The more you know about the history, the better you can design for today. When you learn about the way it was done in the past, you become a better problem solver. From the work that I've seen by students coming out of architecture school, there isn't the knowledge and respect. If I was running an architecture school today, I'd have a lot more required history courses, and they would have to deal with a lot of vernacular stuff. I sound like an old fogey.

When I graduated, the postmodern style was hitting. We trashed the modern style in school. I loved postmodernism because it was based on history and was very humorous. My favorite teachers at Yale were among the best teachers of postmodern architecture in the world: Robert Venturi, James Sterling, and Charles Moore. Their work takes historic arms and twists them, giving us a new way of looking at them. It's a modern way of looking at the past, not taking it too seriously, for example, mixing the Georgian style with the modern style and coming up with some really interesting buildings.

Of course, that's what those McMansions are. But they lack the humor—they take themselves too seriously—and they lack a careful knowledge of history. They have columns that are not supporting beams; they go right up into the roof. The Greeks would throw up looking at that. A column has to hold up a beam, and a beam has to support an entablature. They're designing stage sets for the wealthy, or for the people who want to impress their neighbors.

Do you find any current trends in architecture or design to be particularly intriguing?

Walker: I think we're getting back to modernism, which I'm enthusiastic about. My son, Jess, graduated from the same school I did—Yale. It's very interesting to see what's happened over those thirty years since I graduated. He was instrumental in the last four chapters of my book. He works for Aldo Rossi's office in New York City. Aldo Rossi, who recently passed away, was my hero when I was in college. My son is much more of a modernist than I am. His work is serious, but it has Rossi's humor. It's a little more straightforward than my work; I could get involved in a little bit more decoration than he could. His spaces aren't quite as tight as mine. My buildings tend to be a little more broken up because I like to reduce spaces down to their more perfect size, whereas he'll allow a bulk of space to serve a lot of different functions, which is a kind of modernist way of looking at buildings. And I can appreciate that now because it's less expensive to build. It's an interesting turnaround from when I went to school. He's not refuting the history of all these different periods of architecture either, because architects today do utilize a lot of different styles. But it's a modernist way of looking at them.

What have you learned as an architect from the specific landscape in which you are currently working?

Walker: Any site has very specific problems and highlights. The first thing you do is find out where the driveway is coming in, where the sun comes from, where the wind comes from, and whether it has big trees and views. Where is the septic field going to go? Then you talk to the client. Do you want gardens? Do you want to take advantage of the views? If there are trees on the site, do you want to have rooms that are more private in the trees? The site creates the initial set of forces on the building. Then you take the owner's needs and superimpose them on the site. For example, the living room wants to have the view, the bedroom wants to have the trees, the entryway wants to have the driveway, the bathrooms want to have the septic, the garage wants to have the driveway, the big windows want to be on the view side, and the entryway wants to be protected. You arrange the programmatic requirements of the owner on the site according to the forces that are exerted by the site.

Then you go to the owner and say, do you like this? Do you think all these rooms and spaces are organized in a functional way? Can you live in this house? Is it exciting and interesting? Are the bedrooms in the quiet part of the site? Are the public parts on the public part of the site? So you start to design, and they say this is good, this is bad, and you rearrange the spaces until they settle into a nice diagram. Then you take that diagram and the owner's magazine clippings of the kinds of things they like and you start getting into style, which melds with the diagram that you have. You work them together. You build a model. You do drawings. The owner looks at it again and says I like this, I don't like that, and you start working on it again. The owner is bringing more forces into it. They don't want the flat roof, they want the roof to slope, they want it to be more storybook or modern or whatever they want.

I like to work with the owner because you end up with a house that you couldn't have imagined in the beginning due to all these different forces. You learn about the architecture along the way. And then you end up with something that is usually really exciting because it's this natural progression of what the owner needs and what's structurally healthy for the site. So the landscape, as I say, is the primary set of forces. You can't ignore it. You can talk the owner out of certain things, but you cannot talk nature out of being the way that it is. The nature of the landscape is the driving force between the architect and the building.

Small house in the Boise National Forest, Garden Valley, Idaho

SARAH SUSANKA

"That's one of the fundamental principles
of building Not So Big. We're taking less
and we're making it more."

The bestselling author and cultural visionary Sarah Susanka (b. 1957) is a registered architect, a member of the College of Fellows of the AIA, and a certified interior designer. Her "build better, not bigger" approach to residential design and her Not So Big philosophy have led an anti-elitist movement in residential architecture. Born and raised in England before moving to the United States, Susanka was dubbed "one of eighteen innovators in American culture" by *U.S. News and World Report*.

We feel "at home" in our houses, according to Susanka, when where we live reflects who we are in our hearts. Our quality of life soars, moreover, when we fully inhabit each moment and show up completely in whatever we are doing. People have resonated deeply with her message—over a million of Susanka's books are in circulation.

The Not So Big House (Taunton, 1998), her groundbreaking first book, was followed by *Home by Design: Transforming Your House into Home* (Taunton, 2004). Then Susanka partnered with Marc Vassallo for *Inside the Not So Big House* (Taunton, 2005), which focuses on the built-in details that bring personality to a home, even before interior design. In a second encore, Susanka launched *Outside the Not So Big House* (Taunton, 2006) with landscape designer Julie Moir Messervy. Susanka and Messervy weave inside with outside in twenty examples of simple gardens that surround Not So Big houses.

Sarah Susanka enters the American home conversation agreeing with her colleagues about the benefits of downsizing—"finding the abundance in less material," as she puts it. A properly proportioned home, says Susanka, "offers a much more comfortable place to live, and it reflects more of who you are on the inside."

Since you wrote *The Not So Big House*, you have been partly responsible for a rather dramatic wave of interest in residential design that favors, as you put it, quality over square footage. This philosophy seems to resonate with many Americans. At the same time, there's evidently an implacable, countervailing strain of "bigger is more bang for your buck" in the American psyche. What do you make of this? Is this just the warring of two inherent human natures: pridefulness and modesty?

Sarah Susanka: That's a great question. If we look back in history, this has happened before. During the Victorian era, we saw houses getting bigger and bigger. And then we saw the Arts and Crafts movement come up and offer an alternative, which was a smaller and better-designed house. A hundred years later, the same phenomenon repeated. We had bigger and bigger houses being built, but a segment of the population didn't see themselves reflected in those McMansions and wanted something different.

I had been working as a residential architect with a number of colleagues for many years in Minneapolis and St. Paul. After spending sixteen years serving middle America by putting forth options that were designed for the way people really live, I started recognizing that it was time to explain what we were doing. The inspiration for writing *The Not So Big House* was in some ways self-serving. I didn't want to keep telling the same story over and over when trying to help people understand that what they needed was not more space; it was better space.

The art of this is really to make sure that normal, everyday people understand what connects with their values in terms of architectural design. I think where architects didn't get the picture—until these books came out—was that homeowners aren't inherently interested in architecture; they're interested in a better house for themselves. *The Not So Big House* books are written to say, here's how you make a better house for you. It's not a hard sell on architecture; it's connecting with what people are really looking for.

I don't think we will ever see the complete disappearance of what we're calling the McMansion, but I do think that the audience for the smaller, better-designed house is going to increase as people see that it offers a much more comfortable place to live and reflects more of who you are on the inside. It's a nurturing environment for you and your household.

There seems to be a divide between wishes and needs, if I might borrow a phrase from one of your book jacket flaps. I wonder if you could talk about the difference. In a recent article by one of our producers, she talked about how her apartment had forced her to be prudent about accumulation and for that reason she'd actually become grateful for its limitations.

Susanka: Wishes and needs are a fascinating issue because we have all sorts of wishes that we think of as needs. The wealthier a culture becomes, the more we believe that the things we wish for are absolute needs. You can see that, for example, in cable access. It used to be that very few people had televisions. And now that's one of the basic fundamentals of life. It's no longer in the wish category, it's in the need category. But is it really? I ask people to recognize that when you meet your needs, your true needs, in a way that really supports who you are as a human being, many times the extra wishes go away because you are satisfied. I often say that in this philosophy, less is more. And I'm not trying to squeeze people into tiny houses and have them do with less. It's actually not like the simplicity movement. It's much more about finding the abundance in less material where it's beautifully designed to really inspire you.

Do you think that some of the origin of the philosophies found in *The Not So Big House* comes from an English sensibility, and by this I specifically mean the pastoral ideal that one might find in the Cotswolds?

Susanka: I know that my English upbringing had an enormous impact on my present career because I saw how differently American houses were lived in than their English counterparts, even though we essentially had the same rooms.

What do you mean?

Susanka: Growing up, my family had a house with a formal living room, formal dining room, and a formal entry, but we used those rooms all day, every day. They were the living room and the dining room; we ate three meals in the dining room every day. So part of what allowed me to see that there's something amiss in the American house is that when I moved to Los Angeles, when I was in high school, I looked at how my friends were living in their houses. And I saw that the formal living room and the formal dining room were never used, as far as I could tell. They had the plastic seat covers on. So why build them? It just didn't make sense to me. I think if you don't use it, why do you have it? I came from a culture that didn't have as much; it was important to use what you had and to use if effectively. That's the sensibility that's colored a lot of my work.

I think that your ideas come from a sincere and personal place, but I wonder how much the popularity of your philosophy has to do with how expensive it is to own or build a house.

Susanka: Houses are expensive to build, whether you're building new or remodeling. They're almost always more money than most people imagine. Unfortunately, when the emphasis is on size, which is typically the tool that people assume will allow them to get a better house, no money is left over to make that space really wonderful. So what I've been trying to help people see is that if you take a little of that square footage out of the equation and you use the money saved to add character to the space, what results is something that's far more supportive of you and your family. It's helping people to see that the more-ness they're looking for isn't size. It's actually one of feeling supported by the environment.

One of the slogans I have for Not So Big is that a not-so-big house is about a third smaller than what you thought you needed, but it's just as expensive. That often gets a chuckle when I'm talking in public. It's not about less money. It's about using your money effectively so that you get a house that makes you feel wonderful.

Working with an architect is fundamentally a privilege.

Susanka: Typically, when somebody wants a better house in the way I'm describing, they do need some help to make that happen. And the best help is from an architect, which, of course, costs money. That fact automatically puts it into what we might say is an elitist bucket, which is not what I think a lot of us who are architects would wish.

One of the things I think will happen as we help people visualize well-designed space is the mass market will move toward really good, well-designed architecture. I think over the next twenty years we'll start to have some panelized and even modular and manufactured housing that isn't the bottom of the barrel but is the top of the barrel. I think we'll be able to get high quality at a much more affordable price point. It's not here yet, by any means, but I am working with a number of architects around the country to find solutions that would allow that to happen.

When people ask you for guidance on transforming their existing houses into homes, what are your general principles?

Susanka: Well, in fact, all of the things I'm talking about in *The Not So Big House* and, in more detail, in *Home by Design* and *Not So Big Solutions for Your Home* are really translatable at any price range. Let me give you an example. One of the principles that I describe in *Home by Design* is called "light to walk toward." We are physiologically programmed to move toward light. So we can use that principle to animate parts of the house that we find dull. A lot of postwar houses have a long, dark hallway with a series of doors on either side that access bathrooms and bedrooms. If you put a lighted painting at the end of that hallway, the whole hallway jumps to life because you're pulled toward that light. Not only that, but it starts to make the rooms on either side much more attractive just because you enjoy going down the hallway. It's a very simple remodeling job to put a recessed light fixture above a painting at the far end of the hallway.

That's inspired. Can you give me another example?

Susanka: Another one that's a little bit more expensive to apply but still not out of sight for most families is to actually lower some ceiling areas. In an awful lot of houses, every room is 8 feet tall. So what I'll often do when I don't have a lot of money to spend for a client is to lower some sections of ceiling to, say, 7 feet. Over a kitchen counter, for example, I'll bring what architects call a "dropped soffit" out to the edge of the counter top. What it does is give a sense of shelter around the work area. Now you might think that lowering part of the ceiling would make the room feel smaller. But in fact, it does exactly the opposite. It makes the 8-foot ceiling part feel taller. That's one of the fundamental principles of building Not So Big. We're taking less and we're making it more.

The last question is not so much a question as a musing. Do you know who Sam Mockbee, the founder of Rural Studio, was?

Susanka: Absolutely.

Sam Mockbee wrote, "Everyone wants the same thing, rich or poor, not only a warm, dry room, but a shelter for the soul." I've thought about that a lot because so many of the architects that I've interviewed are problem solvers, and at the same time, they're interested in making an individualistic statement. I wonder if there's a tension for architects between trying to serve their clients' needs while at the same time desiring to build dramatically in a way that differentiates their work.

Susanka: Architecture has a built-in problem. When we're trained as architects, we are encouraged first and foremost to do something unique. The focus is on who *we* are as individuals. I've been very interested in making sure my clients know that this is *their* house.

With every project, you learn about space and design. So you develop a bag of tricks. If I look at my own work, a certain flavor runs through many of my projects. But the character is really dependent upon who the client is. For example, one client walked through one of my contemporary Prairie Style houses and said, "Oh, this is very interesting. I love the feeling of this place, but I can't stand trim lines." So I designed a house for them that is basically white architecture. It's pristine on the inside, but it still has the shaping of space that I have used on a number of Prairie school–oriented designs. So even if your goal as an architect is not to have a specific style that you always design in, it's difficult not to develop a kit of parts and ideas over the course of your career.

I believe very strongly that architects serve their clients best when they get out of the way and really listen to what the person is looking for. It doesn't mean that you can't give design direction, because almost everybody needs that. But to be able to draw from their dreams and not from your own is a very important part of being an architect, I believe.

BARBARA WINSLOW AND MAX JACOBSON

"I think the building does the same thing.
You are sheltered inside, or you're outside
in the world. With the porch, those two
experiences meet, and going between
them makes you aware."

Barbara Winslow (b. 1945) and Max Jacobson (b. 1941) work together at the architectural firm Jacobson Silverstein Winslow/Degenhardt Architects, in Berkeley, California. They coauthored, with Murray Silverstein, *Patterns of Home: The Ten Essentials of Enduring Design* (Taunton, 2002).

Barbara Winslow combines a background in social psychology with architectural design. Her interest in designing for individuals with special needs led to coauthoring, with Ray Lifchez, *Design for Independent Living* (University of California Press, 1979), which addresses the unique design needs of the physically disabled and was a finalist for the 1980 American Book Awards. Winslow, who is a member of the Organization of Women Architects, received her MArch from the University of California, Berkeley, where she served as a lecturer from 1979 to 1987. Her recent work ranges from the design of custom homes, including several for individuals with severe physical disabilities, to fully accessible affordable housing projects.

Max Jacobson was an associate at the Center for Environmental Structure in Berkeley from 1971 to 1974. With Christopher Alexander, Sara Ishikawa, Murray Silverstein, Ingrid Fiksdahl-King, and Shlomo Angel, he coauthored *A Pattern Language* (Oxford, 1977), which remains a primary text in residential design theory. The book points out that in architecture, the infinite variety of designs within a system can be formalized into patterns. These patterns are deeply humanistic and archetypal, rooted in the nature of things.

Front porch of the Dixon H. Lewis House, State Highway 97
(County Road 29), Lowndesboro, Alabama

In 1973, Jacobson received his PhD in architecture from the University of California, Berkeley, where he lectured from 1972 to 1976 and from 1984 to 1986. He has been an instructor of architecture at Diablo Valley College since 1975.

Contributing to the evolving conversation, Barbara Winslow and Max Jacobson discuss the fundamentals of successful home design, including proper circulation, multiple sources of illumination, transitional space, and connection to the site and landscape. They like the fact that they do not have a recognizable signature style to their residential designs. As a firm that caters to homeowners with special needs, they pride themselves on designing houses that are "completely unique to the clients we work with."

Tell us about your book *Patterns of Home: The Ten Essentials of Enduring Design* and why you wrote it.

Max Jacobson: We asked ourselves the question: If you were going to teach a class in architectural design, or if you were to begin a design of a house for a family, what are the ten basic design concepts that would be most helpful to create an efficient, well-thought-out, well-designed living space? It's not like we couldn't come up with four hundred essential items, but what are the ten? For example, one of the most common mistakes when people design houses is that they don't allow rooms to receive light from at least two directions. If you can explain it in a vivid and clear way, it becomes a powerful design tool.

Another example would be that people are always having difficulty with circulation through rooms and spaces. Typically, there will be a big room with doorways on all four walls, and the circulation will crisscross the room. When you analyze it, you realize that there's no pool of quiet in the room in which to place a table or a conversation area. And by illustrating a very simple concept of circulation, all of a sudden, spaces become much more comfortable, settled, and interesting, because circulation is moving through them in an efficient way.

Barbara, you can read the titles of the ten "patterns of home" from the book.

Barbara Winslow: Inhabiting the Site; Creating Rooms, Outside and In; Sheltering Roof; Capturing Light; Parts in Proportion; The Flow through Rooms; Private Edges, Common Core; Refuge and Outlook; Places in Between; and Composing with Materials.

People's experience of the home includes the site that they're on, their surroundings, and how the building fits with that, how it invites them to go in and out, and what sorts of spaces you've created by using the space around the building to create rooms. And it also has something to do with what the building itself feels like. "Sheltering Roof" is a very good example of that because people often come to us wanting a powerful roof. They want the sense of being within something that expresses shelter, and that's certainly part of the image of the building that's coming not from us or from a style, but from some kind of a fundamental instinct to have a sheltering roof.

I think of the home in social, psychological terms. The real essence of a personal relationship, for instance, comes in the moments of greeting and the moments of parting. You settle in when you've been together for a while, and when you're apart, you think about the other person in the abstract. But at the moment when people come together, there's this critical experience that has the essence of the relationship in it. It brings together everything—your fears and your hopes. I think the building does the same thing. You are sheltered inside, or you're outside in the world. With the porch, those two experiences meet, and going between them makes you aware. You're aware of the wind the moment you can get out of it. You have the opportunity to go either way, to make a choice, and the building is expressing that experience.

Why do you think this is such a pleasure for most human beings?

Winslow: It's the quality of choice. You're most aware when you're making a decision, making a choice between doing something or not doing it, being there or not being there. Experiencing possibility. And you only do that when you're at a cusp.

One aspect of your practice is designing for clients with special needs. Let's say that you're creating a house in which someone who is wheelchair-bound has a lot more liberty than in a typically designed house. If someone, such as myself, who is free of the wheelchair, comes into this house, what am I going to learn?

Winslow: Well, for one thing, if you're in a house in which the person who is using a wheelchair is comfortable moving around, you're going to be operating essentially as an equal. Within that house, they have the freedom to function as effectively as you do. This is not the case in a lot of environments. The person who is in a wheelchair is really at a deficit. There are many things they can't do. You become an aide to them; you become the interface. When the environment is the interface, it changes that relationship.

So it's democratizing.

Winslow: It's democratizing. It lets people be everything that they can be and function with others in a different way. I think this applies to a lot of different special needs. We work on housing for people who are aged, people who have mental health deficiencies, and people who in a variety of ways have limited abilities. And giving each of these people an environment that empowers them makes a huge difference. I think it helps each of these categories of people function at their best.

There are many things that can be done to make a space function as an equivalent environment. For instance, if you're visiting an older person who can't climb stairs, if you go up with them in an elevator or an escalator, or if you go up a ramp, you're there together doing the same thing. It's just a different way of being. You're not coming in as the person who has the abilities and the other person does not.

My basic philosophy is that in handling the environment, it's not necessarily the overall gesture but rather the small acts that enable an individual to live comfortably, to achieve his or her own potential within that space. That is what makes that environment transformative for them, and this approach can ultimately extend to society as a whole.

I don't think that buildings as such are a social force, and I don't think an environment can necessarily change peoples' experiences, but what I do think is that designing buildings in a way that enables people to achieve their potential ultimately will become a major social force.

What would you like to see transformed in American residential architecture?

Winslow: I'm thinking back to one housing development that we were involved in, in which the houses were literally called "product." We were working on developing more product, which was kind of a shocking term because that's not the way we view a house. And what was really being said was that we're selling the image, we're selling the material, we're selling the things you see in a magazine, and you can pass that on to the next buyer. We're not selling something that creates an enclosure for your life. And that is what I see as the big difference. I think at one time people built houses to encompass their lives and create this same kind of potential that you have with people with special needs. They created the potential to live a life they wanted. Now they create a universal potential for the standard family that can be sold to the next buyer.

Jacobson: Coming from our experience with Chris Alexander and the writing of *A Pattern Language*, we entered our professional practice with the attitude that we were going to try to help people become a part of the design process, while providing what technical skills they lacked. Whatever resulted in the design of the house emerged from their needs, their personalities, and their aspirations. As a result, our work doesn't have the stamp of us as authors. It's simply a collection of very unique and unusual homes and other buildings designed by our clients. They have tremendous range.

So, your design philosophy is client-centric. How would you say that is different from the approach to residential design of the last seventy-five or a hundred years?

Jacobson: Instead of every time you see one of our projects, you say, "Oh, there's a house done by those guys," the houses are completely unique to the clients we work with. What we end up with is a bunch of clients who would say, "Wow, what an experience that was working with these guys, and look at this house we've created with them, which is ours."

Normally, architects view their work as a contribution to society from themselves. I would say that what we're trying to do is extract the creative spirit from our clients.

HADLEY ARNOLD

"I have gone through the mental exercise of if you replicated this model indefinitely, what would be the result, and I actually believe in courtyard architecture and courtyard urbanism as a viable model."

Hadley Arnold (b. 1964) is an architect and an educator. Reflecting a progressive-minded moral code, her work emphasizes the importance of morality and ethics in the design of the built environment. Like Susanka, Arnold believes in living small indoors but living large in the landscape, a philosophy shared by her husband, Peter Arnold, whom she met while studying at SCI-Arc (Southern California Institute of Architecture). For the Arnolds, moderation is "essential for a sustainable nation."

Hadley and Peter are the founding directors of the Arid Lands Institute, a self-sustaining education, research, and outreach center dedicated to issues of aridity, climate change, and the design of the built environment. Their design work has been recognized by Los Angeles's MAK Center for Art and Architecture, the Architecture and Design Museum in Los Angeles, and the AIA's Los Angeles chapter.

While living in a 650-square-foot wood-and-glass home designed by Cliff May in 1941, they bought the house next door—a 1947 home by Rodney Walker, who would go on to design three Case Study houses. After remodeling the badly rotted Walker house, they moved into it and turned the May house into their architectural studio. The design of both homes encourages seamless indoor-outdoor living, one of the perks of Los Angeles living.

Hadley Arnold picks up the discussion of finding beauty in restraint and austerity, and expands the conversation to include the ethical question of a home's footprint on the environment and within its community. As she puts it: "'Home' is something larger than the house that you occupy."

Certain rules, patterns, and qualities of style in residential architecture endure. What are the things that you hope will endure, that matter to you?

Hadley Arnold: When I think of what constitutes home and what I would want to endure, it is rarely architectural. It begins for me in two other things: the landscape and, for lack of a better word, the urbanism. Above all, home for me is a participation in and a loving of the landscape that you're a part of. Out of that rises a way of building that reveres, enhances, or respects the landscape, or magnifies that which we love. Looking at the pantheon of buildings, I love seeing the genealogy unfurl and the little bits of DNA mutate and carry forward, some of them enduring and some of them going off on their own. But I immediately want to place them in their location.

In part, I am looking at how it is that a house could be from a certain place and no other, how the landscape informed the architecture, and how it's adapted to a particular climate, whether it's in the thickness of the walls or the placement of the chimney radiating out. The second part is all the paraphernalia that goes around houses that connects them to and separates them from others.

What's an architecture that makes you love a landscape and allows you to participate in and cultivate that love? I don't really know. Here in Los Angeles, I think courtyards are a part of that. I believe in the courtyard house as a building type for Los Angeles. And I think that's different from a front yard, from an idea of a commons. I don't think this is a particularly popular notion. The front yard is hallowed ground; you read articles in the paper about wars in West Hollywood over the height of fences and hedges. I actually think of the courtyard as a kind of engaged retreat from Los Angeles, which is healthy and allows you to cultivate a love of the climate and the land itself. And that's really important if you're going to care about this abstraction called a city. Looking around here at what helps make this home and why I think it's enduring, I'd say first and foremost is the strong enclosure.

In a sense, you're saying that our response to the landscape is an enduring issue in creating a home.

Arnold: I think so. Also important is creating a commitment to a place so that "home" is something larger than the house that you occupy. It is also part of the settlement—the community and the ecology you're participating in. And you have to look at the footprint you're leaving behind.

Facing: View from the balcony into a courtyard at the Stoltzfus-Humphries House, 6855 La Valle Plateada, Rancho Santa Fe, California

You have built a small compound with your office next door to your home. Why did you design it in this way?

Arnold: Obviously, we didn't see in this site what a lot of people did, which was to build to its maximum floor area ratio and maximum building envelope, and realize its greatest economic potential. We could have put three 2,400-square-foot family residences on this lot. And lots of arguments could be made for that being appropriate, or even necessary, in terms of scale and density. But that's not what we saw. Work is there, home is here; that makes sense personally. It makes sense at a policy level, too. It's where Los Angeles is going, and it's something that we would advocate—getting people to more density-clustered centers near where they work and live, getting them out of the car. Small was necessary but also seemed appropriate and even affirmatively good.

It sounds as if you were swimming upstream in that respect.

Arnold: Right. Certainly the marketplace, the major driving force behind our culture, says 2,400 square feet is what a young family needs and what the market craves. And we're building it at 835 square feet. Why? There were economic necessities for doing that in terms of making use of an existing slab without triggering expensive retaining wall ordinances. But I think that working with how something can give abundantly within what appear to be the constraints of austerity or scarcity is the creative challenge that appeals to us aesthetically and ethically.

Ethically? How can you be an ethical architect?

Arnold: I think there are lots of ways to be an ethical architect. I don't want to make any pretense to being one. I guess you could just say it's being mindful about consumption and overconsumption, although there isn't an objective case where one can draw the line and say what you have is appropriate, necessary, and enough. It's important to us that we always be questioning and testing if what we own, what we purchase, what we make, what we consume, and what we dispose of is necessary and sufficient. I think that's an engineering principle—that which is necessary and sufficient—but it's also not a bad ethical one if you're just trying to measure equitable consumption.

This is a response to a general feeling that the society is overly consumptive?

Arnold: Right. It's a critique of consumer culture. Capitalism—consumer culture—is an illusion of abundance that will ultimately create scarcity. It's not just about some kind of puritan self-denial. To be in this space is to have a lot of luxury conferred in the form of light and air, the integration of the outdoors, and the observation of the seasons. Can one provide aesthetic luxury, the highest standards of excellence, without size being a function of it?

In a sense, you are expressing different criteria for luxury.

Arnold: Yes, and I'm suggesting that it's totally possible within restraint. We accept scarcity and are more interested in exploring abundance in something that appears to be scarcity or restraint—scarcity of size, restraint of power and materials, the discipline about what gets used in the making of the house and the resources that are used to heat, cool, and run it. Those constraints squeeze us and yield a kind of richness that is surprising and delightful to us; it sustains us.

How would you characterize it? What's on the list that defines abundance that emerges from those constraints?

Arnold: For me, so much of this is less and less about architecture and more about trying to live a life and beliefs. If we keep acting on an assumption of prosperity and abundance, we're going to run out of fossil fuels, water, decent soil quality, and an appropriate level of naturally occurring greenhouse gases. Scarcity is going to come up out of an attitude about abundance. I think over a slow process of checking out from the comforts of the culture—in terms of information, stimulation, entertainment, and possessions—we could do just fine on much less.

In a way, I feel like I am sharing with you what are my most deeply held beliefs. It's amazing how powerful the interior voice is for me. The Thom Maynes and the Greg Lynns of this world are speaking a much more sophisticated language; I feel intellectually impoverished by sharing my beliefs. I know they're small and personal at this point.

But they're not. This house is your response to the notion of scarcity. Why? It's not about being proud, or pretentious, and it's not about being holier than thou.

Arnold: No, it's actually about creating a home. It goes back to the question of making home possible for us in this city—in this particular topography and climate at this particular time. Reflecting on the basics—the underlying fundamental blessings of just being here—becomes the generator of something as seemingly trivial as an architectural style. It required knocking down a wall to allow for that retreat to happen and then it required a transparent architecture that engages the outside.

And I'm not suggesting it's enough. I'm really interested at the moment in the issues of what is enough in anything. Being in this particular climate and canyon

49

topography requires that we harness our energy from the sun, put every drop of water that falls onto the site back into the water table, be careful about the materials we choose, and limit our energy consumption.

I think that what you do with this kind of architecture, in your small but firm way, is to resist the ramrod consumer culture, which wants us to build big spaces and fill them up with stuff. It seems to me that you are striving to open up a greater awareness of the natural landscape.

Arnold: There is some link between putting that skylight in the roof and trying to create a sense of a durable home, not only a well-made house but a sense of participating in a landscape and a community in such a way that you could imagine the next generation wanting to take care of it as well.

I moved in here alone while my family was still next door because I was sick and didn't want to be coughing on them. And it was a total blessing. I was lying flat out on the couch, looking up through the skylight, for most of those few delirious weeks. It was the rainy season and quite a memorable one; we hadn't had that much rain in 150 years. It was black, and sheets of water were coming down onto that 6-by-6-foot skylight that's 3 inches thick and weighs 700 pounds. It doesn't really have a good reason to be there except we wanted to be able to watch the sky. It made me so aware of the fragility of our little purchase on this place. I was seeing something that hadn't happened in 150 years; I was witnessing part of the process that caused huge problems and misery for a lot of people—mudslides, runoff, and pollution in the bay. I was witnessing a small act of trying to mitigate that damage by how the water is shed off the hill, off this roof, and into a carefully graded yard that isn't putting water back into the bay, isn't running down the slope.

Your practice begins with an elemental principle of the illusion of abundance and how to respond to that in your work and the way you lead your life, intertwining the two.

Arnold: It's funny because, on one hand, it has nothing to do with architecture. It has to do with landscape and how architecture fits within that landscape and creates this thing called settlement. But the truth is, my heart really warms when I think about the first architectural act allowing, promoting, fostering, and nourishing this thing that makes a landscape and a community worth living in. First and foremost, you have to love it. It's architecture that allows you to love something—or not love it. We mostly build architecture that separates us from the natural world, from our neighbor, from creation, from a sense of connectedness. By puncturing that roof and peeling away these walls, we are reconnecting to that landscape. I have gone through the mental exercise of if you replicated this model indefinitely, what would be the result, and I actually believe in courtyard architecture and courtyard urbanism as a viable model. What starts as love, architecture makes happen, and then out of that you can start to have a conversation about the environment or about cities.

When I started our conversation, I thought, architecture has nothing to do with it; let's talk about those other things. But upon reflection, it's actually architecture that tends that little flame and makes things possible.

There's really just one word in there that's the critical one—"love." If you don't feel something about that landscape or that sky or that sun or that tree or the child that is playing in it or what that might bring alive in her, who cares what the architecture is? And if you're not one to take a risk to make an architecture that causes that love, I don't think the other conversations are going to get off the ground about what we do about our overtaxed, overstressed landscape and cities, which are the same things ultimately.

PART 2

History, Tradition, Change

To look forward, architects must look back. The designers in this section—keenly aware of those who came before—discuss the dynamic tension between established forms and innovation. Some are modernists, some are postmodernists, some are traditionalists, and all of them know their history.

LaRionda Cottage, 1218–1220 Burgundy Street, New Orleans, Louisiana.
It was built around 1810 and has served many functions.

ROBERT VENTURI AND DENISE SCOTT BROWN

"How do you define the function of a building
if it has housed a range of different activities
over perhaps five hundred years?"

Robert Venturi (b. 1925) has been described as one of the most original talents in contemporary architecture. He graduated summa cum laude in 1947 from Princeton University, where he also received his MFA three years later.

In 1964, Venturi designed a home that has been called the first postmodern building—or in fellow architect Frederic Schwartz's words: "the first postmodern anything." The Vanna Venturi House in Philadelphia—named for his mother, who commissioned it—was featured by PBS in "10 Buildings That Changed America," and it set the stage for a movement away from glass walls and the minimalism that had defined the 1950s and 1960s.

Around the same time his building was rocking the architectural landscape, Venturi published his first book, *Complexity and Contradiction in Architecture* (Museum of Modern Art, 1966), which has been honored with the AIA's Classic Book Award. Six years later, he came out with *Learning from Las Vegas* (MIT Press, 1972), a postmodern classic, written with Steven Izenour and Denise Scott Brown, that describes how the Las Vegas Strip is emblematic of a new architecture. As *Vanity Fair* puts it: "They celebrated the virtues of the ordinary, everyday buildings that most architects were taught to disdain. 'Main Street is almost all right,' they famously said."

Venturi's teaching, lecturing, and writing have received widespread attention and critical review. His awards include the Pritzker Architecture Prize (1991) and the Presidential National Medal of Arts (1992). The founding principal of VSBA (Venturi, Scott Brown and Associates), Robert Venturi retired in 2012, after over fifty years in practice.

Denise Scott Brown (b. 1931) began her collaboration with Robert Venturi in 1960. When the two were married in 1967, they lived for six months in the attic room of the Vanna Venturi House before finding their own place not far away.

Scott Brown participated in the broad range of architectural projects at VSBA and was principal-in-charge for many projects in urban planning, urban design, and campus planning. Her years of experience in interdisciplinary work and teaching contributed to the firm's unusual breadth and depth in architectural design. Since retiring from VSBA, Scott Brown continues to publish and present her work. Her ideas and work as an architect, planner and urban designer, theorist, writer, and educator have influenced architects and planners worldwide.

The couple never considered themselves to be postmodernists, however. As Scott Brown famously said: "Freud was not a Freudian, and Marx was not a Marxist."

"We feel we are modernists," states Robert Venturi, unequivocally.

Robert Venturi and Denise Scott Brown enter the conversation by discussing the importance of learning from historical precedents in architecture (especially when you are intent on overturning them) and the idea of planning for change—the evolving roles of buildings over time.

Denise, I'd like to begin by quoting something from a lecture you gave in 2001. Speaking of an educational sojourn in Venice, you said, "On our travels, our views on function in architecture were again rocked, this time by buildings that had been in use for hundreds of years. Many historic buildings no longer serve their original purposes. How do you define the function of a building if it has housed a range of different activities over perhaps five hundred years? How functional is it to plan for buildings' first uses—the client's program—and not consider how it may adapt to meet change in the unforeseeable future?" What I appreciate in this quote is the presumption of the architect's rather dramatic responsibility in the long-term process of change, especially since I'm interested in thinking about questions of the home over a stretch of time.

Denise Scott Brown: I began thinking of this question of function many years ago as a student, and it came to a climax when I spent a couple of months in Venice. I realized that houses in Venice from the twelfth century were still being lived in today. We architects have a philosophy of function that I think is a wonderful one. We really want to be true to function; we want to make sure our buildings work well. But if you begin to ask what does working well mean when a house is going to be occupied by so many different kinds of families and people over so many years, it can't be the same thing as talking to one family and planning as if they would occupy it for all eternity. What can it be? How can you plan for changes that you can't foresee?

And this isn't, of course, only in houses; it's very much in cities as well. This seemed to be an unanswerable conundrum, but eventually, when I studied city planning, we thought about the fact that you can indeed plan for change itself. And you can make buildings in a certain way so that it will be easier to change their functions over time. One of the things you can do is give enough space. An abundance of space means that you've got greater leeway to change what you want over time, but that's a rather expensive way. Another way is to keep the spans of the structure broad enough so you're not always running into columns when you want to change walls. Another is to keep the structural system mainly near the outside of the building, allowing leeway on the inside. Yet another is to keep the mechanical systems separate from the use spaces to some extent so they can change to serve different kinds of uses. We've evolved the term "generic" to explain the kinds of buildings that do in fact change over time. For example, I'm speaking to you from an old warehouse. We think it was once a roller skating rink from the way the floors are organized, but it has mainly been used for storing goods, and maybe there were some industrial processes here. As architects, we love the generous column base, the even lighting along the perimeter through the walls, and the big high ceilings. It gives us everything we need by way of flexibility. We can try out very large models, and we can get the light we need as architects. No one thought of putting an architect's office in here before, but it serves the purpose beautifully because of the way they planned it.

Robert Venturi: I think I could add a little to that, if I may. With modern architecture in the last century, there was an emphasis on function. The famous phrase "form follows function" came out of the Chicago school. And modernism said that the main idea behind the quality and the form of architecture is function. Now we are rediscovering the idea of the generic loft building, like the building we're in now, which could go from industrial to professional. And there's a long tradition of loft building even in the form of housing, for example in the Italian palazzo of the Renaissance period, starting in the fifteenth century. It was a residence for a noble family that later could become a museum, library, governmental building, embassy; it could evolve over time.

We like to make the analogy of form follows function. It makes me think of the glove that fits over the hand, where every finger is accommodated, versus the idea of the mitten, which is a more general covering of the hand where the fingers can wiggle inside, so to speak, and change. Sometimes form follows function in a literal sense, but I think in general the older tradition of form accommodating functions is more appropriate. The loft building has a long tradition of that, whether it be an industrial mill, a noble palace, or a building like Nassau Hall at Princeton University, which was partly a dormitory and partly classrooms; it was this and that over time. So we should look at function in many ways.

Scott Brown: There are other ways of thinking about function. Mies van der Rohe started out, I think, by talking about general space, although he didn't use the term "general space." Louis Kahn called those general spaces "master spaces," and added to that "service spaces." (He called them "servants spaces," but they really were service spaces.) I began to think in a funny way that those service spaces can be the most public and civic in the building, because very often the corridors become the streets. This can happen in a house, but particularly in academic buildings, where there's never enough common space. So now you have public space and private space as two functional categories, which are much more general than bedroom, living room, dining room, etc.

I think you could look at styles of houses and analyze how each of them mixes public space and private space. In most houses, there's a sequence from the outside, which is public, through the front porch, the front door, and the living room to the private spaces behind and above and then into the private yard in the back, which is different from the more public front yard. I think you could look at all housing sequentially and analyze the relationship between public and private.

This second question also derives from something Denise said, although probably either of you could have said it. You've constructively criticized architects for their belief that "every problem must have a physical solution." You argue that this can lead to a disconnect between ideas and results. May I invite you to come up with a broader definition of the architect's role in addressing urban problems that would include what will always be part of their identity—the desire to find physical solutions for social problems—but might be more realistic and rigorous?

Scott Brown: Architects have this tendency to propose a physical solution for everything because that's what they do and that's what they love. For example, take a school district that has great education problems and also an ancient set of buildings. It may very well be that you would put money first into teacher training and teacher awards rather than into refurbishing the architecture, not because you don't need both, but because the teaching is even more important than the architecture. I think architects fall into trouble when they start using their skills beyond architecture and propose too many physical solutions when their role is at a more statesmanlike level, and they should be thinking of lots of different kinds of physical, social, and political solutions. It takes great creative imagination to build in a very economical way when there are dire problems. And my feeling is real beauty comes once you tackle hard problems in a sober way.

This next question is for Robert. You seem uncomfortable with the label of the intellectual father of the postmodern movement. I thought I'd simply ask you, in what ways is your thought and work *not* postmodern? And how do you think your work will endure and remain current beyond identification with a particular movement?

Venturi: I'd love to quote Denise Scott Brown on this subject. She says, "Freud was not Freudian, and Marx was not a Marxist." And one could say Christ was not a Christian. I think there is a tradition of being misunderstood and being identified with a movement that you're not sympathetic toward. So postmodernism does not make me happy at all. And I think it's a misunderstanding simply for this reason: I'm a modern architect and thinker. I began, in midcentury, to refer to historical examples of architecture, to make historical analogies. It could be called comparative analysis. It was unusual then for modernists to do that. For example, I can refer to the columns of the Parthenon being a certain way and you can learn from that, and that idea can be applicable—not directly or literally, but still effectively—to a modern situation in planning. The comparative analysis is historical. But where postmodernism is literally reviving historical styles, that has nothing to do with what I was saying.

I think also the neomodern architecture that's very fashionable today is a sort of baroque version of the abstract expressionist modernism of the original period. I love the original modernism. I learned from it. If we have any historical reference in our work, it's not literal; it's not direct. It's almost written on the building, so to speak, rather than being a three-dimensional sculpture on the building. So postmodernism has nothing to do with us, and it involves a misunderstanding of what we were saying in our various writings, which was that we could learn from historical reference.

When we went to Las Vegas and wrote our book *Learning from Las Vegas*, we went from emphasizing form—which was a modernist idea—to the idea of symbolism and signage. The signs of Las Vegas taught us the symbolic element that has always been part of architecture: the stained glass windows of cathedrals, the hieroglyphics all over ancient Egyptian architecture, the use of mosaics in Byzantine architecture. We are reacting against the purity of modernism, which says you cannot use ornament and you cannot use symbolism. That is extremely important, but it involves being misunderstood. I think very often if you have good ideas, they are misunderstood.

Through your writing and especially your architectural work, you encourage the return of contextual historicism. It seems that you are arguing for the architect to be inserted into an ongoing conversation with those who came before and those who will come afterward. When

work is mannered and iconoclastic, how is it also in conversation with the intellectual forebearers of the landscape and context you are working in?

Venturi: You will find that most of our answers to questions are complex and contradictory, and that leads to mannerism. Mannerism is a trend in art that we relate to very much. It was historically evident over centuries that where you acknowledge exceptions to the rule, to the convention, you dodge ambiguities. And that's been understood and talked about by critics and artists over time.

The idea of context is an interesting one, and I rather like the idea that I can say that I brought back the idea of context into architecture. I remember when I was a student and I was looking at a book of Gestalt psychology where there was a definition of meaning deriving from context, and I said, "Eureka," a fascinating idea. No one in modernism had talked about the importance of context. Le Corbusier and Frank Lloyd Wright were vital enemies, but they both fed you design from the inside out, meaning the exterior of the building derives only from the reflection of the functions inside. And that means that what's around the building is insignificant. There is a great tradition of buildings being part of a larger context, having an effect in their design on a palazzo or piazza in Rome, and that's a very valid tradition. The idea of context was a new idea then. And it was very relevant and important.

Again, this idea was misunderstood. My great teacher in college said harmony derives from contrast as well as analogy. I like to say you can wear a gray suit with a gray necktie and it's harmonious, analogous. You can wear a gray suit with a red necktie and that can also be harmonious. Or you can be more complex and mannerist and wear a gray suit with a gray necktie with red stripes on it. The context idea was misunderstood as meaning you must absolutely be analogous to what's around you when you design. But it wasn't that. You could be contrasting to it. Very often, it does make sense to evolve out of what's there. But there are moments when it makes sense to be revolutionary instead of evolutionary and to make your new building very different from what's there. All of these things are valid. Context is important, but I think it's been overused and misunderstood by purists who have taken it up.

Scott Brown: I'd like to add that if you think of context as not just the physical surroundings of the building, but the economic, cultural, social, and political as well, and then you think of them not as static in the way we were taught to consider context but as changing, the building changes and the context changes. Now you can think of yourself as surrounded by a set of urban systems that are the context—economic, activities, transportation, etc. Sometimes the systems don't all mesh. They're obeying other rules, and by the time they reach a local site, they can be clashing considerably. Now, whose rules are you to obey in the building? You bend and break quite a few of them to get a building at all; that's just realistic.

So out of that again springs mannerism, the breaking of the rules. In those kinds of situations—and most urban situations are like that—you produce something that is unmannerly, that is bad mannered; it breaks the rules as a mannerist. Maybe the people in the conversation think you have bad English because your conversation is not as literate as they'd want it to be, but it's also accommodating a lot of complexity, satisfying a great many different systems.

> **I realize you have written a whole book to answer this, but I'm going to be shallow and brazen and ask you to please describe for me what you mean by arguing for architecture as "sign and systems for a mannerist time."**

Venturi: Well, let's start with the mannerism. We are in a mannerist period that has to acknowledge complexity and contradiction. There has to be a system, there have to be conventions, but then they have to be broken, and art can derive from that. German historians of art invented the idea of mannerism in the mid-nineteenth century. T. S. Eliot wrote about the importance of ambiguity in art and creativity.

Signs are also important. We like to remind people that "space" was the word you used all through the twentieth century and the modernist period: "architecture as space." And space is important. But there is also the issue of symbolism; the forms that you use aren't just abstract. Significantly, when you talked about architecture as space and not as signs, you also forgot shelter. Even more important than making space is to make a place that can keep out the cold weather, the hot weather, the rain, and all that. So the idea of shelter is important, and the ideas of reference, symbolism, and signage are important. It was so thrilling to go to Las Vegas and learn about signs. Now, when we talk about Las Vegas, we should emphasize that we are talking about the old Las Vegas that we saw in the late 1960s and early 1970s. It's entirely different now, deriving directly from Disneyland.

I think Denise should go from the signs to the systems.

Scott Brown: By adding systems, I was trying to talk about the sober side of architecture, of our work. As modern architects and functionalists, we are into producing shelter that works, that's economical, that's proper. I called the shelter part "systems" because I had augmented it to include all the laws and rules derived from economics and sociology that we have learned about the city. One of my rules has been to take this kind of thinking inside buildings. We do land use and transportation planning inside buildings, particularly in the large complexes that I'm involved with. So systems, in our case, derive from urban disciplines, which we then use creatively as artists to make beautiful architecture.

Do you have any comments on the subject of residential architecture?

Venturi: One of the tragedies of architecture and urbanism over the last century is that there has been no real and effective dealing with the idea of residential architecture. When modernism took over in America, it was essentially a style that came from Europe. The early modernists were mostly Europeans that came here: Walter Gropius, Marcel Breuer, and so forth. The irony was that a lot of their modernism was inspired by American industrial architecture, so it got mixed up.

When I was young and working for an architect, we had to do some governmental housing for low-income people. Automatically, we did what was modern and what the Europeans did at the time, which was to make slab high-rise apartment buildings. They were essentially derived from the wonderful invention of slab buildings by Le Corbusier, the first one being Unité d'habitation in Marseilles, in the early 1950s. We designed a slab building, and it turned out that the low-income people in America did not want to live in that kind of building. They wanted to live in single-family houses. They had hoped that they could improve their condition and become bourgeois. The irony was that, in Europe, the proletariat was distinguished as low income and they would live in high-rises. In America, there was no proletariat class; it was believed that those people were temporarily low income, and they would increase their wealth and their standing and then they were going to move into houses. And it's so interesting that the building I designed, which is only about a mile and a half from where our office is now, was blown up. It was one of those buildings that had to be blown up because they were not appreciated by the people who lived in them and could not be maintained. Now sitting on that site is a low-rise building that connects with the American suburban ideals.

Another significant question is the ideal of Le Corbusier's Cité Radieuse [Radiant City], where you tear down the whole city and begin all over again. You built a great big park and then you put these independent high-rise buildings all over the place. That never worked in America in terms of community. People living in those places were not part of a community; there was no Main Street. There was a wonderful writer who brought this idea back—Jane Jacobs. She wrote about the significance of the everyday. I also got involved in that in my writing. The idea of an architecture that can encourage community was, to some extent, lost. One way to make community is not to make independent high-rises sitting in parks but to make streets. And another way to make community is to encourage signage and enhance the opportunity for communication. Those are things that continue to interest us.

Scott Brown: There's a question I'd like to answer. Wasn't there anything good about postmodernism? And the answer is yes, of course there was. After World War II, there was enormous religious and philosophical questioning of values. People said that after the Holocaust, there can be no innocence left in society. Someone wrote a book called *God Is Dead*. There was an opening up to values of people other than oneself and a questioning of the fact that people like architects felt they had the message and everyone else was wrong. So that side of postmodernism—being open to values, being remorseful and afraid of false innocence, questioning vision, being very socially concerned—we were part of that, and we came out of that. We were also responding to and part of a growing interest in popular culture, trying to understand the complexity of the social mix in this country. But the architectural side of postmodernism got taken up by completely different people and agendas and was basically commercialized.

Venturi: I think that is a good point. We're accommodating low culture, high culture, many kinds of culture. We're not imposing one ideal, upper-bourgeois culture on everybody. The great sociologist Herbert Gans, who moved into Levittown (New Jersey) and wrote books on it, taught us a lot about that. When we did our study of Las Vegas, we shocked people by saying, "Hey, let's look at this. Let's not just be snooty about it." Denise and I want to emphasize the importance of the social dimension of architecture, which can be lost so easily.

Pueblo Ribera Court, 230 Gravilla Street, La Jolla, California, was designed by
Rudolph Schindler in 1923. It was inspired by Native American pueblo villages.

KENNETH FRAMPTON

"Another aspect is the tension in the modern movement between avant-gardism and the idea of a home."

Kenneth Frampton (b. 1930) is a prominent British architect, critic, historian, and professor of architecture at Columbia's Graduate School of Architecture and Planning. The leading design firm Knoll has described Frampton as "architecture's sharpest and most prolific lecturer and writer."

Frampton achieved notoriety (and influence) in architectural education with his essay "Towards a Critical Regionalism" (first published as part of *The Anti-Aesthetic: Essays on Postmodern Culture*, Bay Press, 1983). In his essay, Frampton assumed a critical stance toward postmodernism, with its whimsy and ornamentation; but he also derided the placelessness and lack of identity of Internationalism. Instead, he proposes architecture rooted in the modern tradition yet tied to its geographical and cultural context. By becoming more "local" in its forms, a home becomes more connected to regional weather patterns. As Frampton put it in his essay: "Critical Regionalism necessarily involves a more directly dialectical relation with nature [.]"

He has authored many books, including *American Masterworks: The Twentieth-Century House* (Rizzoli, 1995) and *Modern Architecture: A Critical History* (Oxford University Press, 1980). A collection of Frampton's writings over a period of thirty-five years was published under the title *Labour, Work and Architecture* (Phaidon, 2002).

Frampton studied architecture at the Guildford School of Art and later at the AA (Architectural Association School of Architecture) in London.

Kenneth Frampton, on the issue of tradition and change, discusses the tension between avant-gardism and nostalgia. He points out how the work of Frank Gehry and other star architects, while impressive, have "a strange kind of spectacular rootlessness." Innovation has a price, says Frampton, but so does kitsch sentimentality. Looking toward the future, Frampton suggests we may need to abandon the notion of an individual home altogether in favor of more communal, high-density housing.

At the risk of being reductive, as you have been richly and diversely prolific, one might characterize your work as that of an architectural historian engaged in a project to define American architectural modernism in immutable terms. Do you think American architectural modernism has gone "off message"? And if so, what has that meant for housing?

Kenneth Frampton: Of course, one could say it's not just American architectural modernism that has gone off message. But if we concentrate for a moment on America, I think it's good to think about the Case Study House Program, which was launched by John Entenza in Southern California after the Second World War, and the postwar idea of the good life in California in relation to those houses. A lot of the young families that were clients of the Case Study houses and similar houses of that period were very ready to live a modern life, which was perhaps easier to do in the climate of Southern California than elsewhere. It's very clear that the modern American domestic tradition in the twentieth century reached some kind of fulfillment in Los Angeles in the forty years between the mid-1920s and the mid-1960s. On the East Coast, upwardly mobile or middle-class people with money tend neither to live in modern houses nor to have a particularly modern lifestyle. Robert Stern will do buildings that are recognizably modern with a capital *M*. But most of his upper-middle-class clients, at least as far as residential architecture is concerned, want a pseudo-colonial house. And that's what they get.

One might add that the so-called New Urbanism has advocated the same nostalgic imagery, basically. And it's fused with the American home-building real estate industry in terms of what is salable. I believe that certain banks, on the East Coast anyway, have second thoughts about loaning money to build modern houses because of their perceived lack of resale value. So a kind of middle-class and upper-middle-class consensus has developed about what is a desirable residence. The imagery is more or less simulated, but the actual details of the windows, the entrance, and all the rest are very crudely handled. They're not refined works.

Another aspect is the tension in the modern movement between avant-gardism and the idea of a home. Frank Lloyd Wright was very successful at creating a progressive, middle-class American image of the home without being kitsch. He brought this to a particularly high level in the Usonian houses, between 1932 and 1940, more or less. He must have built, in his life span, something like two hundred

Usonian houses. I've often said to students that I think that house was the last attempt to render the American suburb as a place of culture for middle-class people with relatively limited means. There isn't a continuation of that culture in quite the same way as Wright intended. We could think of that as "going off message," to use your terminology.

Your question made me think of Clarence Stein, who, in the 1950s, published a book called *Toward New Towns for America*, which was about the greenbelt resettlement towns that were built under the Roosevelt New Deal. They weren't Wrightian, but they were remarkable middle-class communities. Collective housing of that quality is very hard to find in the United States at this moment.

What do you mean by saying that Wright created an "image of the home without being kitsch"?

Frampton: What I mean is that the imagery should not be nostalgic. It should convey a sense of well-being through the organization of space, the quality of the materials, the refinement of the detailing, the convenience of the arrangement of fittings and furnishings, and the refinement of the landscape in relation to it being a closed, domestic domain. I think one could specify all those values without any of them being overdetermined from a nostalgic point of view.

When you were writing *American Masterworks: The Twentieth-Century House*, what criteria guided your choices? What formal considerations and design expressions were you collecting together in the book?

Frampton: I've often asked myself, "What is it that justifies including a particular house in the book rather than another?" If you think about what is produced, lots of houses could be characterized as modern. So why select a certain one? It's not just intuition. Part of it has to do with image, in that all thirty-four houses represented in the book have a very striking and immediately apparent image. In talking to students and other colleagues, I've always been rather loath to use the term "image," but this question of an image of a work is important. It's not sufficient for the work to have a strong image if when you go closer and get inside it, there's nothing else. I thought about including a John Lautner house, but what's disappointing about Lautner is that while the image is powerful, when you go deeper into the houses, they're rather loosely formulated. There's not much care taken with the details. There's no follow-through with Lautner houses. They're all rhetoric, both inside and out.

I coined from my own usage a concept of "micro space." I think the way the interior of the space is articulated in relation to the human body and in relation to the overall frame of the house is extremely important. A particularly good example of that is Rudolph Schindler's Kings Road House, where however delicate (sometimes to the point of fragile) Schindler's furniture is, the relationship of the scale of that furniture to the light and to the windows is all very integrated without being oppressive.

Those qualities are very evident in the houses of Frank Lloyd Wright, of course. But they are also present in Richard Neutra's work. Neutra and Schindler were both, in a way, acolytes of Wright. But apart from Wright, and together with Gregory Ain and others, Neutra and Schindler created the Southern California style. Certainly Pierre Koenig could be included in that group, but I am also thinking of someone more of Ain's generation—J. R. Davidson maybe. In Esther McCoy's book on California architects, *The Second Generation* [Gibbs Smith, 1984], she deals with this generation that came after Wright, including Raphael Soriano and Harwell Hamilton Harris. These people aren't Wrightian, but they follow the line coming from Wright. They pay extremely close attention to the hierarchical space inside the house, the sequence of spaces, and the scale as the body moves through the house.

For the book, I tried to select houses where that was the case, where the impact of the image was manifested in what happens afterward. I included a Craig Ellwood house, Frank Lloyd Wright's Usonian house, Steven Holl's house in Texas, and an art deco residence in Cranbrook by Eliel Saarinen, which is the first in the sequence. All of them have this quality, I think.

I suppose if you tried to push back a bit further, you would come to the English Arts and Crafts house and to architects like Richard Norman Shaw, where the character of the house is to some extent an expression of both the architect and the client, and also of a way of life. I think one could argue that the English Arts and Crafts house was to a certain degree nostalgic for a vernacular that no long existed and was some exemplification of a "country life." Both the architect and the client valued that country life, and the character of the house was very much bound up with that.

Perhaps one could say the same of the American architect Henry Hobson Richardson. But the image of Richardson's houses is slightly different. It's more patrician than the British Arts and Craft house. It seems to me that Richardson, after the Civil War, has a very clear idea of what could be an alternative American civilization. That is what Wright inherits from Richardson. The greatness of Richardson lies in the fact that after the Civil War, he is able to imagine and realize both public buildings and domestic works that represent the United States as something other than a secondhand version of European culture. The European Romanesque becomes the vehicle for Richardson to express an American culture both publicly and privately. Wright builds on that and tries to take it further with more originality—much more, of course.

A lot of your work studies important individual architects, often highlighting emerging innovators. What is it about our times that we are suddenly celebrating our more accomplished architects as cultural stars? Their prominence seems to be based on the hope and expectation that they

are solving some social challenges for us. Are they addressing the right problems?

Frampton: Recently, I was asked by Thames and Hudson to write an additional chapter to the book *Modern Architecture: A Critical History* to cover 1985 to 2005. An enormous production of architecture has taken place worldwide in those twenty years. It was virtually impossible to select what to include and what to exclude. I mention that because in the introduction to that chapter, I talk about this question of the brand or the celebrity architect—the star architect—and the way such architects have a tendency to become almost commodities in themselves and the problematic character of the work. These people are talented, of course, but the work has a strange kind of spectacular rootlessness. Frank Gehry is the prime example, but there are other figures, of course, like Rem Koolhaas and so on.

Are they addressing the right problems? Well, I don't think they're solving any social challenges. They're simply doing spectacular work. It is dramatic, theatrical, at its best a sort of overwhelming spectacle. It's particularly true of Gehry, for example, of his Guggenheim Museum in Bilbao. When you enter the building, there's nothing in it. It's really a substandard structure inside; once you finish with the spectacular skin and the shape, the building has no quality. Disney Hall, in Los Angeles, may be the best building of that genre that he's done, but he's also stuck with that genre.

The system of star architecture takes place at a price. All over the world are very talented architects who could do superior work, but some clients aren't even open to the possibility. They simply want the name. And going for the name is a closed circuit.

Sadly, the competition system has always been rather weak in the United States. Whereas in some European countries, for example, in Scandinavia in general and Finland in particular, also Spain, a lot of public building is decided by competition. It may be changing now, but it was a very different cultural proposition in which municipal governments of medium-sized communities would hold a competition for a particular public building, either a completely open competition, which wasn't always a good idea, or a limited competition, which would often produce better results. In the United States, people just don't hold competitions. Trustees decide to hire an architect, or the developer wants a certain architect. So there is no competition; the person is just commissioned.

The problem is at the level of architectural culture in the society as a whole. Newspapers ought to be able to do that job of evaluating architecture and educating the public. But it's very difficult to develop in the society a culture of architecture that is broader, less prone to manipulation by the media, and less subject to fashion. The whole question of intercity competition with brand architects is a closed loop. I don't want to say that buildings of quality never get produced that way. The Guthrie Theater, by Jean Nouvel, in Minneapolis, for example, might be better than usual. I don't know; it's hard to judge by the photos.

There are good architects in this country: Steven Holl, for example. I suppose he is on the edge of being a celebrity architect, but he's an architect of real quality. Michael Maltzan is a young Los Angeles architect who is of considerable quality. I think he's much more interesting than Frank Gehry.

In *Studies in Tectonic Culture*, you suggest that modern architecture is as much about structure and construction as it is about space and abstract form, and you study a long history of architecture as a constructional craft. Please talk about the theme of the book and its relationship to our present moment in residential design.

Frampton: In the end, it comes down to the idea of relative autonomy, of certain artistic fields versus others. One of the aspects of architecture from the point of view of relative autonomy is that it is constructed. This makes it very distinct from figurative art and even from quite a lot of abstract art. It's very distinct from film, theater, dance, and so on. You could say that the fact that it is constructed is fundamental. The subtitle to *Studies in Tectonic Culture* is *The Poetics of Construction in Nineteenth and Twentieth Century Architecture*. And the attempt, in writing that book for teaching purposes, is to constantly emphasize this question of the constructed work and the poetics of that discourse of structure and construction as a modern tradition that goes back a long way, and as some kind of guarantee, in a sense, that one would resist the reduction of architecture to superficial images, to cinegraphic form, and to spectacle. So even though I use the term "image" in relation to the house—and I think the image work of architecture has importance— that image should be integral with its spatial organization, its structure, and its construction. It should be inseparable from those other dimensions. That's what *Studies in Tectonic Culture* was trying to argue for.

As for this present moment in residential design, I've often said to myself (and sometimes to students, but not so much publicly) that one of the problems that the architectural profession and schools of architecture face is that the true challenge of residential design is ignored or refused. The challenge is how to imagine a viable land settlement pattern for a modern middle class that is capable of giving the image of shelter, security, and home but is not kitsch. It's a complex question that has to be formulated on a wide front.

You could argue that the individual house is a problem in itself. In the end, I would argue that one shouldn't live in individual houses; one should live more collectively. In the past, I've been involved with low-rise, high-density housing, and I still believe in the concept. But it is very difficult to convince the society that one can live a valued middle-class life like that. Such is the unreal premium placed by clients, banks, and mortgage companies on the individual private house standing on its own ground.

LEE MINDEL

"I would go back to the Shakers because of their celebration of light, simple materials, and honesty. They were driven by function, but they celebrated craftsmanship. Each thing they put their hands to was a joyous experience."

Lee F. Mindel (b. 1954) is considered the most prominent interior designer in New York, with clients like Ralph Lauren and Sting. Combining borderline minimalism with a warm sense of welcome, his work has been called "compassionate" by the critic Joseph Giovannini. Mindel's innovative ideas about how we conceive of home have led him to be inducted into the Interior Design Hall of Fame.

He loves, among other things, to travel. "Rome is one of my favorite cities because you can see where it all began," says Mindel. He always stays at the Hotel Hassler above the Spanish Steps with its breathtaking overview of the city. Deeply reverential of historical precedent, Mindel packs a minimum of four cameras to record inspiration where he finds it. He describes openly weeping in front of buildings by Louis Kahn, deeply moved "by their simplicity, their rigor and restraint."

Mindel established Shelton, Mindel & Associates in 1978, two years after receiving his MArch from Harvard University. The firm (which changed its name to SheltonMindel after Peter Shelton's untimely death in 2012) has been awarded many honors for its work in the field, including numerous awards for interior architecture from the AIA and the Society of American Registered Architects, a Progressive Architecture citation, three Roscoe awards for product design, and the American Architecture Award from the Chicago Athenaeum in 2004 and 2009.

Attic of a Shaker Centre family dwelling, north of Route 68 and State Route 33, Harrodsburg, Kentucky. It is part of a National Historic District known as Shaker Village at Pleasant Hill.

Lee Mindel, when asked for historical precedents that have influenced him, begins with Stonehenge: "Then I would have to skip forward to Lou Kahn." He avoids the word "style," however, for it implies a certain rigidity that is frozen in time. "It shouldn't function as a style; it should function as problem solving. As long as it really solves the problem, it becomes authentic." The issue of style, furthermore, is subjective, according to Mindel: "Everybody's references are based on where they tap into history."

I told you a little bit about the project. It is inspired by the book *American Homes: The Illustrated Encyclopedia of Domestic Architecture*, by Lester Walker, which is basically a visual survey of American homes.

Lee Mindel: That is a fantastic book. You know what it reminds me of? It's the Al Hirschfeld of architecture where in one line, instead of getting Marlo Thomas's nose job, you get the whole Queen Anne. It's the economy of line and the economy of that discourse that can be conveyed in a line drawing. We have always used that book in the office, because definitions have gotten screwed up as to what things are. Take, for example, your generation, who grew up during the period of postmodernism. That is probably your definition of classic architecture, which it really isn't. Everybody's references are based on where they tap into history. As a result, the definitions have no meaning anymore. I'll give you an example. We've nicknamed a style in Manhattan "Jewish Colonial," which is a whole thing that happens on Park Avenue. But it is happening everywhere since there isn't a Vitruvian education. The lexicon out there is not the classical education of the history of architecture and art that you might get in Europe. And I remember loving and being thirsty for H. W. Janson's *History of Art* and James Ackerman's *Distance Points: Studies in Theory and Renaissance Art and Architecture*. But I was a lucky guy to get to do that; it really helped me understand the history. But if you grow up in the pop culture now, the references do not go back to the origins. That book *American Homes*, thank God, at least was a tangible thing that you could put in front of somebody's nose and say, "What do you think of that? What does that mean to you?" So it almost became a translator to understand what people understood and how you could communicate that.

People will come in and say, "I want it to look like it was always there. I want it to be clean, modern, and contemporary, but I want a traditional overtone." All that stuff means absolutely nothing. But when you put it in animation or in a book and synthesize what its purest state was, that gives people a quick education. I'm all for *American Homes* because it's a reference that's authentic and not editorialized. When you look at Walker's drawings of Richard Neutra or Le Corbusier, or even go back to a Shaker, Federal, or Queen Anne house, in the economy of line, he has distilled the idea, and that's really helpful. It's like getting the dictionary out and understanding what the styles really mean.

Do you think that since so many older styles are being built now, people don't realize what's really traditional and what's not, and when a style began?

Mindel: Style—and I hate the word "style" by the way—really ends up being the vocabulary of an idea that gets extruded out. But when any of those styles were created, they were not traditional because they were breaking from something and inventing something new. Looking back, they seem traditional because they are sanctioned fifty or one hundred years later. So, in a way, nothing is traditional but everything becomes traditional. We had clients who just bought a house, and they said, "It's traditional eighties." Now there you have it.

It's a big world out there. There are people doing historic work and people doing challenging work. But there's the pure and good of everything. It depends on how it's done, the context, the authenticity, and the intent. It shouldn't function as a style; it should function as problem solving. As long as it really solves the problem, it becomes authentic. The penmanship might find its way into a style or vocabulary, but it's solving a problem that differentiates interesting work.

How do you think the Web has changed design?

Mindel: The Internet is a good thing and a bad thing, as everything is. The bad thing about it is the instant gratification that has reduced the attention span to that of a double click. The good thing is how you can use the double click to attain information and have a bigger attention span. People ask me what my favorite book is. I certainly don't read enough, but my favorite book is the Internet. I can sit with my laptop, which is a book, and I can get any information. I'll be scratching my head, thinking that this thing we're doing is reminiscent of Le Corbusier's Villa Schwob, which is logged into some latent brain part. Type "Villa Schwob" into Google and there's the elevation. Yeah! Before, you used to have to go into the library; you were focused, not so distracted. Now it's harder, but if you can channel it in the right way, the accessibility of the Internet is unbelievable.

What styles have influenced you?

Mindel: I hate to call them styles, but I would say that a broad education of appreciating architecture as an expression of a time and a place has influenced me. I wouldn't say there was one style that I would dismiss. Postmodernism is a little hard to swallow because of the cartoon aspect of it. But then again, Robert Venturi and Denise Scott Brown's idea of "complexity and contradiction" and their book *Learning from Las Vegas* take something of the magic of the popular culture of that period and extrude it into bizarre caricatures. But in its purest state, postmodernism came out of strict modernism. Robert Venturi, thank God, said, hey, wait a second, there's something in the culture that shouldn't be eradicated, and that may be worth celebrating. I'm thankful for that. But postmodern shopping malls are unbelievably depressing. I'd almost prefer a 1930s post office extruded out into a strip mall to broken brass arches and all kinds of other stuff going on.

I don't have a favorite; there's something to learn from every one of those periods of architecture. And that's what's so interesting. You take each of those pictures in Walker's book and a whole story unfolds. It's larger than the style. The early Federal-style buildings had to do with heating, conserving, and enclosure. Then things opened up and technology changed. Each of those approaches gave people a vocabulary and the ability to do different things. When they are abused, they are my least favorite; when they are in their purest form, they become my most favorite—whether it's a beautiful and authentic Georgian house or the magnificence of Chandigarh, both by Louis Kahn and by Le Corbusier, or the High Museum of Art in Atlanta. Each one of those things is magical because it's an expression of something pure in that moment and time. We cherish that as part of the culture.

Whose work has influenced and motivated you, and how has it informed what you do?

Mindel: I would go back to the Shakers because of their celebration of light, simple materials, and honesty. They were driven by function, but they celebrated craftsmanship. Each thing they put their hands to was a joyous experience. That has influenced so many people, including Donald Judd and Luis Barragán.

Of course, you go back to Stonehenge, because that's the most honest thing of all: How do you get something off the ground and support it? It's fantastic. It's so old, but it's timeless. Palladio and Vitruvius tried to document something. It was about order. It gave people a reference tool, a guide that standardized things. Proportion and its relationship to the human body were really thought out.

Then I would have to skip forward to Lou Kahn. He was working in a moment when everybody was running in a different direction. They were consumed with style, and he was consumed with Stonehenge, a kind of primal response. They weren't always successful buildings, I don't think. Raymond Meier, the Swiss photographer, has the most beautiful book on Kahn's buildings in Bangladesh [*Louis Kahn Dhaka*, 2004], and you've seen Nathaniel Kahn's film *My Architect*, I'm sure.

I would throw into that Alvar Aalto and the Scandinavians. "Decoration" and "ornament" are dirty words among modernists. It's still the same old conflict over ornamentation being "sissy stuff." Don't fall prey to ornamentation of things in space because they demean an idea; they're dirty and impure. I really respect Eliel Saarinen, out of Cranbrook. He and his son, Eero, were weavers and craftsmen. I think it is inspiring that they considered every part of the environment as an opportunity to reiterate their design philosophy and make a space better.

And then you have McKim, Mead & White. I find their work a little grandiose, but civically it was fantastic because it looked to Stonehenge, it looked to Vitruvius, and it asked, "How do we exude that kind of power in our new society in America?"

And when it's used to a civic end, it's really amazing. When it's used to a residential end, it's a little bit *Lifestyles of the Rich and Famous*. I can't imagine New York without the Metropolitan Museum. The Metropolitan Museum is like a gateway, a formality, to Central Park. Frankly, I think the best building in New York is Central Park, because it creates a void that's magical in the whole density of everything. So I think I have to throw Frederick Law Olmsted in there, too, for using landscape to create a space without which there would be utter chaos. When you walk through it, you think about everything in there being brought in by man. It's overwhelming to think of the purposefulness and power of architecture and design.

Richard Meier—we can't avoid the contribution he has made. He's his own worst enemy in a way, because the work is so pure that it sometimes precludes anything else from happening. But then most of the time nothing else has to happen; you don't want anything else to disturb what's going on there. It's unbelievably strong, poignant, and beautiful. There are so many people—Zaha Hadid, Richard Gluckman, Herzog & de Meuron, Glenn Murcutt from Australia, Frank Gehry.

When you're staring at the blank canvas of a site, what inspires you?

Mindel: I always think if you go into an open field, there's nothing that gives you a gauge by which to understand perspective. The minute you take a frame and put it in the field, what you see through the frame and around the frame is different. Architecture frames the environment. When the environment is dealt with well, architecture can transform the environment.

Process, to me, is more important than result. It's the process that we grow from, that we learn everything from, that we share with each other, and that we communicate. And that's what it's really all about. It's a way of communicating your time and doing something connected to your culture, and that's really exciting.

ERIC OWEN MOSS

"Every house doesn't have to be Fallingwater. . . .
So Fallingwater by example might illustrate
what's technically possible in a complicated
environment."

Architect Eric Owen Moss (b. 1943) has been called a "game changer" by *Metropolis* magazine. Philip Johnson referred to him as a "jeweler of junk," thanks to his gift for twisting everyday materials into eye-catching forms. There are ten published monographs on the work of Moss's office, EOM, founded in 1973.

"'Making It New'—the aspiration to uncover new ways to think, to feel, to see, and to understand architecture—is the departure point for Eric Owen Moss Architects. . . . We avoid traditional organization strategies, standardized design solutions, and any notion of architecture as simply a repetitive style," as stated on the firm's website.

Moss received his BA from UCLA in 1965 and MAs from Berkeley (1968) and Harvard (1972). He has taught at SCI-Arc, and was appointed its director in 2002.

The Moss-designed Lawson Westen House has been called "a geometric amalgamation of concrete, steel, glass and wood . . . engineered as livable modern art" by the *Los Angeles Times*, which goes on to sum up the structure: "A jigsaw puzzle of large poured concrete blocks suggests a baker's hat with a large tilted window carved out of its center."

Throughout his career, Moss has been passionate about revitalizing decaying urbanity—particularly in his own Los Angeles neighborhood, Culver City—with exciting, whimsical forms, whether in home design or parking structures. But it is whimsy that respects context: "Building has an obligation, always larger than itself, to the city and the culture it intends to join," as stated on his website.

Frank Lloyd Wright's Fallingwater, on State Route 381 near
Mill Run, Pennsylvania. The house was designed in 1935.

For Eric Owen Moss, architecture is an ever-flowing continuum—"It doesn't follow that whatever lesson is learned has to be replicated. As long as the exception continues to exist, it stretches the framework of the discussion." Like Lee Mindel, Moss cautions against the use of a particular style when designing a home: "I think that using learned styles actually takes away experimentation, originality, and individuality." The exceptions and experiments are what make architecture interesting. And it changes constantly, according to Moss, who quotes Heraclitus: "You cannot step into the same river twice."

Describe some of the ideas and trends in architecture that you think should be redressed or confronted critically.

Eric Owen Moss: I think a lot of architects, Norman Foster, Marcel Lods, and Renzo Piano, to some extent, used technique and technology not only as a means to an end but as an end in itself, as an image of what buildings ought to be. Here's a new light, hang it on the wall. Here's a column, here's a beam; make the building out of that. Make it look like an oil rig in the North Sea. I think there came to be a love of the language of structure and industry and assembly line and technology—all of which are specious and dubious, all of which need to be debated because they don't get you to the end that I think the people who use them thought they might. As a matter of fact, by this point in time, I don't think anyone is thinking that the language of industry is necessarily progressive. It might have been in 1930. I think that language is style. You can be a new modernist, you can be a deconstructivist, you can be a New Urbanist, you can be all of those things. I think that using learned styles actually takes away experimentation, originality, and individuality. And to a large extent it divides architects into camps: Like this, hate that; vote for this, vote against that. You can see it in the discussions about rebuilding in New Orleans and the Mississippi Gulf Coast, with all of the debate about New Urbanism.

I just interviewed Robert Ivy yesterday, and he has a lot to say about New Orleans and the issues of style and ecology.

Moss: I know Ivy. I don't know what he has to say about it, but, for instance, my office is in the very early stages of designing a city called Balandra, on the Sea of Cortez, which is an ecological discussion but not an ideological discussion. Meaning, let's make it ecological, but what does that mean? If we bulldozed the hell out of the site, stuffed in the building programs, and then put the site back so you could barely see it, is that ecology?

Our site, which is next to a town called La Paz on the coast of the Sea of Cortez, is about 8 by 5 kilometers. It's huge. It's about an hour and a half from Cabo San Lucas. It's completely unbuilt, so it's a beautiful site. The paradox is that we're trying to find a way to take advantage and to inhabit, to some extent, what is uninhabited. If you didn't go there, you wouldn't know it was beautiful. If you go there too much, it's not beautiful anymore. The question is how to preserve the qualities that make it extraordinary, or even exaggerate those qualities, and still make it possible for people to use it as a resort, housing, office, research and development, as any number of things.

On top of that came a requirement from the owner, Miguel Alemán, that it be Mexican, which is another interesting point. Alemán is the grandson of the first civilian president of Mexico. The road you take into Mexico City is called Viaducto Miguel Alemán. The family is in media, they've got an airline, they've got politics, all of that stuff. We got into a discussion about what is Mexican, what is global. He said please don't make it Ixtapa or Cancún or Waikiki or Monaco or Jamaica. But we didn't know what Mexican was, and by saying it's Mexican, he's introducing an aspect in this global discussion that is not conventionally addressed. When somebody talks about "global," I think they're talking about Americans in Western Europe getting on airplanes to Johannesburg, or to St. Petersburg, and bringing themselves with them.

How can residential work be socially transformative?

Moss: Every house doesn't have to be Fallingwater. I think when architecture and city making get interesting, it doesn't follow that whatever lesson is learned has to be replicated. As long as the exception continues to exist, it stretches the framework of the discussion. So Fallingwater, by example, might illustrate what's technically possible in a complicated environment. But somebody could look at that and say, "Get the hell out of there and leave the waterfall alone." That's an argument, a Sierra Club argument.

When we worked with Alemán, he essentially said, "I don't know how to do this but I've got a lot of ideas, and what I don't want to do is come in as a card-carrying environmentalist saying: build less, environment better; build more, environment worse." Therefore, we looked at different approaches. We gave him four options for making the city, four very different ways of examining that discussion. In an intellectual sense, the options we presented have to do with a tension between possibilities.

I think the experience of being alive has to do with tension. I think that's where the interesting possibilities are, in the contradictions between possibilities. For me, it's much more interesting than saying, "I'm a deconstructivist. I would never make something symmetrical. Couldn't do it." I would never say that. I think the tension between those possibilities, a space that balances in a traditional sense and imbalances in a less traditional sense because they're both hypotheses, they're both aspects. They're part of the circumstances in which we live. Environmentalism is the same way.

Ninety percent—I think this is right—of the creatures who have ever lived on Earth are gone, and you can't write that off to Enron or Exxon, in spite of their flaws. Or George W. Bush, in spite of his flaws, which are colossal. It's not so much the progressives' idea that there is a solution somewhere at the end to leukemia, to pollution, to environmentalism; there actually isn't. There are only provisional paradigms, and they come and they go. This is my experience of the world. So your life is provisional if you want to live it that way, and it's possible to build in very contradictory aspects in buildings.

Would you say that the urtext for this was Robert Venturi's *Complexity and Contradiction in Architecture*?

Moss: I think both Charles Moore and Robert Venturi are reactions to Lou Kahn. I think the best, most interesting students turn over what they've learned. In a sense, both Moore and Venturi said, "Well, what the developers do isn't that bad, maybe we learn a little bit from it. It doesn't have to be Mondrian red, blue, yellow, black, white, and gray, Bauhaus, thank you very much. How about a little magenta? How about a little pastel?" That argument is a very old argument. It doesn't come from Venturi; it comes from Heraclitus, who says you can't step into the same river twice. What I'm saying is that this idea—that the experience of living is not an ideologue's experience; it's a contradictory experience—comes from a lot of sources much deeper than *Complexity and Contradiction*. I would take the discussion out of the context of architecture. I think architecture spent the twentieth century running around trying to copy whatever was intellectually fashionable, to its detriment.

You don't think architecture led intellectually?

Moss: We had a big debate about this when we were talking about the city on the Sea of Cortez. Somebody said Le Corbusier did Algiers. Okay, take a look at the Algiers plan. Now go back and look at Georges Braque, Juan Gris, and Pablo Picasso. It's a cubist image. It belongs to cubism. Nothing wrong with cubism, it's a way of breaking down and looking at the world. I think architecture in that period of time, certainly in Le Corbusier's hands, had something to do with a broader conception of art. Here comes Le Corbusier saying, hey, Henry Ford, great guy, assembly line. Why don't we make houses like that? After Juan Gris, after Henry Ford. My thesis adviser at Harvard was Kenzo Tange. He was a part of the movement called the Metabolists. Tange, Kisho Kurokawa, and Kiyonori Kikutake were part of a number of very interesting, unusually talented Japanese architects whose analog for architecture was this metabolic process of the human body. So we've got Metabolism, Henry Ford, and Juan Gris.

To extrapolate from an intellectual movement to an architectural movement has always been a kind of sloppy intellectual process. So you've got cubism, you've got Henry Fordism, you've got Metabolism, you've got deconstruction. The sources of those ideas that architecture glommed on to are outside of architecture. They belong to a certain idea either of art or of engineering and technical prowess and progress, which are still very much with us. A lot of architects work that way and think the ideal in architecture is an expression of the technology that makes it so. That's a belief system. That's a believer's architecture. I'm interested in it, but I've never been a believer.

I used to give a lecture called "The Square with No Corners." That would be idiomatic of this office, if I could draw that. Can you draw a square with no corners? That comes from a Lao Tsu book that I read. Lao Tsu talks about the square with no corners, which is a kind of contradiction and in a way a resolution of the contradiction. What's interesting is a lot of the stuff you're doing is very intellectual, cerebral, conceptual, philosophical. We could sit in Piper Auditorium at Harvard and debate it, but the experience of the building, it all goes away. In other words, somebody could analyze T. S. Eliot's *The Waste Land* and talk about the sources—Sanskrit, China, Elizabethan literature, the Second World War—but what's remarkable about the poem is that when you're done, it's obviously something entirely new and it's an art piece. It's a lyric. I would say that the lyrical side of architecture is what architecture is. That's how architecture says what it is. But because of people like you, and to some extent people like me, there's always this obligatory side, which is that somehow you have to talk to clients or the newspaper or television or thirty guys in Johannesburg.

You describe architecture as a partnering and negotiation. Are you suggesting that you can't find the same kind of poetry in architecture because it's a collaboration?

Moss: I don't know if it's the same kind. This is another very difficult discussion. It's better in a way for me to say architecture is architecture rather than to say architecture is business or architecture is politics or art or poetry, sculpture, music, deconstruction, any of those things because you're trying to extrapolate in terms of something that is more public, has money, and has a pragmatic aspect. No doubt about it. My sense is that the most powerful architecture finds a way to make the prosaic other than prosaic, which is no different from what poetry does. It takes conventional language and puts it into a frame of reference in which it has very different kinds of meanings. We could debate all day whether architecture is art or sculpture or business. In the end, unless you build for yourself, I think there has to be an amalgamation of interest and shared concern. But the architecture and the architect remain cross-cultural interpreters in a way.

Thom Mayne, who's a close personal friend of mine, has argued in recent discussions, private and public, that the work his office does comes out of the exigencies of very particular circumstances and solving very particular problems. I think that argument is tactically intelligent because it tells the world: You're dealing with somebody who will talk with you and reason with you, and when you're all done, the kinds of insights or solutions that you're looking for—prosaic, pragmatic, and esoteric—will come out of that exchange of opinions. I'm not sure there's no truth to that.

If you dig a little bit deeper, I think that there are probably other kinds of subjects that get talked about very much. For example, Antoni Gaudí worked for the Catholic Church. I don't know who was listening to whom. I've spent days at the Sagrada Família, looking at it. I think it is in some ways remarkable. You know what I like about it? It's incredibly private, subjective, and personal; therefore, it's incredibly public and objective. It's a little like Franz Kafka. Kafka is such a weird guy—bugs, castles, trials, and all kinds of stuff. Who could have a mind like that? And yet what he writes seems to hit a note in all kinds of people. I know he's not Mick Jagger, but in a certain context of culture, art, literature, and music, Kafka is considered to be very insightful. What is very introverted and subjective is also very extroverted and objective. I don't know what the connections are except for the fact that if Kafka were literally what every critic said he was, why would anybody read him? There must be something in it. Gaudí, too, had that private vision.

You're building a city, and in building a city you become a leader. The choices you make are looked at by those who would follow you. For example, in this case, how do you make a place livable without taking away its beautiful and pristine nature?

Moss: You do it how you define livable. All I am saying is my definition is anything that makes the world different has to take on these intersections, different ways of understanding, inside, outside, private, public, all of that. Otherwise, I think you're dealing with style, and in a narrow sense, you're dealing with business and fashion and style. Money won't necessarily get you architecture. I think somewhere in this discussion there has to be an experience. This is what I was calling the "lyrical" side of architecture, and I think that's a good word.

There's a Danish philosopher I used to be really interested in, Søren Kierkegaard. He used to talk about something called the "dialectical lyric," and I would be happy to steal that term. I think what it means is there is a very dense and contradictory intellectual argument but it's superseded in the end by the result of the book or the music or the poem or the building that synthesizes something that, in an intellectual sense, may never be synthesizable. You can argue about contradictions in making something in the language that architecture uses, which is not verbal. Architecture can make you cry. It doesn't do it a lot, but it can do that. It can make you giggle, too.

Did Sagrada Família make you cry?

Moss: I thought it was very funny. It made me laugh. It turned my stomach. In the basement, they have a lot of models, so you could see how Gaudí studied it and how carefully it was done. There's nothing frivolous or accidental about it, and yet there's an inconsistency between the conceptual study and the implementation because of the technique and technology of the construction. It's rougher as implementation. There's always this very interesting gap. You write a word, and you publish it. The word as it's published, unless you have a bad editor, is pretty much the word you wrote. You make a drawing in architecture, glass, steel, space; the results are not necessarily exactly that. It depends. Le Corbusier worked on the city of Chandigarh, between Punjab and Haryana provinces, in northwest India. If you look at the High Court Building that Le Corbusier did in the 1950s, you can see, for example, the results of women walking around with buckets of concrete on their heads and scaffolding that looks like twigs. That actually never bothered me. Chandigarh is a peculiar city for a lot of reasons, in particular because all the buildings look like they were done by Le Corbusier.

When I interviewed Venturi, he was saying Le Corbusier is "it"; you've got to study him.

Moss: I think this is a big mistake for architecture. Le Corbusier was an exceptional architect, but I don't know if he was "it," or if anybody is "it." Bob Venturi is not a particularly reverential guy. If I was going to pick somebody that was "it," I would probably pick somebody like Job, to keep it out of architecture. But I think Le Corbusier had a kind of range and versatility, which has an enormous amount of appeal to me. I think if you look at his work over many years, he was getting more interesting as he got older. There are people who don't do that. In fact, I think the process in many cases in architecture is when you hit it at a certain point—and "it" means some kind of recognizable, conceptual, signed object—essentially you begin to replicate it, and I think that's death. I don't think Le Corbusier ever did that.

You're not concentrating much on building residential architecture?

Moss: We are now, but not single-family homes.

If I carried you back thirty years to the Petal House and other early experiments, I wonder if being a new father would lead you to reconsider certain things. I'm simply asking you to meditate on domesticity and how that may translate into different practical decisions in your work.

Moss: One of the houses we did is the Lawson Westen House. There's a book on it. It was done in the early nineties, in West Los Angeles. It's kind of dangerous; you have to climb up, and you can get very high. The wife didn't like heights and wanted solidity; one railing is solid. The husband wanted it open, but it's a house that doesn't define itself operationally in terms of a Sotheby's house listing in the Sunday *New York Times*. I think that what my son Miller has done for me is encourage me to think about some kind of accommodation for living that would continue to build in the aspect of "I don't know" as opposed to "I know." There are people who come in and say I brush my teeth like this, I sleep like this, I want this dark, this light, this big, this small.

With regard to the Lawson Westen House, the kitchen is the center of the building. It's four stories high. Strangely enough, that came out of a very practical discussion with the owners, who entertain their friends in the kitchen. All their friends come over and they love to cook. I don't think they imagined their discussion would be taken so literally that the house is developed around that central focus of their lives. They are also art collectors, so we had to find a way of allowing them to hang all their stuff.

A TV station did a retro feature on the Petal House, and I went back and looked at it. If you look at the roof, it is taken apart; it opens up. There's a Jacuzzi on the roof that looks over the freeway, which is a very different way of exploiting height. There is not another house in that area that allows the owners to get up on top and understand the world in very different ways.

In the Lawson Westen House, you get it from the floor, you get it from the middle, you get it from the top, you go out of the top, and you look at the city. It's a kind of spatial versatility as opposed to being very regularized and predictable. Somebody could come along and say that the sun comes up differently every day, the moon comes out differently, all you have to do is put something in a room on the table and let the world act on it and it will inevitably be different. My argument is to take a little bit more initiative in what makes it different as opposed to saying God did it, the sun did it, the rain did it. The house is a very active participant in this kind of perpetual exploration. The owners of the house are very unusual people, or it never would have been done.

One of the things Tracy Westen will say is that, as he sits in different places and moves through different places, the house continues to open itself up. You don't get to the end of it. It's like reading a book that goes around and around as opposed to reading a book that starts here and ends here.

And that is an experience for a growing mind?

Moss: I think it's an experience for a mind at whatever level in the chronology you happen to be located.

Home at 1225 Martin Avenue, San Jose, California. Designed by the firm of Wolfe & McKenzie, the house is part of a twentieth-century California-style real estate development.

ROBERT A. M. STERN

"In the 1920s and 1930s, when we built suburbs in the United States, many good architects that you've never heard of—I've never heard of them—designed houses. They were thoughtful and true to certain time-honored, vernacular architectural languages, and they were nice houses."

Robert A. M. Stern (b. 1939) is an American architect and dean of the Yale University School of Architecture. He is also a teacher and a writer. While known for his commercial buildings and large-scale condominiums—he has designed some of the tallest structures in America—many of Stern's early works were private homes, and residential architecture continues to be part of his practice.

His architectural style, which he describes as "modern traditionalist," is generally classified as postmodern with a particular emphasis on context and continuity of traditions. His residential work, in particular, relies heavily on local vernacular. Deeply influenced by traditional forms in home design, Stern hosted the television series *Pride of Place: Building the American Dream* (PBS, 1986).

Stern is a fellow of the American Institute of Architects. His work has been exhibited at numerous galleries and universities and is in the permanent collections of museums across the world. In 1976, 1980, and 1996, he was among the architects selected to represent the United States at the Venice Biennale.

Stern worked initially as a designer in the office of Richard Meier in 1966, prior to forming the firm of Stern & Hagmann. In 1977, he founded Robert A. M. Stern Architects (RAMSA), now a 320-person firm, where he is senior partner and personally directs the design of each of the firm's projects, including many single-family homes. The Brooklyn-born Stern has written a series of acclaimed books about the evolving architecture of his hometown, such as *New York 1900* (Rizzoli, 1983) and *New York 1930* (Rizzoli, 1987), which was nominated for the National Book Award.

On the question of tradition and change, Robert Stern warns against innovation at any cost or, as he puts it, "a kind of fetishization of new materials that often aren't tested in the house environment and are challenging to live with." Many of his residential clients prefer to live in a "traditional environment," and he sees nothing wrong with that: "To abandon the classical or the vernacular traditions is to cut yourself off from a vast reservoir of experience and meaning."

How has the American home evolved over time?

Robert A. M. Stern: First of all, America, more than any other nation in the twentieth century, is a nation of house builders. "The American home" is the wrong phrase, by the way. You can have a home anywhere. You can have a home in a tree or an apartment. Houses are buildings. The various surveys of American houses often are freighted with stylistic prejudices leaning to the traditional styles or to the modernist style. Modernism has become a style and, like other styles, it goes in and out of fashion. One of the attributes of American house building is the wide range of taste, and it's not just highbrow versus lowbrow. People have many different feelings about the character of the house they want. For example, many very sophisticated people who collect contemporary art still prefer to live in a "traditional environment." There are no essential characteristics *except* variety. The Maoist characteristic "let a thousand flowers bloom" comes to mind. Or, a thousand flowers *do* bloom.

I think most Americans prefer a house that doesn't remind them of their office or factory environment. I think that's one reason modernist houses have not generally succeeded. For most people, modernism defines the environment of the workplace, and therefore people hunger to connect with a more craft-oriented, preindustrial environment in their homes.

What current trends in residential architecture do you feel compelled to subvert?

Stern: The current talk of architecture is that we live in a chaotic or fragmented world, and therefore buildings should express that fragmentation by being fragmented. But I believe houses, and buildings in general, should address that fragmentation with images of calming and by drawing people together. Certainly, in a house, I don't expect to have my breakfast with my angst. I'd rather have my breakfast with somebody else's angst on the television. Of course, all modernist architecture is not about fragmentation. But modernism in general tends to be distrustful of the status quo. It tends to search for the Holy Grail of a perpetual avant-garde. It gets harder and harder to be avant-garde because you're like a rat in a cage—you're always running faster and faster, chasing your own avant-garde tail. But I think houses, places where people live, should provide quietude and a state of calm.

Modernism has many sides. The modernism I grew up with, as a young architect, was basically the modernism of the 1920s, rehashed in the 1940s and 1950s. It was very narrow, overly trustful of and bounded by technology, overly dependent on functionality, and short on the psychological demands for enclosure that a house implies. Today's most avant-garde modernism is about fragmentation and the revival of technology. So we get, in our architecture, a kind of fetishization of new materials that often aren't tested in the house environment and are challenging to live with—for example, hard and sometimes even aggressive surfaces. I don't think that's the generally held idea of what a house should be about.

It almost seems as though you feel a moral responsibility to those who will live in the house.

Stern: I get nervous with the word "moral" because I think morality and architecture are not necessarily good bedfellows. And that wonderful, incisive book by David Watkin, *Morality and Architecture*, deconstructed the modernists' claim to a high moral ground for their point of view.

To what extent is it accurate to characterize your work as postmodern?

Stern: The postmodern condition is generally acknowledged in virtually all the arts and probably other disciplines as well. Really, "postmodernism" is the proper term, not "postmodern," because we're still in the modern era, no matter our stylistic inclinations. Postmodernism simply argued that the modernism of the early and mid-twentieth century was over. It had exhausted its energy as it searched for technological and functional solutions, and it had also exhausted its formal capacities because it refused to allow for connections or inventions based on the forms of the past. Now we know that you cannot *not* know history. As Philip Johnson has said, the great modernists of the 1920s, by whom I mean Mies van der Rohe and Le Corbusier, knew their history very well and were always contemplating historical models.

Postmodernism argued that you can go back to go forward, and I still think that's true. In fact, the revival of modernism today is a postmodernist phenomenon, if you can follow that line of reasoning. That is to say, Charles Jencks pronounced modernism dead in 1972, which was as good a date as any. We now find architects, particularly young ones, reviving the modernist houses, such as the Case Study Program houses of the 1940s, 1950s, and early 1960s in California. When I first encountered the Case Study houses, I thought they were thin and diagrammatic, the most boring works of architecture I'd ever seen.

The kind of postmodernism that I have become very interested in is modern traditionalism. Many styles—form languages—have grown up during different eras. Some were willed into being by scholared architects, such as the high classicism of the Renaissance; others grew out of the local soil of the vernacular. And, like any other language, it can be argued that stylistic language does not end when conditions change. It evolves but continues to have its own deeply rooted cultural meaning. To abandon the classical or the vernacular traditions is to cut yourself off from a vast reservoir of experience and meaning. Hence, I am a modern traditionalist.

Now, I don't always do modern traditional buildings. If I'm doing a skyscraper that's 975 feet tall, as I am in Philadelphia, I can assure you my building is glass and sheath and is quite daring technologically and in other ways. However, I'm still thinking about formal models of tall buildings—obelisks and other shapes—that come to us from earlier and simpler times. I also think about the experiments of the nineteenth and early twentieth centuries by various architects who were making super-tall buildings, which we call skyscrapers.

With houses that I design, I'm not trying to rebuild Monticello or a Palladian villa. I'm trying to use the language of Palladian villas, which themselves came from a study of the classical architecture of Rome. They integrated that history with the technology and sensibilities of the northern Italian vernacular to create a new synthesis in the middle-class houses. From that, hundreds or thousands of houses and other buildings emerged, some quite excellently inventive, some more conventional. A continuous chain of events ensued, which could be called a growing, living language of architecture.

I think that self-consciousness with respect to the past is a fundamental modern trait. And it goes back, at the very least, to Palladio. It flowered in the late eighteenth century with the rediscovery of sites in Rome and Greece and the influence of the English architect Sir John Soane, who was one of the most gifted architects who mined the past. The notion that the past is there to be studied, appreciated, and emulated is, of course, a self-conscious act.

All works of art that have any worth are self-conscious with intention. The people who think they should only build to the moment of their own time are not unconscious so much as dead to the larger possibilities, trapped in their moment.

Would you say that the Grove development, at the historical Farmers Market in Los Angeles, is a positive example of modern traditionalist architecture?

Stern: I think the Grove is a very successful environment. I guess it's because I'm such a New Yorker, but it seems to me that everybody everywhere wants to get out of the car or off the subway and be in a place with different scales of buildings with different scales of uses where you can buy fresh fruit, eat, shop, mingle, and so forth. Of course, in Los Angeles, you have to drive to such a place. In some ways, it's a mall, not a street like in New York. But then, even in New York City, Fifth Avenue has Rockefeller Plaza. You can't have only streets. I see the Grove as a sign that the city—or a developer—is addressing what I believe is a largely untapped need for urbanity in Los Angeles.

Contemplating the future, what design directions are you appreciating and engaging in?

Stern: In the 1920s and 1930s, when we built suburbs in the United States, many good architects that you've never heard of—I've never heard of them—designed houses. They were thoughtful and true to certain time-honored, vernacular architectural languages, and they were nice houses.

Many of my clients want their houses to be big and comfortable and meet their program, but be quiet. In fact, that's often why we use the traditional styles. They prefer them, and we try to use them in traditional neighborhoods so our buildings will fit in. Instead of celebrating the moment, they celebrate the place.

Walter Luther Dodge House, 950 North Kings Road, Los Angeles, California. Designed by Irving Gill and built in 1916, the home and garden were razed in 1970. Gill said he left the ornamentation to nature.

SAM WATTERS

"The history of landscape architecture and
house design, particularly in California, is
the mediation between the in and the out.
That's because people wanted to live in
the garden."

Sam Watters (b. 1954) is a historian and critic of art, architecture, and landscape design who has lectured and written extensively about the Los Angeles architecture that has nothing to do with modernism and the Case Study movement. As the *Los Angeles Times* has noted, Watters "chafes at the notion that Modernism began out here with Richard Neutra and R. M. Schindler and that everything else was just a copy of what had been built before somewhere else."

Watters's two-volume set, *Houses of Los Angeles, 1885–1919* and *Houses of Los Angeles, 1920–1935* (Acanthus, 2006 and 2007)—doing for Los Angeles what Robert Stern did for New York—is a re-rendering of Southern California architectural history and a valuable record of houses now mostly lost to later development. Part of Acanthus Press's Urban Domestic Architecture series, the books cover a fifty-year period and reflect a city in search of a past to inform its future.

Watters, the former publisher and president of *The Advocate*, has taught at the USC School of Architecture. His more recent books include *Dream House: The White House as an American Home* (Acanthus, 2009) and *Gardens for a Beautiful America, 1895–1935* (Acanthus, 2012).

Watters was educated at Yale, where he completed his graduate work in English eighteenth-century landscape theory, and at the University of Marseilles, where he studied French and Italian eighteenth-century gardens; he also studied at the Royal Botanic Gardens at Kew.

Sam Watters agrees with Robert Stern that traditionalism has its validity in American home design. "The problem is every conversation about contemporary architecture, about housing and how people live, starts with modernism and then if anybody's interested in traditional architecture, it becomes this big apology." Though Watters appreciates the contribution of modernism to the design of the American home—open floor plans, easy circulation, light and air—he believes it has its limits as a style. "Modernism no longer holds up the social promise that it did in the 1920s," he declares.

When one looks back at the long stretch of architectural history, what are some of the defining qualities of "home" that persist and that we must keep?

Sam Watters: A lot of people end up in houses wondering, "Why doesn't this feel like home?" I think a great deal about the struggle to incorporate what the client wants and what the architect needs. That manifests itself in a lot of different ways because along with the client's desires come some real, archetypal ideals of home as shelter and protection. Architects have a whole aesthetic agenda and idea of what the future is supposed to look like, and those ideas aren't necessarily in sync with what it is to be at home.

There's always an assumption that the houses we see in photographs or illustrations are a house, and therefore we all accept that they function as a house. What if we read the history the other way and said, "Let's find out whether in fact it really functioned as a house," and then found out, no, it didn't? Then what would we think of the architecture?

I'm thinking of a well-known quote by Polly Adler, who was a famous American madam. She used to say, "A house is not a home." [Laughter.] I think that is the big rub. Is a house a home, or a home a house? Would we ever say, for instance, "Oh, that fantastic Richardsonian building. It was a great home." No, we'd always say it was a house. What would we say about a Charles Gwathmey? It was just a wonderful home? Was Frank Lloyd Wright's Fallingwater a home? We have these clear ideas of what great houses are, but were they great homes? I think that that's the relationship that needs to be thought about.

Those houses were built—Fallingwater especially—by corporate guys saying, "Look what I can do. I can hire the master to create a masterpiece." The client probably didn't think too much about "home" anyway.

Watters: I don't know. Edgar J. Kaufmann was deeply involved in the creation of Fallingwater. They had a program. It still had to function. You had to be able to get to the bathroom.

Much of your work and your writing reexamines and appreciates architecture that is overshadowed by the current focus on modernism. When you look at this territory, what has been lost in modernism's wake, notably in Los Angeles?

Watters: If you look at the 1920s and 1930s, you find this remarkable intersection between modernism and historical styles of architecture. You have the Schindler House, and down the block was a Monterey revival adobe house; around the corner from that was an English revival country house. We've drawn these strict lines around these different styles, but why is that? Why did we eliminate one thing and not the other?

I think that those modernist houses, such as the Schindler House, were about a program—a political and social agenda. There was an idea about how we were supposed to live, but it was deeply driven by ideology. I don't think it had anything to do with how anybody actually lived. How functional was the Schindler House? You had badly insulated rooms. It was difficult to move through on a day-to-day basis. Everything was arranged in this peculiar way. How easy was it to live in? I don't think that was of concern to the architect.

I think now we're starting to think about it because the politics of modernism have changed. Modernism no longer holds up the social promise that it did in the 1920s. There is no utopian modernism. We still want to believe that, but after what's happened, are we going to believe that there are any bulletproof solutions to our problems? Therefore, I don't understand why modernism should be a more privileged design tradition than an English country house.

And it also goes back to this idea I have, which is that modernism is about functionality. Now, if you think of it that way, it's a much wider playing field. You can decide modernism now is a style. Well, why couldn't you have a modernist Tudor house or a modernist adobe house? I think that's all going to happen. Maybe we will see a reintegration of those vocabularies back into modernism, as functionality.

One aspect of that vocabulary is modernism's mediation between inside and outside.

Watters: The history of landscape architecture and house design, particularly in California, is the mediation between the in and the out. That's because people wanted to live in the garden. Is modernism responsible for opening all that up? Did style generate that, or was it a push for a new idea of home?

Other valuable things came out of modernism as a style: light and air, open floor plans, and an ability to move around in the house that had not existed before. Older houses always presumed, to a certain extent, somebody doing more work. The kitchen was a place where somebody did the dishes. It wasn't where somebody had dinner. But why does that problem of the kitchen exclude finding ways to incorporate period styles?

What qualities do you treasure in these marginalized historical styles that have been lost?

Watters: It depends on the region. What works in Los Angeles does not necessarily work well in New England. I would say that aspects of the adobe house in California still have enormous potential. Everybody knows they were better insulated against the heat. I think aspects of colonial revival architecture make it deeply suitable in New England because of its ability to shelter against certain kinds of wind, give the sense of protection, and deal with light in a particular way. I think that those regional styles reflected something that was very contemporary. They had an idea; they were very responsive to the environment. I don't see that modernism is responsive to those issues. It doesn't matter whether you build a modernist house in Berlin, New York, a small town in New England, Colorado Springs, or Los Angeles. It's always going to be the same. Why should that be?

I think we have dismissed a legacy of history. I think we missed out on centuries-old solutions to environmental problems that were inherent in the architecture that we no longer have. I think there was a much broader architectural vocabulary prior to modernism. We had two thousand years to develop this vocabulary, then modernism came along and introduced a very rigorous, limited vocabulary.

Remember that modernism was anti-historical. It took what it saw as an endless series of revivals of stylistic idioms and said that we're going to get rid of those. We're going to find a new language with which to build houses. I think we would benefit from reintroducing the idea of keeping history with us, because history is very informative and embedded in style. Modernism was anti history. Look at when it happened. I'm a great believer in not burying our own history, because I think that's a very dangerous place to be, politically.

A lot of things get jettisoned as architecture progresses through history. Are there things in jeopardy of being discarded that you think we should preserve?

Watters: The problem is every conversation about contemporary architecture, about housing and how people live, starts with modernism, and then if anybody's interested in traditional architecture, it becomes this big apology. I really like living in a Tudor house. I'm not supposed to, but I do. I really love these old-fashioned houses with all the woodwork and paneled rooms. I know that I'm old-fashioned. I'm not trendy. The one who likes period architecture is always considered the anti-intellectual. To me, the most anti-intellectual position is to marginalize one group over another.

We're in a period of pluralism. We're not in a period of purity. What happened to the melting pot idea? Where's the melting pot in modernism? It's an extraordinary idea when you think about it. During two hundred years of accretion of all sorts of ideas about architecture, we held on to many different idioms in pure states and hybrid states. Then we get to a period where we have this singular, pan-global taste that is supposed to accommodate everybody. I think that our hegemonic views of architecture in the last thirty years are very politically regressive. Houses are a great reflection of a culture. Maybe we have been in the world in a particularly treacherous way because we have held on to these very pure, rigorous ideas.

Our thinking has to change substantially, because the idea of houses in the future is predicated on the great American tradition of building something new: The cities can be expanded indefinitely, there are limitless amounts of land, and we're going to tear down what already is there because there is always something better in the future. If the subject of how we build on the land is to be addressed, we have to talk about the preservation of what already exists. The minute you start talking about preservation, you start talking about the value of something that already exists. The result is going to be an accumulation of a stylistic heritage.

Inherent in modernist ideas is that technology improves our lives and there are better ways for people to live. Therefore, if what we had in the past can be eliminated, we're going to have this glorious future. Well, maybe that future doesn't exist anymore. We can't keep assessing everything based on what we can tear down. Why can't we take new technology, for instance, and use it to make what we already have built and the traditions we have inherited better? Why can't you have better insulation in a house built in 1890? You don't have to tear it down. It doesn't have to be redone and rethought; it can be reused for another two hundred years. What about that idea? But that's a very difficult idea for people to hold on to because it redefines progress.

A prefabricated Lustron house at 104 State Park Road, Beverly Shores, Indiana. The
Lustron Corporation built more than two thousand prefab homes in the late 1940s.

DOUGLAS GAROFALO

"I would say the other trend, oddly enough, has to do with manufacturing and premanufacturing, which was also an issue in the 1950s, when quite a number of prefabricated prototypes were developed."

Douglas Garofalo (1958–2011) was a Chicago-based architectural maverick known for his pioneering use of computer modeling to encompass his engineering practice. His projects vary greatly in scale and location. They include forms of collaboration that cross both geographical boundaries and professional disciplines. Whether commercial or residential, they push the limits of conventional design practices by taking full advantage of innovations in design technology.

In one of his residential schemes, the Green Bay House, sinewy yellow fiberglass wraps the stacked wings of an addition in an S. In a different remodel, the Spring Prairie House, a rambling red farmhouse gets clad with sensual aluminum roofing in complex, computer-plotted curves.

His public buildings, such as the Korean Presbyterian Church in Queens, are equally daring. With the completion of the Hyde Park Art Center in 2007, for which Garofalo won the Chicago AIA Distinguished Building Award and the Driehaus Foundation Award for Architectural Excellence in Community Design, he became accepted by the mainstream as an important designer of public space.

Garofalo was born in Schenectady, New York, and earned his Masters of Architecture from Yale in 1987. He was a professor at the University of Illinois School of Architecture in Chicago, and was the school's acting director from 2001 to 2003.

The work of Garofalo Architects has been recognized as part of "The New Vanguard" in *Architectural Record* and the "Emerging Voices" program at the Architectural League of New York. His firm's portfolio was the subject of a retrospective exhibition at the Art Institute of Chicago in 2006.

Douglas Garofalo notes the period right after World War II as being one of greater experimentation in American home design due to the sheer numbers of houses that were constructed for returning servicemen. It was also a period of prosperity, which fueled risk and innovation. But mass production tends to fall into repetition, which is more efficient and cost-effective. Today, new technology in materials and digitized manufacturing is affording a new wave of variation in forms and design solutions. "It's a really interesting moment in that regard, and not just in the residential work, it's in all the work," he says.

I think since World War II, our architects of residential architecture have begun to think more progressively about our popular architecture as belonging to everyone, rather than as being for the caprice or pride of a kingly patron.

Douglas Garofalo: I would say post World War II there has been quite a shift from, say, the 1950s to right now. Immediately after the war was a rich period of experimentation in housing in response to the problem of building many houses quickly enough for the shifting population—that is, all these guys coming back home from the war and having families. It led to things like prefabrication. The suburbs boomed and to a certain degree you could say are still booming.

The other thing that plays in is prosperity. As individuals or in groups, people can express all kinds of what you call caprice, or personality. With prosperity comes a bit more freedom to experiment. By the way, I would say there are patrons of architecture, and they tend to be the very wealthy and they build the kinds of houses that make all the architecture journals, but they are not always the most interesting.

I would say that housing is still an issue, but maybe the issues are quite a bit different now. After this period of intense building, since the forties, people are starting to question sprawl. And also, you have the question of style. Why does everything have to look the same? I think the public is more and more aware of that homogeneity, much more so than in the 1950s. But in a weird way, I think there was a lot more variety and experimentation in certain areas of postwar housing than there is now. I think the kinds of developments that go up now are even more expedient and homogeneous. Typically, I mean. I'm talking about the bad stuff.

There's bad stuff and good stuff. Maybe I have a romanticized notion of forward-thinking contemporary architects as being somewhat in opposition to dominant culture. Can you speak to that?

Garofalo: I think traditionally, in the romantic version, the avant-garde would be against the "common market," or would be flying in the face of it. But I think today, avant-garde architects look for ways to operate within the market. I would be more in favor of working against typical developers than I would be against the markets themselves. At this point, developers define markets more than architects, by a long shot, so I would distinguish between the public and developers in that regard.

Do you feel like you have a certain aesthetic mission that you want to bring to your work?

Garofalo: Our approach to residential architecture has a lot to do with thinking of typology, systems, organizations, and forms that go against homogeneity. I suppose that relates to something you were asking me before, about what's enduring across all these styles of residential architecture, particularly in America. I would say it's this notion of individuality, or what I might call heterogeneity. Even as those suburbs get built ad infinitum, one thing that has remained is individualism—an interest in differences. It's what American culture is based on, right? It's the melting pot, but in our version of the melting pot, you keep the differences, you don't make everything gray. You exhibit those differences.

The romantic idea of the avant-garde is to fly against and react, but these days, I'd say the avant-garde is more interested in a both/and scenario where you're producing entirely new things, but they seem to be intimately connected with their contexts. It's a fine line to walk. For example, we've done a lot of work in the suburbs. At first glance, that work probably looks foreign, but if you look at it for any length of time, it makes sense in its context.

Certain suburbs lend themselves to iconoclasm, right? And others less so. Some of the work you've done falls into playful rehabbing.

Garofalo: We've literally not had a house that we've done from the ground up. I don't believe there's ever a clean slate. Even if you don't have a preexisting building, you have a site to react with, to play with. And I think our version of play is to really study the context, research it, and find the kind of idiosyncrasies within it. We tend to exploit those so that they're connected like nothing you've ever seen.

And why is that important?

Garofalo: I think it goes back to not wanting to stick with the status quo and wanting to respond in a very particular way to a context and a client. All clients are idiosyncratic. There's a myth that the suburbs are full of homogenized, like-minded people, and the city is somehow more diverse. When you look into it, those clichés don't hold. So our work tries to respond to the personalities we're dealing with as much as the contexts. I should say the clients are part of the context of the project, so that's why we respond to their whims, desires, and needs—both functional and otherwise. And then we have our own interests, materials, and form.

Are those the kinds of challenges that provoke you to be inventive about materials and forms?

Garofalo: I think those things are part of a larger picture. We're also influenced by the use of computers, not because we're tech heads, but because of our interest in complexity. As I said before, we have this interest in difference or heterogeneity. As architects, we automatically have to think of what organizational systems, geometries, formal systems, and hierarchies can accommodate the most difference or the most complexity. So it isn't just about form and materials, the project mix includes the client, budget, site, and schedule, and our own desires and thoughts on culture and social structure. It's all part of what I call an ecosystem. All those things conflict with one another at one time or another in a project; it's not like they fit together neatly. I think our interest is to add complexity to the project and figure out a way to have the project evolve and take form over time.

The ecosystem is a good metaphor. If you take an ecosystem—a natural region—and you zoom out, you can imagine it as this cohesive, symbiotic, working organism. If you zoom in, you'll find lots of conflict—flora and fauna in direct conflict with one another. It's really survival of the fittest. So both things are true: it's cohesive and symbiotic and also full of incredible variation. That's our wonderful predicament here in the studio—to figure those things out and to make things within that overall sensibility.

That's fascinating. What you're saying is that every architectural challenge, every project, is this holistic cauldron of conflicts that you are in a sense working through to find completion and balance.

Garofalo: I think that's true, and it's only holistic at certain times. It depends on the frame of reference. At a certain point, we're not part of the project anymore. Somebody's living in it and then it keeps going. We think about that, too, although it's out of our control. It certainly keeps it interesting.

I'd like to get back to the first question that I asked you even before we turned on the tape recorder. Instead of thinking in terms of the sweep of residential design history as one of different styles, one might think of it alternatively as responses to emotional challenges. If you were to generalize, do you think that you could make a legitimate comparison between what is being addressed in housing today versus what might have been before World War II, when homes were made, by and large, for more practical needs?

Garofalo: I think I can do that in terms of my own and similar practices. I don't know if I could zoom out more than that because it's pluralistic. I would note a couple of trends right now. One is due, like in the 1970s, to an energy crisis. To me, the crisis never should have gone away. Architecture has a renewed sense of responsiveness to the environment—for both ethical and monetary reasons. I think our response as architects fits right into this ecosystemic model of hierarchy and all the systems and parameters you need to think of with a project. So I think one trend is to make buildings more responsive. But I don't think it's just about function; it's also about aesthetics. We're all engaging in this wealth of wonderful research in terms of materials, textures, color, and lights that's very sophisticated, and that's a lot of fun.

I would say the other trend, oddly enough, has to do with manufacturing and premanufacturing, which was also an issue in the 1950s, when quite a number of prefabricated prototypes were developed. But now it's changed because with computers—digital machinery—everything does not have to be stamped out one and the same. You can have variation in those systems. So an interest of ours is to think about how things are being made and about variation within the repetitive systems of building. Building is a very repetitive industry, and that's how contractors and developers make money—doing the same thing over and over again. But now, with newer digitized machines and methods, it's possible to get a lot more variation, a lot more complexity in projects for not more money. It's a really interesting moment in that regard, and not just in the residential work; it's in all the work.

Both of those trends—responsiveness to the environment and prefabrication—are connected to the past, but I see more sophisticated possibilities than were available previously. Mass production is no longer about repeating the same thing over and over again like a cookie cutter. You can use repetition to deal with some serious issues—for example, public housing—but have variation and individuality within those models.

103

DOUGLAS GAROFALO

TRACY KIDDER

"One of the great things about looking at old buildings, such as old wood-framed houses in New England, is that the ones that remain are usually the ones that were the best built."

Tracy Kidder's (b. 1945) well-known book *House* (Houghton Mifflin, 1985) chronicles the tangled interactions between an architect, builders, and newlywed clients. *House* reads like a novel but is a nonfiction document of the design and construction of the award-winning Souweine House in Amherst, Massachusetts. Its design begins, like any, with proper siting within the lot—or, as Bill Rawn, the Souweine House architect, says in Kidder's book: "A house wants a place."

Kidder's other bestselling works include *The Soul of a New Machine* (Little, Brown, 1981), which earned him a Pulitzer and a National Book Award; *Among Schoolchildren* (Houghton Mifflin, 1989); and *Home Town* (Random House, 1999), in which Kidder, a master of nonfiction, takes us home—into Hometown, U.S.A., the town of Northampton, Massachusetts, and into the extraordinary, and the ordinary, lives that people live there. Exploring what life is really like in contemporary small-town America, Kidder offers an assessment in *Home Town* of how individuals in a community transform a place into a home.

A regular contributor to the *New Yorker*, *Atlantic Monthly*, and *The New York Times Book Review*, Kidder graduated from Harvard in 1967 and served as a first lieutenant in Vietnam from 1967 until 1969, for which he was awarded a Bronze Star. His master's degree is from the University of Iowa Writers' Workshop. Kidder lives with his wife in western Massachusetts and Maine.

Facing: Frame house from the 1800s: Samuel Richmond House, 36 Bowen Street, Providence, Rhode Island

Tracy Kidder delves into how architecture can affect our notion of time: "I think old buildings remind you that there was such a thing as the past and there were people here before you and there will be people here after you." But whether old or new, he believes "people tend to occupy their houses as though they had always been there." We want a feeling of being rooted in the history of a certain place, so "towns and cities ought to think very hard before they tear down old buildings."

When people have their own house built, they begin with a dream. But when the house is being constructed, they often run into the limitations of time and resources. What do people discover about themselves and about the nature of dreams when that dream becomes concrete and contained?

Tracy Kidder: I should say, first of all, that most people don't ever have the opportunity to have a house built for them to their specifications. When I wrote *House*, I was really thinking about a story about social class.

I don't think most people find that their dreams are fully realized in a house. I think it would be a pretty shallow existence if that was all there was to your dreams. But I do think that people, particularly Americans, invest an enormous amount of desire and dreams into houses, whether they have them built for them or not. If you look at tract housing in a place like Levittown, the places don't look the same at all anymore. People change them over time, try to make them fit.

People setting out to build their own brand-new house who aren't extraordinarily wealthy discover that they can't have everything they want. It can be, for some, a bitter experience. I'm told that a lot of couples end up getting divorced after having a house built. That may be in part because people sometimes build a house for one of the reasons that some people have a child—to save a failing marriage. Building a house is not a really good way to save a failing marriage, I would think. You end up having a bunch of strangers doing something really intimate for you, but they're being paid for it. You can imagine all the complicated feelings that would evoke.

We'll get back to the class conflict in a minute. But, for my second question, I want to ask you about this unusual, triangular relationship between the clients, the architect, and the builders.

Kidder: A ménage à trois.

A ménage à trois. I was trying to avoid "three-way."

Kidder: A ménage à trois without sexual connotations.

Can you talk about how these relationships play out as a house is being built?

Kidder: When I wrote *House*, I started out wanting to write a book about carpenters and the building season. Then everything changed. Suddenly, a couple appeared who needed a house, and a brand-new architect—now very famous, by the way—appeared who needed a house to design.

Many years ago, I wrote about an engineer who talked about what's called the three-bodied problem in physics. When you have two heavenly bodies interacting, it's complicated enough, but their effects on each other are fairly easy to predict. You add the third, and it gets much much, more complicated. That's what's interesting to us about triangles.

In the case of *House*, you had latter-day New England craftsmen who cared a great deal about the quality of the thing they were building. They cared a lot about the design that they were executing, but what they really cared about was the quality of the execution—their craftsmanship. And you had homeowners who cared about a whole lot of different things, including how much it was going to cost. Anybody who's ever had a house built or renovated knows that every time you change the initial plans it costs a lot more than you think it ought to. But you also want to be sure you're getting the place you want. And then you had an architect who was new and very talented. There were things he didn't know about house construction. But more than that, architects tend to be at least as interested in the composition of the thing they're making as they are in its functionality.

The carpenters I worked with were funny. If one of the team didn't happen to be there when something went wrong, they'd blame it on the person who wasn't there. So the architect typically would get blamed because he usually wasn't there. It seems like a setup for a lot of fighting.

It occurred to me as I was observing these situations that you could rent yourself out as a go-between—or a go-among, actually—because a lot of the misunderstandings could be rather easily fixed by moving from one party to another and saying that this is the way he feels and this is the way he feels. Someone could be hired to be a diplomat or arbitrator.

Themes of class and of class conflict run through your book *House*. A lot of the individuals you profile are craftsmen and builders by choice, but they are often acutely aware that they themselves cannot afford to live in the kind of house they are building.

Kidder: Jim, who was running the team of carpenters, said that toward the end of a job you realize that they have a house, and you don't have very much to show for it. I think what made this case particularly interesting to me was that all these people were honest, upright people. Yet they still had terrible fights, in part because of their honesty and uprightness. I felt I had in my hands a story for which there was no external explanation that was as good as the story itself. That is to say, I had to tell the story in order to explain it.

I remember the business with the finished lumber that had knots in it. The architect didn't want knots in the casings, but not to have knots in the casing meant buying clear pine, which is much more expensive and was not specified in the contract. The price of the house had been bid with lumber that did have knots in it. The architect was appalled. And the builders would have preferred to use number one pine, clear pine, but it would have cost them a ton of money that would have come out of their pockets.

There's a long history of tension between architects and builders. The builders tend to think the architects are dreamy aesthetes who aren't practical and don't know what is required to build something. Builders, if they're good, tend to be very practical people, although they're aesthetes themselves. And architects aren't always well paid either; it's not one of the great lucrative professions. I think it all leads to a pretty interesting, fraught relationship.

It reminds me, oddly, of a relationship that I observed between scientists and engineers. You would think the scientist would be more likely to be the aesthete, and the engineer the tremendously practical person. But actually, in the couple of cases I know about, it was the opposite. The experimental scientists simply wanted a device that worked. The engineers wanted to build something that had beautiful, technical symmetry and was in a nice-looking box that didn't have wires hanging off the sides.

When people live in the house, how much of the process of it being made do you feel lingers behind?

Kidder: I think that people tend to occupy their houses as though they had always been there. The process of buying an old house and having it fixed up—and doing some of the work myself, practically cutting my thumb off, falling of ladders, and stuff like that—made me interested in this subject. I had no sense, or only the vaguest sense, of the constructed landscape when I got a piece of property myself. It was amazing how, within months, I was staring at houses and noticing things I had never noticed before, particularly the quality of the construction.

In my book, Jim says that what's most interesting to him is where things come together—the joints, for example—which is a kind of wonderful, philosophical statement. What I'm trying to say is that the whole constructed landscape changed for me. Being a really terrible neophyte carpenter myself at that point, I suddenly started to notice how well the carpenters had done their job. And I noticed rooflines, and whether houses were straight and square.

What I was preoccupied with, and had been preoccupied with before in a previous book about computer engineers, was whether craftsmanship could still exist in an advanced, industrialized society. It's a little bit vague, that term "craftsmanship," but what I mean is the opportunity not to do something entirely by rote, but to be solving problems and executing the solutions with skill. For example, drywall in itself replaces a whole bunch of steps that craftsmen used to perform, and it takes the money that used to be paid to craftsmen and puts it into the manufacturing process. What that means for the person who is actually applying the drywall is that so much of the money has already been spent in making this product that you've got to put that stuff up fast. I'm not saying there isn't a lot of skill involved in putting it up fast, taping the joints, and making it look good. But it puts a tremendous pressure on the people who are doing the drywalling. I'm sure this is completely unfair, like all generalizations, but drywall installers tend to be heavy drinkers and to burn out on their job pretty fast.

For the computer engineers that I wrote about, what clearly interested them was the opportunity to be part of inventing something, not that they were wholly inventing. For the carpenters, doing a whole lot of different parts of the job, coming up with nifty ways of doing them, and doing them really well were sources of great pleasure. I felt like I was getting a glimpse at a deeply human impulse. I wonder now if that wasn't a silly preoccupation of mine, given the fact that every job that has to do with working with your hands—except for the jobs of cleaning up or flipping burgers—seems to be migrating out of this country.

Is there anything that you've come to understand about architecture or about your relationship to craftsmanship in these twenty years since you wrote *House*?

Kidder: I find myself caring a lot more about the constructed landscape. I think that the messages that are embedded in architecture were largely hidden to me as a young person, even into my twenties and early thirties. The place where this appears to me as being very important is in schools and colleges. If you look at the campus of a place like Harvard or Smith College, it says to its students: "You are valuable." Whereas what should be our great state university here—which was built, it almost seems to me, on a Soviet model—is falling apart. Its maintenance is grotesquely in arrears. I think it has a very different kind of message for the students: "You're just a number, you don't count, you don't matter very much." It's much more complicated than that, but I think that's the basic message, and I think it's terrible.

I was at a high school yesterday in a city here that is in real trouble and it was a grim place, virtually a penal institution physically. Of course, people can transform any kind of space, but I think it's a terrible thing to inflict on young people and I think it's the visible manifestation of a grotesque unfairness in this country.

I look at the constructed landscape down on the west coast of Florida, where my mother lives in the winter, and what I see is absolutely no regard for what was once one of the most beautiful places on Earth. It's just obscene. We've turned over how the world is going to look—our world—to the people whose only interest is profit. God, I hate it. Who invented the shopping mall? Certainly not someone who cared about how things look.

Another thing I've noticed is that I love New England. There is something to be said about the old towns, like Northampton. I wrote a book about this. It seems to me that towns and cities ought to think very hard before they tear down old buildings, unless those old buildings were badly built and badly designed to start with. One of the great things about looking at old buildings, such as old wood-framed houses in New England, is that the ones that remain are usually the ones that were the best built. We're not seeing all the shoddy craftsmanship. We have this myth of the great New England craftsmen because the buildings that survived were built really well. We don't see the crap.

That's why we have the Great Pyramids, not the minor pyramids, in Egypt.

Kidder: What do old buildings do for you? I think they remind you that there was such a thing as the past and there were people here before you and there will be people here after you. In an odd way, that's a comforting notion, and it's a basis on which meaning can arise. If you live in a place for any length of time, pieces of the landscape acquire very particular meaning for you. There's the veterinarian's where I had to take my dog to be put down. This is the corner where I had that fender bender. A whole landscape can become heavily invested with your own personal history. If you live in a place that isn't all brand-new, you have that sense of ghosts running around.

Look at this culture, the country now; this is the golden age of consumerism. I've been going to a lot of colleges to talk about a book that I wrote a while back, and among a segment of the youthful population, I sense a hunger for something that has meaning outside of fashion and entertainment. And I wonder why does a tiny city like Northampton flourish? In part the answer is that it escaped urban renewal and then found ways to renovate its old downtown. People come from all over, from Connecticut and so on, to have dinner at the restaurants that quite frankly aren't all that good. People flock to places like that, partly because there is wisdom in the layout of an old town that promotes public safety and a kind of vibrancy that people seek.

PART 3

Activism, Sustainability, Environment

The designers in this section know that architecture is much bigger than creating blueprints for buildings. Architects are uniquely equipped to contribute solutions to our most vexing problems—indeed, they have a responsibility to do so. Whether designing affordable yet aesthetically pleasing housing in the wake of environmental disasters, servicing poorer communities, or providing shelter for war-torn refugees, these architects illuminate how their work can make a difference in people's lives.

Row of shotgun houses on the Laurel Valley Sugar Plantation, south of Thibodaux, Louisiana. The homes date from the early 1900s.

MARIANNE CUSATO

"We have to do more than build shelter,
 whether in an emergency situation or not.
 The building industry in the United States
 has moved toward building homes that
 are isolated from community, forming
 monocultures where every house in the
 neighborhood is the same size and so on."

Marianne Cusato (b. 1974) is known for her Katrina Cottage, which she designed in 2005 as a dignified alternative to the emergency trailers supplied by FEMA to the Louisiana families rendered homeless by the catastrophic Gulf Coast hurricane. Cusato was part of a team of architects invited to New Orleans by Andrés Duany, designer of New Urbanist towns across the country, who had been drafted by Mississippi governor Haley Barbour to provide advice on how to rebuild coastal cities devastated by Hurricane Katrina.

Cusato, raised in Alaska, lives in a 300-square-foot apartment in New York's Greenwich Village and believes that even a small space can feel expansive if it's part of something larger. Cusato's prototype Katrina Cottage was displayed at the International Builders' Show in Orlando, Florida, and then picked up for distribution by Lowe's, which sold various models of the tiny house as prefabricated building kits, starting as low as $27,000. (Detailed floor plans are still available for purchase on her website: mariannecusato.com.) Inspired in part by the Levittown homes built en masse after World War II, Cusato's cottages made an extra effort to incorporate local vernacular and historical detailing.

Cusato, who studied architecture at the University of Notre Dame, later collaborated with the British architects Ben Pentreath and Léon Krier, along with the New York designer Richard Sammons, on the book *Get Your House Right: Architectural Elements to Use & Avoid* (Sterling Publishing, 2007). The volume demonstrates how to design houses of any size with appropriately scaled details. She subsequently wrote *The Value of Design* (Plain Paper Press, 2008) with contributions from Andrés Duany and Sarah Susanka.

Marianne Cusato discusses how our responses to environmental disasters do not need to be charmless and devoid of aesthetics. In fact, providing homes that people actually love is key to long-term sustainability.

How did you come to design the Katrina Cottage?

Marianne Cusato: I've been very lucky to be in the right place at the right time in a couple of key moments, and to be able to take some ideas and run with them. Everybody wants to do something that makes a difference. I spent some time doing high-end residential and felt that, although we had amazing budgets and were able to do whatever we wanted to do in terms of details, it wasn't fulfilling, because I wanted to build *places*. So, as I started my own practice, I made a point of taking on projects that looked at the town and community. The Katrina Cottage has been an extension of that, and its success has been thrilling. The project has a lot of angles and different variations but, in the end, it's about putting people in dignified homes, and that's extremely fulfilling.

The Katrina Cottage is an Andrés Duany–inspired concept. We were at the Mississippi Renewal Forum, which was six weeks after Hurricane Katrina. It was the first time that architects, planners, and designers had been brought in while an emergency was still going on to help generate ideas about how to rebuild. We were looking at the short-term and long-term build-out of the coast. It's one thing to solve the immediate needs, but if at the same time you can also look to the needs of the future, then you will have a much better place in the long term.

I was on the team of architects and designers that was looking at buildings, and Andrés challenged us to come up with the Katrina Cottage, a dignified alternative to the FEMA trailer. Because of the scope of the disaster, we were forced to think about things in a different way. We threw out all of the conventional practices and asked: What is an ideal situation? What would I want to live in if I were in this position?

The first thing to highlight about the cottage is that it's an idea, not a single building. So, it's a variation on a theme that really can be adapted to several uses. But it's permanent, secure, and safe, and it's designed to last for many, many years. In contrast, a trailer is not permanent, not necessarily safe—people have to evacuate for tropical storms—and the moment it rolls out of the factory, it is at its highest value. Homes actually go the opposite direction and continue to appreciate in value. If we build permanent homes that are safe and secure, even if they're small, over the long term they are assets on the property.

There are a couple of ways of using the cottage plans. One is to build it free of the footprint of the main house, as an accessory building in the backyard. Once the primary house is built, you move into that house. The cottage becomes a mother-in-law flat or a rental property. It's adding value. It's not something you have to worry about taking away. The other way is for the cottage to be the first piece of the primary house. When you get the plans for the small cottage, you also get blueprints that indicate where the extension would grow. So you may not build the whole house at once, but you know where it's going. When you do build the second part of the house, the masonry, roof, and floor plan continue to work. You're not blocking up windows. You've sited it properly on your property so the extension fits. So it's really building hope. You get the first piece, but it can also be so much more.

We're trying to balance three big variables. Affordability is crucial. Safety and a strong, sturdy building made of good materials are crucial. But so are design and aesthetics. It's easy to satisfy affordability, security, and strength, but then you've got barracks. You're not building places. If we're putting the effort into rebuilding the Gulf Coast, it's a very lengthy process. We need to rebuild communities, because that's what was lost. It's a constant balancing act between these three things to make sure that what we do stays affordable. It's really easy to achieve any two of those qualities. You can have a really beautiful house that's extremely safe, but the price can go through the roof. I think we've achieved all three with the product we've come up with. For example, we chose the three best window designs and standardized their sizes. For all of the different designs, we use a kit of parts so we can get a bulk price, taking advantage of economies of scale.

A lot of the housing proposed for the Gulf Coast region after the hurricane consists of prefabricated buildings that are designed to fit on trucks.

Cusato: The Katrina Cottage is actually not prefabricated. We are doing materials packages—kits—so we're getting great prices on everything that we're ordering. We designed a custom front door, but because we're able to standardize the size of it, we're able to get a great price, and now it's a stock item. So that is how we're able to raise the quality specifications yet keep it affordable.

I think we've come to a really good balancing point where the buildings are secure. They've got Hardie cement board siding, which is rot and termite resistant and hurricane rated. These buildings aren't going anywhere. If you build cheap, you're going to build twice, but if you spend a little bit more and build really well, and build a place that people love and want to be in, then that building is going to be there forever.

How does sustainability factor into your designs?

Cusato: The most sustainable building that you could ever build would be a building that people love and want to be around, because then they will maintain it and cherish it. They'll want to continue to be in it. You can have all the greenest products in a building, but if it's not loved or maintained, or is built in a place that you have to drive a car to, then it is not truly sustainable. You can't make a sustainable building just out of products. The design and the urbanism have to work, or you will have missed the boat.

What have you learned about housing in the wake of the Gulf Coast disaster?

Cusato: We have to do more than build shelter, whether in an emergency situation or not. The building industry in the United States has moved toward building homes that are isolated from community, forming monocultures where every house in the neighborhood is the same size and so on. You can almost tell somebody's résumé and bank balance by reading their address, because every single person in a single neighborhood is the same. There's no mix.

And when you go into your home, it has to be huge because outside your home there's not a community that you can plug into. We sit in cars for an hour and a half in one direction going to work; it's a common thing in this country. Instead of doing that, we could build communities. We could build places that are more than shelter, places that are more connected, where you could be engaged with your neighbors and the street. I think we all yearn for that. We search for that connection in our environment and in our lives. The building industry could help. It could enhance that feeling of connectivity with others and with ourselves.

When we started the Katrina Cottage project, one of the absolute most important things was to create a place of dignity, to create the dignified alternative to the FEMA trailer. It goes deeper than just a single building. It's everything that's connected to that building, the cluster of the buildings and the streets that those buildings are on. Everybody that's been involved with this, from Andrés initially to everybody since that has worked on the project, we all truly believe this. What's so rewarding and validating is the number of people that have come to us and said that the design does matter. What it looks like matters. And that's crucial. Very often, we don't put enough value on that in the built environment. A lot of what we do becomes very functional. We sell square footage; we don't as much sell the details. The Katrina Cottage is affordable because it's small, but it's also beautiful because it's simple. We're not trying to over-ornament it, but rather, through proportion, make it be something that's beautiful and that people can identify with. We make sure the roof slope is steep enough. We make sure the front porch isn't just a gratuitous front porch but a front porch that is deep enough to have several people sitting on it comfortably. We have 9-foot ceilings in our cottages, and that really helps them feel like a secure, proper home.

What's interesting about architecture is that when things work really well, they also tend to look nice. So a vertical window, which looks nice and feels tall in the room, also has value because you can pull down the top sash and get air circulating through the house. The front porch, which looks nice, also helps shade the front room of the house and creates a connection from the house to the street. It creates this semipublic, semiprivate space that allows you to go outside and be raised slightly above the sidewalk. You feel that you can still be in your home yet connected to people walking by. Because the front porch is raised up, you don't feel that people walking by are looking down at you. All of these things contribute to making more than just a building, to making a home. And that's the goal of the cottages.

The first one was 300 square feet. We now have a full range of sizes that goes up to 1,200 square feet. But in 300 square feet, you can still have something that feels like a home. And that's through design. A guiding design principle is that anything we use has to be real and functional. It's not there just because it looks nice. In such a small space and with such a tight budget, nothing is gratuitous. If we're going to put a front porch on the building, it can't be a 3-foot front porch that you can't fit a chair on. It needs to be an 8-foot front porch. On a 300-square-foot house, we still have a 100-square-foot porch, and the building feels much larger because of that.

Have you been surprised by the following that the Katrina Cottage has garnered outside of the Gulf Coast region?

Cusato: The amazing thing about the Katrina Cottage is the number of people that have come to us and said that they see this as a perfect solution for affordable housing, elderly housing, even vacation homes. It fits in a market segment that currently is not being served: people who want to live in 500 square feet. Their options are a condo or a trailer; 500-square-foot houses are not readily available. You can always hire an architect to design something custom. But the cottage is easy and affordable for the broader public. Any time you build a house, it's a big project. But if you're only building 300, 500, or even 700 square feet, it's manageable.

I feel that the Katrina Cottage, which was born out of a horrible disaster, could possibly be a long-term solution for the problem of affordable housing. There's a real opportunity there. It's not a single building; it's an idea that can be adapted to many different places.

An early stone house—built in the 1700s—near Lobachsville,
Pennsylvania, is known as the Keim Stone Cabin.

ANDREW FREEAR

"I hope that what our architecture
does is delight in the everyday."

Andrew Freear (b. 1966) became the director of the Rural Studio at Auburn University in Newbern, Alabama, in 2002, after the untimely death of Samuel Mockbee. The Rural Studio is a hands-on architectural pedagogy that teaches students to design and build charity homes and community projects in some of the poorest communities in rural west Alabama. The focus of the student's thesis year is a community-based project and sustainable materials research. Working in small teams, the students experience the Arts and Crafts "hands-on" building tradition, where they work directly with the community while negotiating designs and procedures with their teammates, creating beautiful and economical structures that are not only unique but also nurture human dignity and sustainability of the natural world. Rural Studio projects have ranged from baseball fields and community centers to a durable house made of cardboard.

Freear is from Yorkshire, England, and was educated at the Polytechnic of Central London and the Architectural Association, London, England. He has practiced extensively in London and Chicago, and taught at the University of Illinois at Chicago and as a Unit Master at the Architectural Association.

Freear has designed, supervised, and built Rural Studio exhibits in Chicago, Cincinnati, Vienna, Barcelona, and at the 2002 Whitney Biennial in New York, the 2005 São Paulo Bienal of Architecture in Brazil, and the 2010 Victoria and Albert Museum in London's exploration of structures of refuge and retreat. His work at the Rural Studio has been published extensively in magazines and in two books by Andrea Oppenheimer Dean and Timothy Hursley.

Andrew Freear, like Marianne Cusato, believes that, regardless of a client's budget, it is important to bring "enthusiasm, delight, spontaneity, and exuberance" into the design process—to make homes that people cherish and feel pride in. For Freear, a discussion of sustainability must also include durability, flexibility in design to accommodate changing families, and using low-maintenance materials: "There is something of a responsibility for us to build houses of cardboard and carpet because we can. If we aren't pushing the boundaries and asking these questions, nobody else will."

How should architects manifest their social responsibility?

Andrew Freear: I hope that what our architecture does is delight in the everyday. Founding Rural Studio director Samuel Mockbee always used the term "to lift the spirits." What our clients most appreciate about what we do is that we have a dialogue at the planning stage about all the necessities of everyday life, that the building is well made, and that we bring a little extra something to it. There's a spirit to our work that's exuberant, that we hope brings them delight and makes them feel special. Our clients' most frequent comment is: "That's unique." What they mean by that is that nobody else has got what they've got, and that makes them feel good about themselves. If you talk to Lucy Harris, for whom we built the Carpet House, in 2002, she knows that she's the only person in the world that has a house made of carpet. That makes her feel special.

We concentrate an awful lot of our time on trying to figure out how to ventilate and condition houses so that our clients are not going to be spending a lot of money on heating and cooling. We also pay special attention to how we bring natural daylight into the houses and community buildings. It's all about seeing those things as necessities in life.

When you start to talk about style, it's an odd thing. I have to say that out here, rarely do I have a conversation with the students about the way the projects look. The conversations are more along the lines of how long this material will last, how that detail can work. There's very little push to be stylized. Hopefully, the stylization comes out of the material use. For example, the Carpet House, which is made from 72,000 hand-stacked carpet tiles, obviously is going to have a different look from a house that's built out of plywood and two-by-fours. The plan of that house is simple. The parental bedroom, which makes a tower, didn't have to be as strangely shaped as it was, but it was an act of exuberance on the part of the students to celebrate the place, the people, and the space. When Lucy sits in bed, she can see the North Star, and that's what she asked for. She didn't ask for a crumpled tower, but the students had a desire to test it, push it, and try it. I hope that "exuberance" is the word to use relative to what we make. I think that even in the most banal of details we try to delight in the everyday, in life, and in being a family and working together, whether it's a group of students or students interacting with clients.

The beautiful thing about the students is that they don't have preconceptions about people. They have no fear, so they don't know to whom they shouldn't be talking. There're no age issues, no race issues, no sex issues. It's simply, well, we've got an opportunity here, and how can we do the best we can? Oddly enough, when you're in an academic situation like this, where the studio has rolled along for fourteen years, the next set of students wants to outdo the last set of students. It's bigger and better and bolder and noisier and naughtier than the last.

How does sustainability factor into the Rural Studio's teaching philosophy?

Freear: For us, sustainability, with a small *s*, is what is the right thing to do for people in a particular circumstance or a building in a particular situation. We're very disappointed with the contemporary world for the way sustainability has been taken and commercialized and used in a way that it doesn't mean anything anymore. What we mean by sustainability is thinking about our client having a small pot of money and figuring out how we can stretch this money as far as we possibly can and give them an environment that will be as durable and as long-lasting as possible.

Most recently, what's really become an issue for us is flexibility, how sustainable a house can be relative to the changing demographic of the family unit. There are a lot of single parents. There are a lot of families with children who, after they grow up and leave, end up coming back and living at home and having children of their own. Three or four generations can be living in a single house. And families continually evolve. For example, we'll be building a house for a family with three children and by the time we're finished, it's got four children. We've really tried to look at the forms and plans of our houses and the spatial implications of families reducing and expanding in scale. We look to bedrooms that are relatively small; we look to making pieces of houses that can be cut off so that you don't have to heat them. Most recently, we've looked at L-shaped buildings where you can close off a complete wing if all the children leave home.

Again, I think the term "sustainability" always comes up, and we look at it on a number of levels, whether it's the way the space is used or the utilities. How can people afford to pay for them? How can they also maintain them? So often the high technology of today's sustainable world is completely and totally irrelevant to what goes on in a place like Hale County. For example, we're often criticized for using septic systems, but quite honestly, the septic system is the most maintainable way to deal with that stuff in west Alabama.

How have the buildings made by the Rural Studio evolved since it was founded by Mockbee in 1993?

Freear: In the very early projects, there was a lot of color. More recently the projects have become less colorful because we are focusing on making these things last as long as possible, which assumes zero maintenance. At the simplest level, you want materials that will weather well and not require repainting. And that begins to suggest a sort of palette. Our most recent palette consists of galvanized aluminum, stainless steel, and cedar. Cedar is beautiful. It goes a beautiful light gray color, and you don't need to finish it, you don't need to paint it.

Whether it's a house or a public building, that's our emphasis. Don't do silly, superficial things that can harm an inhabitant or require being fixed or rebuilt. Honestly, the toughness of that conservation is, from our point of view, about self-preservation. Samuel didn't have to fix any of the buildings that he built in the beginning because he dropped dead. It's his joke on me, quite frankly. I'm the one having to fix them all.

At the beginning of every year, I take the students out and we go around to the houses and the different projects. We don't have a library at the Rural Studio, but we have a library of buildings and projects where you can wander around them and look at how they touch the ground, how to finish the roof to the wall, how to deal with all these things. Which ones are successful, which are not, which work, which don't work, and really ask some tough questions about them. From a student's point of view, you make this decision and the client's got to live with it, so be smart and choose your moments.

How does working in a rural community affect what you build and how you build it?

Freear: In places like Chicago and New York, in all of the big cities, the codes have become the standard design practice. Out here, there's kind of a social agreement. You and I decide to drive on the right-hand side of the road so we won't drive into each other. That is the wonderful situation that we've got down here.

When we decide to build what we do, we sit down with our clients and we start to talk about things like handrails and the nature of the construction, and we'll say to them, what do you feel about this? And most of the time they agree with our approach: this is life, this is the real world. We're not in a litigious situation down here. One day we might be. One day somebody will come along and bang their head and that will be it and the house of cards will come down. But at the moment, the first thought on anyone's mind is not "I'm going to sue you." At the same time, we have no desire to put anybody in danger. I would like to stress how I believe that to take on all of that responsibility is a big deal. We don't have a rulebook; we invent the rules and decide where the line is, and it's quite terrific to be able to do that.

In some respects, there is something of a responsibility for us to build houses of cardboard and carpet because we can. If we aren't pushing the boundaries and asking these questions, nobody else will. I take the responsibility quite personally to say that there's an opportunity here, and let's push the envelope.

I think that one of the downsides of the Rural Studio is that every student comes here expecting to build something, that building is the answer. Often, it isn't necessarily the right answer. In rural communities, land costs much less than in a city. The careful use of rural land is a challenge when it's so plentiful. I hope that at the end of the day, when our students go into the wider world of practice, they take with them the ethical view that there are not boundless and limited resources, and that there's an appropriate way to do things. But you can do things appropriately and also do them with enthusiasm, delight, spontaneity, and exuberance.

Most recently, we've been looking at doing a $20,000 house, which is $10,000 in materials, which is incredibly small. Every detail and every square inch of space is pored over, and it preaches an ethic to ourselves and others that space is of value. Small is good. Big is not necessarily better.

Cities produce the dilemma of suburbs, where people have these sprawling 5,000 and 10,000 square feet of housing and they don't talk to each other. I think the beautiful thing about living in rural areas is that we encourage people to talk to each other. We believe in the front porch and front stoop and all of those things that are about the public realm. We believe in human connection and compatibility and people enjoying being with each other. I hope the students take that optimistic attitude when they go off and work in the city.

How has the Rural Studio pedagogy developed in recent years?

Freear: When I showed up at the Rural Studio, my first reaction to the place was to listen, watch, and learn. Really, I've done that for seven or eight years. The South is not my culture; I'm learning about it every day. I'm certainly not here to change the world. For me, it's about small victories. We get a few opportunities, small projects to make the world a better place, and that's about it. We will work with anybody in the community, whether black, white, pink, or green, as long as they're doing something that we see as being positive. I've encouraged the studio to take on larger public projects so that they can touch more people.

At the end of the day, I hope I haven't brought my style to it at all. We have many, many hundreds of thousands of hours of rigorous conversations about the right and appropriate thing to do. It's not "What can we do?" but rather "What should we do?" I have about three things that I tell the students. They're sick of hearing them. Our conversations really are mainly about what's the material I can use here; what's the appropriate thing to do in this situation; let's make sure it doesn't leak.

What's wonderful about this situation out here is that it's an education that allows every conversation to be architectural. It doesn't become about style, it becomes about how are people going to interact with this, how are they going to understand it, how are they going to use it, how are they going to engage with it. Therefore, are we making the right decisions about this? It's all about sustainable with a small *s*, things that will last a very long time, and people will appropriate them in their own way. You can never guess the way a client will use a house or a community will use a building. The most wonderful part is when they appropriate it and take it on as their own. They care for it, and that's all that we ask. A beautiful social exchange comes into play here. Really we just ask clients to be good and trusted people who are interested in the project and give us honest responses, not responses that we necessarily like, and are honest about what they feel, and we respond to that.

It's a fantastic teaching situation. I have the students in the middle of nowhere. There are no good bars, no good restaurants, none of the accoutrements of city life. They come down here, and they focus on an opportunity, and they grab it most of the time with both hands. And they really dream of doing the best that they possibly can.

CAMERON SINCLAIR

"A lot of people are vying for a replicate of the shotgun house. The shotgun was invented in Ghana and brought over by Africans. It's an adapted vernacular that has become a truly original African American architecture."

Cameron Sinclair (b. 1973) is the cofounder and former executive director of Architecture for Humanity, a nonprofit organization promoting architecture and design solutions to humanitarian crises and design services to communities in need. He was trained as an architect at the University of Westminster (BArch [Hons]) and at the Bartlett School of Architecture in London. He coauthored (with Architecture for Humanity cofounder Kate Stohr) *Design Like You Give a Damn* (Thames and Hudson, 2006), a compendium of innovative projects from around the world that demonstrate the power of design to improve lives. Since its founding in 1996, Architecture for Humanity has built and developed projects in forty-nine countries, including England, Mexico, Russia, South Africa, and the United States. Projects range from school building and tsunami and hurricane reconstruction to developing mobile medical facilities to combat HIV/AIDS.

Currently, Cameron Sinclair is the director and principal designer for Small Works, a social impact design and development company that focuses on post-conflict reconstruction.

Sinclair is a recipient of the American Society of Interior Designers (ASID) Design for Humanity Award and the Lewis Mumford Award for Peace. In 2004, *Fortune* magazine named him one of the "Aspen Seven": seven people changing the world for the better. As one of three recipients of the 2006 TED Prize, Sinclair called for "open-source architecture," where designers could share blueprints and collaborate on solving the world's housing crisis, in which one in seven people live in either a slum or a refugee camp.

Row of houses at 300–306 North Canal Street, Natchez, Mississippi

Cameron Sinclair discusses the socially transformative power of architecture and what he learned from Architecture for Humanity's mission. He talks about "bottom-up" architecture—the idea of enabling people to participate in the practical designing of what they need.

Architecture for Humanity takes a very principled approach to helping people. Can you describe that for me?

Cameron Sinclair: Architecture for Humanity brings architects and designers into humanitarian situations and gets them involved in responding not just to crises but also to systemic issues. Our work ranges from dealing with long-term reconstruction after natural disasters to issues such as homelessness in our cities. We've done a number of projects dealing with developing healthcare facilities and tackling HIV/AIDS in sub-Saharan Africa.

Our role after Hurricane Katrina began very early on. As an organization, we do not impose an architecture, nor do we fly designers into the field à la Doctors Without Borders. Rather, we really try to understand the long-term needs of a community and bring together a collective of experts who will work alongside that community.

Although we arrived on the ground in Mississippi and Louisiana less than a few weeks after Hurricane Katrina, we've only just begun to start construction on housing. The role of an architect is not only to push the boundaries of what can be built but also to figure out what is relevant to be built. So it really is important that our designers come up with pragmatic and scalable solutions.

How did you approach the situation on the ground in New Orleans after Katrina?

Sinclair: We saw our role early on as not to come in with large-scale planning exercises and present them to a community that had neither the capacity nor the funds to implement them, but rather to work one-on-one with families to figure out what they could afford to rebuild, how they could find the funding, what were the long-term strategies of those families, and then come up with real models for regrowth, because those models could then be scaled.

The most successful of these is the Biloxi Model Home Program, where rather than coming up with designs and presenting them to the community, we selected a dozen architects from around the country who were chosen based on their skills and their involvement in the region. We asked them to come up with a technical solution to issues facing residents. How do you build a low-income house for a family that integrates disaster mitigation and code issues? Those architects were invited down to Biloxi to present their ideas to the community as a whole.

127

What the architects did not know at the time was that we had been working for months with specific families and we had brought together funding to allow us to build housing for them. Those families interviewed the architects and selected the one they wanted to work with. The families then entered into an agreement with the architects to develop their ideas into something that would suit their specific needs. Rather than just building a model and presenting it, we are building the actual housing. And at the end of the process, we're going to be releasing the construction documents of those houses to anybody.

Rather than trying to come up with the snazziest, best-looking housing solutions, we're asking what can really be built for less than $90,000 in the South that deals with the issues of an area that is prone to hurricanes. That's a very tight agenda. Coupled with that, we also helped work out a forgivable loan system so that the families could afford not only to have these houses but also to maintain them.

How do these houses relate to the historical idea of "home," particularly in the South?

Sinclair: What's interesting in dealing with post-Katrina are the conversations about the aesthetics of how we build a house. What is the look of a house in Mississippi or Louisiana post-Katrina? A lot of people are vying for a replicate of the shotgun house. The shotgun was invented in Ghana and brought over by Africans. It's an adapted vernacular that has become a truly original African American architecture.

When you look at the post-Katrina context and apply the new height restrictions requiring you to raise these houses 9, 12, or 14 feet off the ground, you end up with these stilted shotguns that no longer work as a home. So you need to address these houses in a more appropriate way. That doesn't mean creating some slick, avant-garde, abstract solution. It's about integrating local materials and appropriate construction techniques, and creating a housing type that can be replicated and, more importantly, that will generate business.

One thing that a lot of architects do not focus on is the idea that reconstruction is a form of renewal within a community, and that your building not only serves as a solution to a housing need but could actually become the start of a new business model within that community.

What did you learn about the kinds of homes people want?

Sinclair: When we did the Biloxi Model Home Program, we brought these architects down, and they presented their home designs to the community. We didn't tell the community that they had to accept them. We just asked for their input and for their views on which homes they would prefer. This was a very harsh process in the eyes of the architects because we invited a dozen architects down, but we only had funding for seven homes. So it meant that five architectural firms were going home empty-handed. They would hear loud and clear from the community about what was wanted.

We were quite stunned by their choices, which were actually quite modern approaches to housing. Rather than large, McMansion-type houses, they selected very pragmatic, space-utilizing housing. For some of these architects, this was the first time they were able to work with clients such as these. I think we're going to create some remarkable architecture as a result.

How can residential architecture be socially transformative?

Sinclair: If you really want to effect change in the world, you have to understand that utopia is dead. And the reason for that is that there is no silver bullet for the housing crisis, and we are closing in on what will be a global housing crisis.

So how do you tackle what will be one in three people living in illegal, inadequate housing? You're not going to do it with some grandiose idea that we're going to create some kind of holistic community where we all live in peace and harmony. What we need to do is be very pragmatic in our response to localized issues and localized problems that arise based around the idea of home. The architects that we work alongside and support understand that. And more often than not, they are from those areas that are looking for solutions.

The face of our architect is not the face of the star architect. It's somebody that lives within the country, understands the context and the culture, and is looking for partnerships with people that can bring in new forms of technology and expertise to address their needs. It's really about partnership. If you can empower the local community to be a part of the design process, then you'll come up with realizable and scalable solutions.

What are the biggest social challenges facing architects?

Sinclair: When you look at housing, we are verging on a global crisis that hasn't been addressed. I am stunned by the numbers. We've certainly talked about the need for sanitation and clean energy. But the idea of adequate housing never really gets addressed on a global basis. When you look at the response of the architect on a global level, it's very, very small. Less than 2 percent of new housing in America uses an architect. Here are two great challenges: How do we address housing needs on a global level, and how do you make architecture relevant today?

We've gotten to a point where our profession is becoming more and more marginalized from the real needs of the community. Part of that has to do with a technology push within our profession that has priced out a lot of potential innovators from being a part of the design process. What I mean by that is when you're working in Kenya or Ghana or anywhere in South Asia, in order to run an architectural practice that can get funding to implement these projects you have to have $100,000 in computers, software, manpower. But what if you created a system that was completely open? What if you not only create a repository of proven ideas that are local solutions, but also you gave away implementation tools to allow teams to work collaboratively and to implement those solutions and share those projects with one another?

What we're looking to do is to create this network that will bring together architects that believe in sharing their ideas and distributing their ideas for the greater good. When the foremost thought on your mind is not financial gain and it's more about doing good, then you're much more open to a sharing community, which brings us to the idea of intellectual property: How do you share your ideas but still protect certain rights?

That is why we are partnering with people like Creative Commons to come up with a new licensing system for architecture and design. This will allow design professionals to regain copyright control of their designs and distribute their ideas based on their own set of criteria. For instance, let's say I design the perfect housing solution for low-income communities in sub-Saharan Africa and I want to give that idea away. Well, by adding certain Creative Commons licenses, I can give away all the construction documents, I can give away all the concepts, but I can retain control in the developed world. If somebody adapts the solution to a housing situation in the West, I can be recompensed for that. It's the idea that you're not giving away all your creative rights but you're giving them away to whomever you want.

What is the impact of technology on your organization's work?

Sinclair: Architecture of Humanity is a web-based organization. We started with $700 and no support. We realized that most design competitions and projects need tens of thousands of dollars just to cover operating costs. But by utilizing the Internet, by working with blogs and social networking sites, we were able to build one of the largest nonprofit sites in the world.

Now how do we takes those advancements in technology and allow nonarchitects to be their own inventors, to take those innovations and spread them? What I'd like to see in the future is that, rather than looking at a slum and seeing 400,000 people in desperate need of help, you see 400,000 potential innovators whose ideas and solutions could be developed and supported through microfinancing. Eventually they rebuild their own lives rather than being dependent on a top-down solution.

What are some of the ideas in residential architecture that you think should be redressed or confronted critically?

Sinclair: In terms of housing, many people don't fully understand the level of community involvement in our projects. The community members are not only partners in the design process but also, because we've come up with an appropriate solution, they're part of the construction process. What that leads to is a community that not only is empowered but also has huge ownership over the buildings that are created. Certainly, post-tsunami, this happened time and time again. The reason this is important is that if you love the home that you're in, you maintain it. If you take the top-down solution, where you're given this kind of concrete block house with no air conditioning—we call them chicken coops—and the attitude is that we're giving you this house, you should be grateful, well, chances are that community doesn't feel proud of the house they're in. It's not addressing their specific needs. It doesn't get maintained and then it fails. For a home to be fully sustainable, it really has to involve the resident in the construction and design of it.

131

A typical New Orleans home from the early 1800s with shops on the ground floor and living quarters above. At 638 Royal Street, the house is in the heart of the French Quarter.

ROBERT IVY

"New Orleans, in its past, was a cosmos unto itself. It was a self-contained universe circumscribed by water, a fragile floating place in which a very particular culture emerged over centuries."

Robert Ivy (b. 1947) is the chief executive officer of the American Institute of Architects (AIA), the premiere organization representing licensed architects and professionals in the design and construction industry since 1857. Highly regarded as a thought leader in the field, Ivy was formerly the editor-in-chief of *Architectural Record*, considered the touchstone professional architectural publication in the world. Under his leadership, *Architectural Record* received publishing's highest honor, the National Magazine Award for General Excellence, in 2003.

Since assuming the management of the AIA, Ivy initiated important investigations, in partnership with the Clinton Global Initiative, into the role of architects in society and the future of architecture, including a decade-long effort to make design a catalyst for improving public health.

In 2010, Alpha Rho Chi, the national architecture fraternity, voted unanimously to name Ivy "Master Architect," a title he shares with only seven other people, including Eliel Saarinen, Mies van der Rohe, Buckminster Fuller, and I. M. Pei.

A frequent spokesperson for the profession of architecture, Ivy travels extensively as an advocate for many of the most important social, political, and environmental issues affecting the built environment. In 2002, the Department of State appointed Ivy as United States Commissioner to the Venice Biennale of Architecture. He holds a master's degree in architecture from Tulane University in New Orleans, where he serves on the advisory board, and a BA (cum laude) in English from the University of the South.

Robert Ivy feels strongly about the role of architects and architecture to shepherd society in socially responsible and sustainable ways. With increasingly cataclysmic weather events and earthquakes, Robert Ivy believes that architects play a vital role in finding forward-thinking solutions that can have life-saving consequences. My conversation with Ivy begins with the rebuilding of Katrina-ravaged New Orleans, a city close to his heart.

Let's talk about the Gulf Coast. I know that you are a New Orleanian and that what happened to that city and what will happen in the future are very important to you. I, too, lived there for a time, and I think I can relate to its powerful and mysterious sense of history and sensuality. I can think of no other place in America where the visible presence of the past through its built environment is as core to its identity and the way people experience the city as New Orleans. Can you lay out some of the issues that city planners and designers need to consider in the wake of the disaster?

Robert Ivy: New Orleans, in its past, was a cosmos unto itself. It was a self-contained universe circumscribed by water, a fragile floating place in which a very particular culture emerged over centuries. It will not be easy to replicate the layers of history, intermarriage, intercultural association, depth, and odor that resonate within that city. They still exist to a certain extent, but have been eviscerated and dispersed across the United States. There are few people left; 150,000–200,000 people remain. The high ground remains. The historic architecture that has defined the well-known tourist city remains. However, that vastness that allowed an individual to be lost in an unending sea of small houses, I don't think we'll readily get that back. The people have scattered, their economic, social, and personal interests have spread out across the country. They will not quickly return, and if they do, it will be more like clusters of urbanity than the sea of urbanity that defined New Orleans. It was like the water, and you would rock and roll from neighborhood to neighborhood, from the Ninth Ward to St. Charles and on and on. That will not be easy to reclaim. I don't know that it can be artificially designed, per se, because it grew by accretion like moss. It was like scales.

You have written movingly about what we might call the "fabric of place," which is to say, all the nuances and poetry that are in jeopardy in large parts of New Orleans and other parts of the Gulf Coast and that might not be addressed by efforts to rebuild and restore it because they are not immediately part of the language of construction. You have spoken about the legitimate and highly rational nature of the engineers, developers, planners, and designers who respond to this disaster earnestly, but who don't share a common understanding about "the fabric

of place." What language and tools should architects be aware of in order to address how the built environment offers a sense of connectedness to place and the past?

Ivy: I'll work my way into it, perhaps. Let's think about what makes the Gulf South unique. I mean by that the urbanity or the buildings of the Gulf South. They are in part dictated by rational means. Historically, when it was done successfully, construction responded to earth, wind, and sky. Buildings offered shade from the broiling sun and addressed the humidity. We can identify certain building types that were unique to this place. One example is the raised cottage, which lifted the inhabitants above the humid, damp ground up to where there was hope of catching a breeze and sheltered them by large roofs from the omnipresent sun. Those buildings worked. That is rational. The suprarational, the metarational, and even the poetic take us to how these buildings, when they were put together over time, interlocked with the individuals and with one another to form something else. The challenge is that so many of the small-scale, fine-grain, independent businesses and freestanding houses, and the neighborhood associations that went with them, have been destroyed.

The best that we can do is save what remains—and there's a great deal that does remain—and be absolutely assertive about saving the shards that hold those elements of human history. Having said that, what is new can remember what was there and respond to it. We can't build back what we've lost, and in some cases, we shouldn't. In some cases, those buildings were ready for renewal. I think our challenge is that we have to devise a new urbanity while maintaining a sense of history.

How can that be accomplished?

Ivy: I think it means holding on to remnants where they make sense or where they touch us in a special way. But I also think, to counter that argument, that there are large, low-lying areas that were built on more recently that were never meant to be built on. Perhaps that land should remain natural, passive, filled with live oak trees. That's going to be a very difficult thing to achieve.

There are other disasters around the world, and how we approach the issue of large-scale loss is really the question. What do we do when what we had is no longer there? Do we build it back? Do we build a faithful reproduction? Do we interpret, or do we go on from where we were before? Storms like hurricanes can affect us in different ways. The Mississippi Gulf Coast, for instance, was obliterated. Very few buildings remain. It's as if a giant Cyclops marched ashore and knocked everything down with large cartoon hands. It defies human understanding that water rose to the height of 28 feet with overtopping waves and ground to powder anything in its path. Certain towns no longer exist. The only things that still stand are live oak trees that grow by torsion and were able to twist in the force of the water, but there are no buildings under them anymore. New Orleans sat in 9 feet of stinking water and essentially rotted, a much more complex situation. How do you approach these two very different places? And what meaning does that hold for other places that might face similar loss? Tornadoes seem to be increasing in intensity; we read about and see on television, almost weekly, straight-line winds that take down anything in their paths.

The devastation is absolute.

Ivy: The loss of a single house is a very straightforward event. An insurance policy typically covers the physical property. People typically will rebuild exactly as they had before. I think of the Sam Walton family, which lost its house, designed by the architect Fay Jones, to fire. This was a superlative example of an American residence, and it was the home of what ultimately became the wealthiest family in the country. When their house burned, they moved an Airstream trailer onto the site and rebuilt the house almost exactly as it had been built before, making minor corrections and modifications to what they had known and felt comfortable with.

When a city is lost, or a segment of a city is lost, we face something that's more complex because it isn't about the individual unit. It's about the relationships of the pieces and parts. It's all the things in between that are lost. It's the space between the buildings that held the movement and the life. The value of these nuances— the built-up odors and tactile and sensory experiences—is very difficult to argue for in a rational and economic sense. And the way we built in the past is sometimes harder to justify economically. That is, low-scale, high-density construction is sometimes more difficult to justify than high-density, high-rise construction. That's a challenge that threatens many cities across the county. People argue about it all the time. They're having massive fights about that right now in downtown Brooklyn.

Did you have a particular passion for the architecture of Fay Jones that led to your book _Fay Jones: The Architecture of E. Fay Jones, FAIA_?

Ivy: The work with Fay Jones began with an invitation by a publisher to meet Fay and to consider the book. I had heard him speak and, frankly, he had shown hundreds of slides and I had thought, gee, that's a lot of wood and stone. Let's say, I was not particularly moved. But the moment I got off the airplane and met this extraordinary man and walked into one of his houses, I knew this was architecture with a capital _A_, the kind that moves you, the kind that changes things. It was the real thing. From that moment on, I was hooked.

Fay was an apprentice of Frank Lloyd Wright, and he is one of many architects influenced by Wright. Do you think we can plot a genetic course from Wright to the present?

Ivy: Absolutely. Many architects that have followed in Frank Lloyd Wright's wake, including Fay, give explicit acknowledgment to that unparalleled architect. Wright influenced more than one generation of architects. And Jones is one of the few people to have worked with and learned from two of the great American masters: Wright and Bruce Goff, who was a wonderful teacher and architect in Oklahoma at the time Jones knew him. But Jones really deserves our attention where he broke out of the Wrightian mold and went beyond it. But much of Jones's early work, and some of his latter work, is explicitly Wrightian in its organization, materiality, and the ideas that underlie it all.

I think the great lesson is to find what is of value and immerse yourself in it—which Jones did with the lives and works of Wright and Goff—and then filter it through your own consciousness and allow something new to emerge. Don't try to invent something out of your own consciousness—very few people are able to do that. There's much to learn from others.

Describe some of the emerging ideas and trends in American residential design that you are enthusiastic about.

Ivy: I think we've reinvented the meaning of home, for instance, in some of the elements of the home. Historically, one of the hallmarks of residential design has been an energy source. That energy source has varied from the fire in the earliest domed houses in Cypress and the cave dwellings to the fireplace hearth, to the television set (pardon me very much), and to the home entertainment center or the kitchen today. That source of heat and light is constantly being renewed, and we're always rethinking what it consists of in inventive ways that reflect the way we live today.

Another is our relationship to the outdoors. It's possible now to build houses that are membranes, that invite us to know nature and to participate in it in all of our daily lives. We can shower outside, we can let light in our bedrooms, we can have closets that are not dingy, and we can have entry spaces that are inviting, all by placing ourselves in the knowledge and presence of nature. Proximity to nature has been in our history of design for a good 150 years, and it shows no sign of abating.

I heard Ellen Gilchrist talk about waking up and the first thing you encounter is an oak tree, as opposed to a wall. Today we can live that way, in touch with the world around us. The relationship of humankind to nature was a tenet of the International Style but also of organic architecture, and both of those have roots in the early-nineteenth-century writers like Emerson. Today, the buildings that we describe as modern, that you see in *Dwell* magazine, for example, are International Style in origin but hark back to nineteenth-century ideals. They are positive ideals that I think are happy-making for the human psyche.

Conversely, what trends should be redressed or confronted critically?

Ivy: I think artists are strengthened by limits. A great failure or weakness that the American artist and architect face today is limitlessness. A tighter budget produces more invention, which often creates greater work. The open checkbook produces too much of a good thing. Today we routinely see mega houses on sprawling acreage that lack definition. They don't ultimately present us with the most serendipitous accommodation for living, to coin a euphemism. They offer us too much choice, too much space. They don't offer us the intimacy, knowledge, and security that come with shelter. Instead, we're presented with a dizzying array of choices of places to be in spaces that are ill-differentiated. A certain gloom accumulates around such grandiosity.

How long do people keep such big houses in a world in which we routinely shed spouses, in which families break up, in which the social order seems to be tenuous at best? They're despoiling the landscape, they're greedy of material, means, method, place, and labor. I don't think they reflect well on who we are and how we think. They're not particularly inventive. So what do I dislike about where we're going? I'd say bigness is not a virtue.

How would you suggest we capture the zeitgeist of residential architecture?

Ivy: That is a good question. From my perspective, and as many others have said, architecture is a language. It is discreet and material in its expression, but it is a language. It uses rules as explicit as grammar, but it uses them in three dimensions with solid objects. It exists in part in theory but primarily in expression. When we're looking at a building, we're looking at what we think. It's that simple. So we should be able to look at the buildings we're currently making and take the temperature of who we are. We've been able to do that historically for thousands of years. I think we can still do that.

The larger question is what lies beyond where we are right now. This is a very tentative moment in residential design, but a heroic and inventive moment in other kinds of design. For instance, I think of how digital media have completely unlocked human imagination and our ability to create new forms. We don't see a concomitant change in residential design. The question is why not.

CHARLES GWATHMEY

"I think why architects still love to do
houses is that you can think about all
the formal issues, think about multiple
strategies, think about different materials,
and you can experiment . . ."

Charles Gwathmey (1938–2009) was a founding principal of Gwathmey Siegel &
Associates. The firm's extensive portfolio includes a 1992 addition to the Guggenheim Museum, the International Museum of Photography, and the Astor Place
condominiums—all in New York. A house he designed in 1966, for his artist parents
on Long Island, has been consistently named one of the most influential buildings
of the modern era. Along with Richard Meier, Gwathmey was a member of the
New York Five. His work strongly adheres to the tenets of early-twentieth-century
modernism (exemplified in Le Corbusier's buildings of the 1920s and 1930s), tem-
pered with pragmatism and an almost playfully experimental approach to design.

Gwathmey was born in North Carolina and received his MArch from Yale University in 1962. In 1970, Gwathmey was honored with the Brunner Prize from the
American Academy of Arts and Letters; he was elected to the Academy in 1976. In
1983, he won the Medal of Honor from the New York Chapter of the AIA, and in
1985, he received the first Yale Alumni Arts Award from the Yale School of Architecture. The Guild Hall Academy of Arts awarded Gwathmey its Lifetime Achievement Medal in Visual Arts in 1988. That honor was followed in 1990 by a Lifetime
Achievement Award from the New York State Society of Architects. Gwathmey
passed away on August 3, 2009, after battling cancer for several years.

Charles H. Baldwin House, Bellevue Avenue opposite Perry Street, Newport, Rhode Island.
Built in 1878, it was described as "a very tasty appearing villa" in contemporary newspapers.

Charles Gwathmey, taking the long view, considers how architects must now deploy material innovations, particularly in the mechanics of energy use, in anticipating global warming. He sees sustainability in house design as an ethical concern, explaining, "By continuing to explore architecture through the house model, one not only learns a great deal about process but is also able to apply that process to larger-scale and more complex problems."

Your firm has created many major projects for real estate developers, schools, and museums, yet you maintain a thriving residential practice. Why do homes continue to interest you?

Charles Gwathmey: Residences have been a kind of prototypical architecture; historically, they have been the critical building type. If you think of Palladio—and we all go back and look at his buildings—they inform Architecture with a capital *A*, and yet they were mostly houses. I think why architects still love to do houses is that you can think about all the formal issues, think about multiple strategies, think about different materials, and you can experiment with—rather than through—your clients to determine whether your ideas are legitimate, interesting, provocative, enriching, and can also apply to other work. So I think as a microcosm, the house is totally fulfilling in the hierarchy of complexity, the hierarchy of public and private, and the ideas of arrival and sequence, orientation and view, and circulation. It embodies all the elements that architecture has to deal with.

I think today it's unfair to isolate the house as a unique or small or non-content kind of work. It's never been, at least in my mind, about size; it's always been about content. By continuing to explore architecture through the house model, one not only learns a great deal about process but is also able to apply that process to larger-scale and more complex problems.

Where do you see your work in the history of residential architecture?

Gwathmey: I don't like to speculate about things like this, but I think the house I did for my parents, which I now occupy, was a groundbreaking moment in modern residential architecture in America. In particular, I think it changed the whole idea of American vernacular to a more European-based reference. And I think that house and Richard Meier's houses at the time together changed the landscape of how architects—forget about clients—started to think about residential architecture. What's amazing to me is that it's a wood house, not a steel or concrete house, but it embodies all the formal strategies that are essential to modern architecture.

Which architects have most influenced your approach to architecture?

Gwathmey: I think of Le Corbusier and Frank Lloyd Wright, for different reasons. Corbusier for his planned graphic and the composite idea of plan and section for being simultaneous. And Frank Lloyd Wright for the architectonic and material ethic, the architectonicness of furniture and everything being considered simultaneously and being integrated. And the way he used natural materials. Both architects impacted how I thought about residential architecture.

Do you see any technological innovation on the horizon that will have a significant impact on homes being built in the United States?

Gwathmey: I think two interesting phenomena are finally being acknowledged as real issues: the environment and the ethics of green architecture. The Europeans are way ahead of Americans in that area. The investigations of double-layer façades and different materials that act appropriately are opening up new opportunities and possibilities that are both aesthetic and environmentally sensitive. I think the environmental issues are gigantic and not being pushed enough. They're not being marketed to the degree where all the people that should be are concerned and aware. Something has to give, and it shouldn't be an earthquake.

The second thing is the notion of the mechanical systems and what kind of fuel one uses and the economy of means. All of that would impact the aesthetics, how you make buildings, and what you make them out of.

We were at a conference on environmental issues and global warming recently. If you really hear the facts, it's astounding. And it's not so far away. Maybe far away for me, but it's not so far away for you. And it's definitely not far away for people who are being born today. I think architects have obligations about this. Like anything else, when you first begin to respond, there are going to be trial and error and unknowns, and there's going to be an economic impact. But as we research and find appropriate solutions, they'll become a part of the language and a part of our responsibility to address.

Someone was telling me that the source of all the water in Los Angeles is going to run out in fifteen or twenty years.

Gwathmey: This global warming problem is gigantic—the carbon monoxide emitted into the atmosphere, fuel shortages, and energy issues. Architecture to date, especially in our century, has exploited the notion of applied comfort. But while you're air conditioning to make yourself more comfortable, you're destroying the atmosphere, you're getting bad air, and you're using fuel. It's a contradiction. We can make buildings that are self-ventilating and cool their own air by allowing it to move naturally from low to high and through spaces. All these things are going to impact aesthetics and become part of the "next technology." And the house—by being a prototype and offering the opportunity to learn and experiment—is the ideal scale project to discover how to manipulate this stuff.

And it's not even being done very much.

Gwathmey: Not yet. Not here.

Do you think that using a computer, as opposed to using your hands and eyes, changes the way people think and create?

Gwathmey: Teaching today, I realize that the computer is not a tool. From my point of view, it's an integral piece of the process now. And it's causing a problematic conceptual gap between how one creates with the hand and eye as opposed to the seduction of this technological achievement. The computer doesn't allow for the frustration of the self-editing process that you have to go through to come to a refined determination of an idea. It's too loose.

I think there's a huge learning curve that is becoming wider in the difference between how one thinks and how one understands. The two should be simultaneous. When I teach now, I refuse to let my students use a computer, which is a killer because not only can't they draw, they can't build models. And it's getting worse. I don't want to sound like an old-school guy who can't deal with the future, but I think it will take time to integrate the computer as an extension rather than as the center of how people think about making things.

The young architects we get here don't have a clue, not a clue. I guess one could say, "What's the big deal about making things?" I still think that architecture is made and detailed and has an obligation over time. And I wonder, on another level, whether certain kinds of buildings being made today have any longevity whatsoever, both in terms of self-maintenance and applied maintenance. Because it still rains, the sun still shines, the south is south, and that's not changing so fast. Buildings expand and contract, they leak, and they have obligations over time. What's going on right now is a little facile and idealized. It's in a vacuum.

143

PART 4

Cities, Suburbs, Regions

In this section, we explore the house in its context—the organization of homes within communities, from the master-planned towns of the New Urbanists to the regional vernacular of the Midwest; from ambiguous Los Angeles manifestations of "authenticity" to the challenging and all too real climate of the Pacific Northwest.

Monkey Fountain at the J. Paul Getty Museum, Ranch House, 17985 Pacific Coast Highway,
Malibu, California. It is a replica of a Florentine fountain from the sixteenth century.

PAUL GOLDBERGER

"The Getty is a wonderful lens through
which to look at authenticity."

Paul Goldberger (b. 1950) is an American architectural critic and educator and a
contributing editor for *Vanity Fair* magazine. From 1997 to 2011 he was the architecture critic for the *New Yorker*. According to the Huffington Post, he is "arguably the leading figure in architecture criticism." Goldberger is the author of many
books, including *Why Architecture Matters* (Yale University Press, 2009); *Building Up and Tearing Down: Reflections on the Age of Architecture* (Monacelli Press,
2009); and his chronicle of the process of rebuilding Ground Zero, *Up from Zero:
Politics, Architecture, and the Rebuilding of New York* (Random House, 2004). Most
recently he wrote *Building Art: The Life and Work of Frank Gehry* (Knopf, 2015), his
first biography.

Goldberger's architecture criticism at the *New York Times* was awarded the
Pulitzer Prize for Distinguished Criticism. Mayor Rudolph Giuliani presented
him with the New York City Landmarks Preservation Commission's Preservation
Achievement Award in recognition of the impact of his writing on historic preser-
vation in New York in 1996. In 1993, he was named a Literary Lion, the New York
Public Library's tribute to distinguished writers. He is a graduate of Yale University.

Paul Goldberger talks about cyberspace and public space. He discusses the loaded
concept of authenticity, using examples of Los Angeles public spaces like the Grove
and the Getty Villa. In this discussion, he considers the changing nature of the city
concurrent to the rise of a pervasive virtual experience. If work is less contingent

on place, if the city isn't primarily the place we live because it is the place we work, "Is the city going to be a theme park where everyone walks around and goes to festival marketplaces and nice boutiques, and then goes into their nice glass condos?"

In a speech you gave at Berkeley in 2001, titled "Cities, Place and Cyberspace," you considered the contradictions that we are "torn between believing that the city is irrelevant in the age of cyberspace, and believing that it has more urgency than ever—or that place matters more than ever." You also observed, "We like to play at urbanity, without getting ourselves messed up in it. We want controlled environments, because that is what we have become used to in a world of private space, and it is what the computer has made us even more accustomed to. And we call this urbanism." Have you reached any further conclusions on this topic?

Paul Goldberger: Well, I think that when the concept of cyberspace was new, there was a lot of fear that the virtual would somehow drive out the real. I think we've realized now it isn't going to happen. The real has a compelling urgency to it. We want to be in real places. We crave them. We will always be in them. We're not going to allow virtual space to drive it out. But there are subtle shifts in the way technology affects real space, and we're continuing to absorb them and deal with them even now. The great concern several years ago was that technology would somehow replace real community with virtual community and that people would choose to communicate and socialize primarily online through virtual communities. The second part of this concern is that the replication of space through technological means—both in the substitution of face-to-face community and human interaction with online communities of people and the replacement of real physical architectural sensation by a simulated technological illusion of such—would replace the real experience. Both of those phenomena continue to exist, but they have not amounted to what we feared they might. As Freud once said, reality insists upon itself. It keeps pushing itself back through, even if its form is somewhat altered and compromised.

Technology has always affected the nature of public intercourse, discourse, community, interaction—call it whatever you will. All entertainment once took place in public. The inventions of the phonograph, radio, and television have gradually been making these experiences more private. But in the end, other things arise to create new forms of public experience because we're not going to allow ourselves to live without it.

I remember, a few years ago, the widely predicted end of retailing because between the Internet, toll-free calls, and catalogs, who needed to go to the store? Well, in fact, shopping as a physical act is a bigger preoccupation in this culture than ever. What happened is that the store morphed into a form of entertainment. People don't go purely to satisfy their needs for commodities. People still do that when they go to the supermarket, but they also shop as a means of entertainment and sometimes as a means of socialization as well. The mall is certainly not the equivalent of the old Main Street, but it does serve similar functions. We've seen a reaction against the mall environment and a resurgence of the pseudo village environment.

Like the Grove, in Los Angeles.

Goldberger: The Grove, absolutely. The Grove is the new form of mall, which in Los Angeles probably began with CityWalk at Universal Studios and Rodeo Drive in Beverly Hills. Both are strange conflations of the village and the theme park. With CityWalk, you don't really know if it's a city street pretending to be a theme park or a theme park pretending to be a city street. We've seen the environment of the theme park and the environment of the "real" city—and I put "real" in quotes there—come together to become increasingly the same thing.

It all began fifty years ago with Disneyland. Charles Moore's "You Have to Pay for the Public Life," from 1965, is possibly the greatest essay written not just about Disneyland but about urban space in California. When Disneyland was only ten years old, Moore wrote that Disneyland was the public space of Southern California and that people went there to pretend they were in a city and to have a conventional urban experience. They would drive along the freeway, park their cars, get out, and pretend they were living in a more traditional place. Increasingly, we create these artificial, vaguely urban experiences. In a way, Disneyland or Universal CityWalk may be the low end, the Grove is the middle, and the Piazza at the Getty is the high end.

> **In your Chicago Forum speech, in March 2004, you said, "We live in an age in which we have come to expect a much more sophisticated visually and emotionally engaging public realm." You expressed concern that this profound cultural shift, along with its attendant ubiquitous design culture, threatens "individuality and distinction of place, offering instead the homogenization of places."**

Goldberger: Those are related but slightly different phenomena. The latter point was referring as much to the most serious and intellectually ambitious architecture as to everything else. The former point, which is maybe the better one to talk about first, is really about the risks of success in design. I believe we live in a time in which the dream of the Bauhaus—that modern design of decent quality is not only available but also actively sought by the mass market—has been fulfilled, in effect, by IKEA and places like it. The price we are paying is that as we are raising the floor, we're also slightly lowering the ceiling. Of course, extraordinary, distinctive, and idiosyncratic design still exists, but it becomes harder to do those things and make them noticed.

The Grove is an interesting example on this score as well as in terms of urban space. You walk around there and you don't see a lot of junk. If you go into places like Banana Republic, J.Crew, and the Gap, it's all pretty good. And some of it is very good—Pottery Barn and Crate&Barrel, as well as IKEA. The mass market produces things at a level that is very different from what was produced a generation ago, not to mention significantly longer ago. You see far greater interest and sympathy for design in the marketplace, but it does push us toward a kind of homogeneity. This stuff is ubiquitous. Look at a company like Design Within Reach, where once high-end, difficult-to-obtain pieces of classic modernism, the very possession of which connoted a certain elite, can now be gotten as easily as you can get a bed-spread at Bloomingdale's.

Some call it Design Out of Reach.

Goldberger: Yes, it's expensive. But something has changed in terms of the society, both culturally and economically, that supports that business. An Eames chair was even more expensive relative to the dollar thirty and forty years ago, and much less available. The success of Target is significant, too. None of the things we're talking about are without exceptions. But the center of gravity has moved, and that tells you something.

You have stated that you value _authenticity_. How would you define authenticity as it relates to architecture?

Goldberger: "Authenticity" is an essential word to talk about, and yet there's no simple way to define it. I moderated a roundtable discussion at the Getty Villa in Malibu with a bunch of architects and scholars. The theme was the architecture of the Getty and the expansion that had just been completed. The Getty is a wonderful lens through which to look at authenticity. Was the Getty's fake Roman villa from the first century that was recreated in 1974 more authentic in its 1974 version or its 2006 version? In 2006, it was made slightly more historically accurate in some ways, and less historically accurate in numerous other ways. Historical accuracy itself is a matter of conjecture. And are the modern buildings that surround it, designed by Machado and Silvetti, more authentic? They themselves owe a significant debt to historical examples of modernism. In some ways, one could make an argument that the Getty Villa is a more original and creative work than the Getty Center in Brentwood, by Richard Meier, which owes huge debts to the modernist aesthetic of the 1920s. The Getty Center is arguably as much a piece of historical derivation, albeit creatively altered, as the Getty Villa of 1974 was. In other words, the authenticity discussion becomes a cat chasing its tail, yet you can't avoid it either.

Authenticity is crucial, yet our sense of what connotes authenticity changes over time, and it changes as a result of our own experience. All kinds of things in cities today feel authentic to those of us who had a certain upbringing in a certain culture, yet might not be to someone else. One might even say that those standardized stores in malls that we're bemoaning represent the authenticity of our time in a certain way. How we define authentic means a lot. Certain things give us a gut sensibility of representing something genuine that connects closely to real human beings doing things on their own. I think that's often what we mean when we say "authenticity." Things that are created by vast corporate enterprises do not feel authentic, although they authentically represent vast corporate enterprises. We often use "authentic" as a code word for meaning small, comfortable, and connected to the sensibility of an individual, all of which are very valuable things. But authenticity is a bigger and more complex issue than that.

You have written extensively on the role of residential housing in regenerating cities.

Goldberger: Today we are seeing and experiencing cities very differently from how we once did. The city is not as essential economically as it once was. It would be nice to believe it is, but it isn't. We don't need it for manufacturing, we don't need it for transportation, and we don't even need it for commerce in the way we once did. We do need it culturally, though. I don't mean that we need it as a place to have an opera house and the symphony orchestra, although we often do. I mean something much broader and subtler than that. We like the culture of cities. We like being close together. We like the excitement that generates; we like the serendipity, the surprise, and most of all the stimulation—many of us do, at least. Increasingly, an educated upper middle class seeks cities and chooses to live there even when it's not absolutely necessary. As manufacturing institutions move out, people move into the city, just for the fun of it. That creates all sorts of problems. Is the city going to be an artifact? Is the city going to be a theme park where everyone walks around and goes to festival marketplaces and nice boutiques, and then goes into their nice glass condos? Maybe. We don't know yet.

I find it a very important sign of our time that right now some of the tallest buildings and the most interesting skyscrapers being proposed in many cities are condominiums, not office buildings. That's a really new development, and it symbolizes the shift of the city from commercial to residential. It's never going to go entirely in that direction. Certainly, a city like New York, which is home to many creative people, is also home to creative industries and communication industries, and that will remain so. It's not going to disappear. But cities are less and less places that are home to manufacturing industries and the people who work for them.

Elias Olcott House in Rockingham, Vermont, overlooking the Connecticut River Valley

JEREMIAH ECK

"Most of the houses we see today
 are plopped rather than sited."

The architect-author Jeremiah Eck (b. 1945) is a partner in Eck | MacNeely Archi-
tects inc., in Boston, Massachusetts, and a fellow of the American Institute of
Architects. The author of several books—*The Distinctive Home: A Vision of Timeless
Design* (Taunton, 2003); *The Face of Home: A New Way to Look at the Outside of
Your House* (Taunton, 2006); and *House in the Landscape: Siting Your Home Naturally* (Princeton, 2010)—he is especially interested in making a house "work" as a
home through the relationship of the house's setting in the landscape to its interior
design. A lover of the Northeast, he is also an accomplished landscape painter.

Disheartened by the absence of design aesthetics in most suburbs, Jeremiah
Eck believes that too many American homes lack the "spiritual quality that homes
should have . . . people will go out and buy houses from developers with little or
no idea where the house came from, what's inside it, or how it is built." He feels
that distinctive homes are a result of a balance between site, floor plan, exterior
elements, and interior details.

Eck is a former lecturer at Harvard University's Graduate School of Design,
where he continues to offer professional development seminars on house design.
In addition, Eck sits on numerous public service committees and speaks frequently
about how architects may better serve their clients.

Jeremiah Eck picks up the discussion of "authenticity," examining what makes a house "real" and the principles and hallmarks behind how you get there—including the importance of siting and the synergy between parts. He talks about the problems with suburbs, where too much emphasis is often placed on a home's "curb appeal" and not enough on design and material quality. In our accommodation to dramatic city growth, have we forgotten what makes a good house?

You have said that, in the twenty-first century, we Americans don't feel comfortable in our houses.

Jeremiah Eck: My personal opinion is I don't think our houses are authentic anymore. When you look back over the history of the American house, there are certain icons or periods in which houses had a certain kind of meaning that was so strong that we actually even today try to reinvent it. I have in mind, for instance, a center-entrance colonial, which, for a number of years, was the most popular house ever built in the twentieth century. Something about that image and the feeling of that house was so strong that developers and spec builders were able to carry it over, even though the house inside bore no resemblance to the original. We seem to be searching around for some language, some sense of place—of house—and we don't have it right now.

If you go out into the suburbs and look at houses right now—which I do a lot and I'm sure you probably do, too—most of them are ugly. They're too big; they're disproportioned. They often don't even have plans that make sense to people. They aren't well built; a lot of them are going to fall down in twenty years. We all seem to know that, yet we trade them on the real estate market and they're worth a lot of money to a lot of people. But they seem to be more about entertainment than authenticity. I think, as an architect who does houses for a living, that there are some missing ingredients. Before we can go forward, we need to go back and look at what houses really mean to us and how to make better houses. The issue of style is irrelevant.

Personally, I don't care if you do modern houses or traditional houses. I think it's a waste of time to worry about it. I think if you like modern houses, fine. If you like traditional houses, that's fine. Even if you like big houses, I think big houses can be beautiful, too. But a more serious matter is quality, authenticity. What makes a real house, and how do you get there? What are the principles and hallmarks behind a good house? We seem to have forgotten that.

On a more positive note, what makes a home distinctive today?

Eck: First of all, I don't mean to be negative. I've been doing this for almost thirty years and I love it. I hope that other people will, too. I'm optimistic that we can all make better houses. I don't think it's negative to say we need to reinvent the issues.

Now what makes a good house? In my opinion, first of all, it's siting. Most of the houses we see today are plopped rather than sited. When I talk to clients about issues such as the sun, they act surprised. But it's fundamental. It's been an issue in houses and other buildings for thousands of years. The other siting question is what's around you: what's the vegetation and what climate are you in. It's disturbing to find New England houses in Florida or on the West Coast, because they don't belong there environmentally. So siting is probably in my mind the most mysterious but most important way to have a beautiful, distinctive house.

The second critical issue is the plan. The plan really has to work for the way people live today. If you look at the history of houses in this country and you put aside how they look on the outside, I could probably tell you within thirty or forty years when that house was designed, just by looking at the plan. The plan is a very important element in designing a good house. When you think about it, the plan is where people start asking what rooms do they need, how do they relate to each other, how do I really live, what's really important, what's not, what's formal, what's informal, what's public, and what's private. All these issues are the first order of questions when you start to design a house, and they place you in your century, in your time. In my own lifetime as an architect, the kitchen has become the premiere room in the house. When I grew up, it was off to the side. The living room was the most important room, and yet you never went there. You weren't allowed to go there. What happened was the TV. All of a sudden a—I love this term—"rec room," as if you spell it "w-r-e-c-k," or family room, became the place where people were spending their time. Women were working outside of the home just like men. People said, "Where do I spend my time?" In the kitchen. So why don't we make the kitchen part of the house? Now you have rooms like the hearth room, or what I call "living hall," which contains a kitchen and family room—informal space. Even in my relatively short lifetime, the plan has changed. So plan is the second most important ingredient.

The third issue is what it looks like. I use the words "ugly" and "beautiful," and I use them definitively, because I think we don't use them enough. I think people are afraid to say "ugly" in our culture. They seem to think that it's a word that only certain people can use or that no one has the right to decide what's beautiful or what's ugly. I would say that the complementary colors have always been complementary as far as I know. What's wrong with making judgments, if you're trained to do so, about what's beautiful and ugly?

A house is a shell, if you will, surrounding activity, penetrated by openings, facing a certain direction, and made up of certain spaces that you have to roof. The sum total of all that is a metaphorical piece of sculpture that you're twisting and turning to adjust to the site and to the plan, and you make an object that has to be beautiful. You look at a lot of the houses built today and you wonder what's going on inside. They're an amorphous accumulation of parts that don't seem to have any meaning. So the third most important part of making a house distinct is to make the outside be balanced, the mass good, the scale good, and make it beautiful. And it is something you can train yourself to do. I don't think it should be left up to everyone to decide what's beautiful. That's just my not-so-humble opinion. I often think there ought to be aesthetic police, but I won't get anywhere with that, I'm sure.

The fourth is the details. When you think of houses that you love, often it's just about a few details. You might go into a house and see a beautiful fireplace or a wonderful staircase or the ways the windows are handled or the way one room has certain paneling. So you have to make sure the house has a few details of quality.

All four of those principles are blended together. They interact with each other. One is not independent of the others.

Do you have a pithy aphorism that expresses how those components should work together to add up to something more than the sum of their parts?

Eck: Integration is a synergy between the parts—wholeness. Authenticity comes from wholeness. You can't imagine a good house that would be poorly sited or had a terrible plan. If you look at any great house, it will have all four of those qualities. Take most development houses. We're talking about over 50 percent of all the houses that have been built in this country in the last thirty years, single-family houses. That's been in my architectural lifetime, so to speak. Most of those houses, the vast majority, have hardly been designed at all. So when we're talking about architectural houses and the kinds of icons that Lester Walker's *American Homes: An Illustrated Encyclopedia of Domestic Architecture* shows, those are prototypes for a particular style and rarified types. But today there are so many bad houses. It's hard to know in a hundred years what Lester would draw to represent the suburban house of the late twentieth and early twenty-first centuries. There is no clear picture of what it should be. Again, I don't mean to sound negative; I'm trying to reverse the trend. I think ultimately the answer to all of this is art.

When you talk about balance and wholeness, is there something you consider universal and timeless?

Eck: Again, to go back to the principles, I believe strongly that this is not about size or style. So the only word I can use is "authenticity," which becomes timeless. When you look at a good house, you hardly worry about when it was done. What you look at is a complete package, and my thesis is that the reason it holds together is that it has a bit of these four principles. Now compare that to today's suburban tract houses. I won't judge the plan because I haven't walked into the house. But I can look at the outside of most of those houses, and they don't look sited. They look plopped. And they don't have the third principle, which is a beautiful exterior that is balanced and well proportioned.

These terms are not difficult for people to understand. People go to Marblehead, Venice, Paris; they stay in these houses and they see beauty and say, "Isn't this wonderful?" Yet, they'll come home and not expect it in their own backyards. And that's unfortunate. I think this problem is not associated with any single profession or person. It's a universal problem that needs to be resolved universally by all of us, by reexamining what a house is.

I come back to art as the answer. I think it starts with our children. They have to learn more about the right brain, not just the left brain. Even our presidents in speeches stress math and science all the time, and they never talk about art. Art is seen as somehow not useful in our lives. But I would argue that it is probably one of the most useful things that we do. In the nineteenth century, they understood that true education involved both art and science. And if you look at the sketchbooks of nineteenth-century schoolchildren, you'll see drawings that are very similar to the beautiful buildings of the nineteenth century that we all admire. I challenge anyone to go out and look at the sketchbooks of contemporary American kids. You won't find that because it's not taught. So a beautiful house is not just these principles but putting the principles together in an artful fashion.

One thing that stands out in your book *The Face of Home: A New Way to Look at the Outside of Your House* is how the exterior of a house has a huge impact on a person's experience of the interior of the house. How do you think that works, psychologically?

Eck: Well, that's a very interesting question. I chose the metaphor "face of home" because it's always struck me that you see someone in the distance coming down the street and you recognize their outline, the length of their hair, and how tall they might be. As they get closer, you begin to recognize more about them, what they have on, the complexion of their skin, and the details of their face. I think it's the same with houses. You see them from the distance, and you see them close-up as you arrive. You see them really close-up, and then eventually you walk inside. We tend in this culture to disassociate the outside from the inside, and I don't know where that came from. We have these notions such as that "curb appeal" sells houses. What exactly does that mean? It may look good from the curb, but is that where it stops?

My book points out two problems. One is when you say things like "curb appeal," you're associating house with surface, yet there's more to it. The outside should say something about the inside and vice versa. Secondly, the labels have become meaningless, the way we describe houses. Lester's book is beautiful in the labeling of certain iconic house types. If you say to yourself it's a Victorian, in your mind will probably come an image of a Victorian that is much like he's drawn it. There are many different Victorians, yet that label is appropriate somehow for that type. Today we don't have meaningful labels anymore. We have things such as "modern French château." What the heck does that mean? I think we have to understand that houses look a certain way for a reason. They look that way because of the plan. We have to reexamine the meaning behind the house in order to understand how it looks on the exterior. I'm not saying labels have no use, but we should say to ourselves, "What is it about this house that I really like when I look at it? What is it about the outside that makes sense to me and why? Is it authentic in the sense that it says something about the inside? If it does, then it's probably going to be a beautiful house, and it doesn't matter what you call it. That allows for incredible diversity. You don't have to say you like modernism or you like traditional houses. You can like anything as long as it's authentic.

So what kind of responsibility do you think all that places on the architect of a new home?

Eck: I would not place the responsibility on architects; I would place the responsibility on all of us. As I said earlier, the vast majority of houses are designed without architects. If we, as buyers, begin to be more discriminating in our houses, sooner or later people who build these houses will start to be more discriminating in the way they are designed and built. I think all architects can do is serve as examples of what can be. Ultimately, the responsibility lies on all our shoulders to make a better house. They're all going to fall down soon anyway, so we're going to have the opportunity to reinvent the house in the next twenty years.

I'm amazed when we talk about environmental friendliness and these other notions as if they're abstract questions, when in truth a good house is environmentally friendly and would probably make all of us feel healthier. I honestly believe that. One could argue that part of the disillusionment of our culture is about the disillusion of our houses.

I happen to believe sprawl is an issue, too, but if our houses were beautiful, it would be less of an issue. I don't believe that cars will survive as the sole tool of transportation. But I don't think that means that there won't be houses anymore. I'm not going to argue that single-family living is better than urban living, but I do think there will always be room for the single-family house, and we can make more beautiful houses. That's the reason for writing all of my books, really.

Could you elucidate the elements of a good exterior, as set forth in _The Face of Home_?

Eck: The first is that site and house are one. That's the simplest way I can say it. That can be true in the city, suburbs, or subdivision. I'm not just talking about the beautiful house overlooking the ocean; that's not my concern.

The next thing is that the house has to have a balance, what I call "mass in scale." This is not a new notion by any stretch of the imagination, but I think it needs to be reiterated that the mass of the house has to feel appropriate for its size. If it doesn't, it has to be broken down into smaller parts. And you have to feel like it has a human scale; when you go up against it, it feels appropriate.

The next principle is what's behind the face, and that goes back to this notion of the plan. I happen to believe that the exterior of the house should reflect the interior. In a sense, if you were to take the plan of a house and turn it up on its side, you ought to be able to see the plan in the elevation. These rules are not hard and fast but, for instance, if there is a large room in the house on the left side and it has a high ceiling and you turn it up on its side, there ought to be on the outside a larger window in scale to the rest of the windows or something else that says that's the room inside. Again the face metaphor, everybody has something going on behind the face. We're all heavies. Same for a house. It is an accumulation of how people actually live behind it.

Then what I call "face-to-face." You're facing the front of the house as you might be looking at someone walking down the street—you, for instance. I see that you've got glasses and beautiful earrings on, and I can see your hair is cut in a certain way. The same is true for a house. I can see the starkness of the stucco, the muntins on the windows, the trim boards that might be wrapping around the roof, or the texture of the chimney. I begin to see a lot of details, and that detail has to fit the mass and the scale that I talked about earlier on. If you imagine it with no detail whatsoever, just a concrete or stucco box, it would have a completely different feeling than if it had decorative shingles or was white versus red. So as you get closer, as you get face-to-face, you begin to see something closely.

And then the final one is what I call the "complexion" of the house. I'm stretching the metaphor of face a little bit, but it's about the detail. When you go beyond the mass, scale, and materials, you begin to see certain details—edges, brackets, and columns on the exterior that add up. And they have to make sense with the rest of the exterior of the house. In other words, you would never put a great Doric column on an Arts and Crafts house. It would be silly. That's an exaggeration, but if you're trying to reinvent a new look, which I think is wonderful if you can do it, then the column should say something about your reinvention.

I grew up in a foursquare house in Ohio, and I have fond memories of that place, the alley out back, and people sitting on the porch out front. You open the door, and the neighbor is next door. It's hard for me to imagine that kids who grow up in the suburbs today have that same quality of life.

It sounds like you didn't exactly grow up in the suburbs.

Eck: You could argue that I grew up in a kind of 1940s suburb, although the houses were much smaller and closer together and they had a kind of rhythm to them. The "new urbanism" of back alleys and porches was all there for us. Nobody designed it; it came naturally. A park was related to each section of town—West Park, North Park, East Park—and the alleys connected to the parks, so everybody

159

JEREMIAH ECK

had a common space. There was a rhythm of life and a connective tissue that doesn't exist now. We're now at the end of a yoyo string in relation to the world. It's no wonder people want big-screen TVs and Jacuzzis, because what else are they going to do with their lives? It's lonely. You go in and lock the door, set the security system—you're afraid of the world—and then you sit there and watch people killing each other or having promiscuous sex on TV. It's kind of absurd when you think about it.

TOM KUNDIG

"At its core, residential architecture is shelter. It's the most primitive, basic need, right after food."

Tom Kundig's (b. 1954) designs successfully combine art, craft, and the human experience of space. Kundig's award-winning houses are celebrated for their rugged yet elegant and welcoming style. He is internationally recognized for his big American West landscape sensibility.

Kundig is known for holding to a tradition of art fabrication; integration of elegant architecture with the exploration and reinvention of parts of architecture, such as doors, windows, or stairs; and for his use of kinetic architectural elements.

To date, Kundig has been awarded a total of twenty-six AIA awards, including four recent National AIA awards (for The Brain, Chicken Point Cabin, Delta Shelter, and Tye River Cabin). A monograph on the work of his firm, *Olson Sundberg Kundig Allen Architects: Architecture, Art, and Craft*, was published in 2001 by Monacelli Press, and in 2006, Princeton Architectural Press released *Tom Kundig: Houses*. Kundig earned his undergraduate and graduate architecture degrees from the University of Washington. He is a recipient of a 2007 Award in Architecture from the American Academy of Arts and Letters.

Tom Kundig identifies how the Northwest landscape informs his architecture, yet how good design can transcend regional boundaries. How does that dynamic tension between vernacular of a region and the "playfulness" he is known for coexist? "Whether you're from the Northwest, Southwest, Australia, or Europe, you find a common thread of problem solving the idiosyncratic situation of a

Joe Pfeiffer Homestead in Grand Teton National Park near Moose, Wyoming

place. That place may be desert, forest, mountains, or the shore, but at the abstract level, they're all problems we're trying to solve. We're all trying to resolve the landscapes." In this conversation, Kundig reminds us to ask ourselves, "What are the peculiarities of the landscape? What are the peculiarities of the climate—now and further down the road?"

What are the essential qualities of residential architecture that you think will endure over time?

Tom Kundig: At its core, residential architecture is shelter. It's the most primitive, basic need, right after food. It's survival, and because of that it has meaning to all of us at the most visceral level. It's not just personal lifestyle. It is our protection from the elements; it's our place of refuge. Around the world, we all share the same thing. We need food and we need shelter.

In your opinion, what aspects of residential design need to get thrown out or subverted?

Kundig: I'm not sure anything should be thrown out because it is so close, so personal. Home is not only its "shelterness"; it is also a reflection of the culture. So you could be skeptical about a lot of the stylistic machinations that have occurred over time. Some of them have been absurd, some ridiculous, some wonderful, and some brilliant. Some of them have affected our larger cultural institutions and are very important. Houses are like a breeding ground for the culture because it is where the culture is at its most elemental, human level. So to say you should throw anything out is a little bit dangerous, because you don't know if you're throwing out something that's very important to our future, our humanness.

That said, some of the experiments that have happened at the residential level over the years have been absurd, and yes, in hindsight, were probably mistakes. But they are experiments, they are risks, they are an indication of a changing, moving, and thinking people.

Can you elaborate on some examples of experiments or risks that people have taken in residential design—good or bad?

Kundig: There has been a tendency to oversize homes. I'm seeing more and more a tendency to bring back the scale to a more human, personal scale. It seems like there's a size for a family unit that makes sense, where you feel in contact with your family members, spouse, or relatives. I think it's also genetic. There's a limit to what we feel connected with, and in the past our personal spaces got too big; not only in the recent past but also in the distant past, with the royal palaces and some of the earlier, large residential buildings.

Then there are all sorts of other little minor affectations that came up during different eras, like the sunken living room in the sixties, to pick on an absurd one. Basically, a sunken living room was a perfect place for somebody to trip and fall.

Style is an issue that is pregnant with meaning and differences of opinion, and some stylistic evolutions and experiments were not particularly successful for a place to be with yourself and your family.

What is your guiding light when you design?

Kundig: I've always understood architecture as a profession of problem solving. Essentially, it is understanding the issues in front of you—of shelter, style, lifestyle, comfort, and the particular issues of the client. There are also issues of landscape, site, weather, structure, and safety. For example, how is this building going to react in an earthquake, or with winds hitting it and snow on the roof? How is this building going to heat and cool? How is this building going to effectively meet a budget? All these variables work their way into an equation, an algorithm that you're trying to figure out. You collect all the issues into a big, rough draft, then solve this unique place.

The bottom line is about solving a larger problem, and the more successful and the more elegant, clean, light, agile, and beautiful the solution, the better the architecture.

Do you think that being in the Northwest gives you a specific vision?

Kundig: We're always asked to talk about regionalism and how it affects the design we do. I used to think that regionalism had a lot to do with the way we design. I'm in a transition period now where I'm not exactly sure if I think that anymore. I've met so many people around the world in different cities and landscapes, and I've found that we all share a global sensitivity. Whether you're from the Northwest, Southwest, Australia, or Europe, you find a common thread of problem solving the idiosyncratic situation of a place. That place may be desert, forest, mountains, or the shore, but at the abstract level, they're all problems we're trying to solve. We're all trying to resolve the landscapes. What are the peculiarities of the landscape? What are the peculiarities of the climate—now and further down the road?

Being in the Northwest has made me appreciate how wonderful the landscape is, and how much the natural landscape can inform my work. The study of the environment is, in fact, the study of us; it's the study of earth, physics, science, and chemistry.

If you're making an algebraic equation out of your house designs and the landscape is one of the variables, isn't a different landscape going to create a different answer to your question, even if you're using the same equation?

Kundig: You're absolutely right. If it's a sincere, authentic algorithm, your architecture will be affected by the local conditions and reflect the local materials, local building technologies, and local systems strategies in the building. In other words, when you work in the desert, your desert house is going to have mitigation strategies for the sun that are different from your strategies, for example, on the north slope of Alaska. Issues in both of those extremes should affect the look, feel, shape, and strategy of the house, the logic of the house.

Ultimately, your question suggests that a residence in the Northwest will have a different feel than a house in the high desert of Utah. But it is also asking, if the landscapes are relatively similar, for example, if you compare the temperate forest landscape of the Northwest to New England, do they have to be different? No, they can be very similar. There may be a stylistic expectation, for example of a salt-box style in New England and an Asian Northwest contemporary style in the Northwest, but those cultural influences may have been appropriate for the land. A building that works effectively in one environmental condition could look very similar to one in a comparable environment.

How much do the cultural mores of the region affect your clients' tastes, and therefore impose themselves upon you as a designer?

Kundig: Interestingly, about 80 percent of my work is not in the Northwest. We're being hired by people who are attracted to the work we did in the Northwest because they feel that somehow it's appropriate for their parts of the country, and in fact it can be, whether it's in the mountains of North Carolina or northern Idaho.

Do you ever have clients who wish to emulate something they like of yours, but you feel it's completely inappropriate for their landscape?

Kundig: Hardly ever happens, and I think that's because the people who hire us are very sophisticated about buildings and they understand what the possibilities are. They wouldn't even ask us to build something completely inappropriate. Sometimes, when you're published, people will call you who may not understand what it is that you do, but those aren't necessarily the people who ultimately hire you.

It doesn't matter if it's a very expensive house or inexpensive house. Frederick Cabin is a very inexpensive house built for a very sophisticated client who understood the possibility of something very small and discreet in the larger landscape.

I want to ask about the playfulness for which your work is known.

Kundig: Playfulness is really important to me. Maybe it's because I grew up in northern Idaho and eastern Washington in a small community of artists and architects. The core group of personalities there lived life to its fullest. I recognized that the art and some of the architecture could have a sense of playfulness and wonder. I think that is missing in many houses. For me, if you are living in a home, why shouldn't it be fascinating? Why shouldn't it always test you or delight you in different ways? It's your home. I always say it should be a place where you come home and you smile. Whatever makes you smile, whether it's a little gizmo that morphs the room in a certain way or if it's a little wink and a nod about a little design detail that you didn't see the first time but you discover the second or third time. Bob Venturi called it Second Glance Architecture, which I think is a terrific way of describing what happens that second or third time you look at something, or maybe the fourth, fifth, or sixth time. Maybe it's something you didn't even recognize for years.

One of the most wonderful things for me is when I get a phone call from a client after they've lived in the house for two or three years, and they say, "Aha! I get that now." That's like reading a terrific novel that you have to re-read two or three times, or a movie that you have to buy on DVD because you want to watch it time and time again because every time you look at it, it gets a little richer and more delightful. Playfulness is part of that; it's part of the story.

You're very in demand. Do you find it difficult to maintain that playfulness for yourself?

Kundig: I'm known for my gizmos, and people will say, "We want a gizmo." Well, gizmos don't just happen; they come out of the process. It's back to that algorithm idea. You're solving this whole thing, so you can't go into it thinking, "I'm going to get something playful here," because that's like adding something from the outside that's not authentic to the process. It would be almost like saying, "I'm going to write an Oscar-winning screenplay." I think the trick in the creative process is to be ready and facile enough to recognize the moments in which something inventive and wonderful can happen. But to predict or anticipate what that will be is like using a note in a musical score that doesn't fit. The most concerning part is that those moments are quick. You have to be there and you have to grab them. You don't want to miss them because that's the best part.

ELIZABETH PLATER-ZYBERK

"Mass production is no longer about repeating the same thing over and over again like a cookie cutter. You can use repetition to deal with some serious issues—for example, public housing—but have variation and individuality within those models."

Elizabeth Plater-Zyberk (b. 1950) is an American architect and urban planner. In 1977, with her husband, Andrés Duany, and architects Bernardo Fort-Brescia, Laurinda Hope Spear, and Hervin Romney, Plater-Zyberk cofounded the Miami firm Arquitectonica. The firm was renowned for its dramatic and expressive "high-tech" modernist style. Duany and Plater-Zyberk later founded Duany Plater-Zyberk & Company (DPZ), also in Miami, with a mandate to replace suburban sprawl with neighborhood-based planning. Indeed, DPZ is a leader in the national New Urbanism movement, which advocates the master-planning of "traditional" towns and retrofitting livable downtowns to help end urban disinvestment. The firm first received international recognition as the designer of Seaside, Florida, which was inaugurated in 1981 (and later featured in *The Truman Show*, the 1999 film by Peter Weir). Since then, they have completed designs and codes for over two hundred new towns, regional plans, and community revitalization projects. The firm's method of integrating master planning with design codes is being applied in towns and cities for sites ranging from 10 to 10,000 acres throughout North America and in Europe and Asia.

Plater-Zyberk is dean of the University of Miami's School of Architecture, where she has taught since 1979. She has coauthored two books: *The New Civic Art* (Random House, 2003) with Andrés Duany and Robert Alminana, and *Suburban Nation: The Rise of Sprawl and the Decline of the American Dream* (Macmillan, 2010) with Andrés Duany and Jeff Speck. A member of the first class of women

Techwood Homes, at 467 Techwood Drive, Atlanta, Georgia,
was the first public housing project in the United States.

to graduate from Princeton University, she received her undergraduate degree in architecture and urban planning from Princeton and her MArch from the Yale School of Architecture.

Elizabeth Plater-Zyberk examines the principles of New Urbanism, the importance of maintaining the integrity of human-scale neighborhoods, the "ecological transect," and the relationship between sprawl and the "American dream."

You are constantly fielding calls from journalists asking the same old questions about New Urbanism. What are the canards of New Urbanism that you would like to redress?

Elizabeth Plater-Zyberk: I have several. New Urbanism is greenfield building and therefore it's not addressing the curtailment of sprawl. It's not infilling existing cities and it's not transit-oriented. All of that, of course, is false. Another myth is that New Urbanism is only for the wealthy. I think most New Urbanist firms would show you practices that are quite the opposite of those misconceptions.

What are the principles of New Urbanism?

Plater-Zyberk: Embedded in the charter of New Urbanism are the goals of diversity and an understanding of an urban structure that should be of benefit, access, and quality for all people, regardless of income or occupation. The implementation of any of the New Urbanism principles is not easy. But many of us are involved with current methods of implementation that are specifically funded, such as affordable housing and otherwise subsidized projects. I think one of our best engagements as a group has been with Hope VI in the remaking of public housing to include diverse homeownership as well as rental housing. There are lots of good examples that have already resulted from that. And I think we'll be seeing some post-occupancy studies before long.

What's important to understand is that there are several tools. In the case of affordable housing, design can take you a certain distance, but policy is also needed so the design principles reinforce diversity in close proximity. One example is the ancillary unit above a garage in a single-family neighborhood, something that codes generally outlawed until we started rewriting codes. Another is producing new models for apartments above shops, the downtown residential type that's not a high-rise or a single-family house. A whole new panoply of building types are coming out of New Urbanism that promote diversity, including live/work, a type of unit that didn't exist a decade ago. The live/work unit encourages workplace and residence to coincide. Generally, the workplace would be on the ground floor with the residence above.

But there's only so much that design can do when real estate prices are escalating, and very often, as you know, real estate prices have nothing to do with the demand and supply of housing or of any of the products but more with investment forces. There are many cities in the United States that have become unaffordable where only a decade ago they had few concerns about affordability. That's the point at which policy comes into play. Whether it's inclusive zoning or special funding like tax-credit programs, public sector intervention is required to re-level the playing field.

Maintaining the integrity of a walkable, human-scale neighborhood, which is one of the tenets of New Urbanism, while offering modern residential and commercial "product" to compete with conventional suburban development seems to be a difficult balancing act. In teaching young architects, what are some of the design mistakes you see here?

Plater-Zyberk: I think the question about erring on the side of commercial conventions while trying to introduce new paradigms is of course always a risk and an issue for the New Urbanists. The goal is for a developer to consider assembling a program as a Main Street environment rather than a strip shopping center. For example, how do you take the strip shopping center and the apartment complex next door and make it into a two-block-long Main Street instead?

What we worry about the most is the hybrid. Outside of Orlando, for instance, everything around you is strip. And then you look in one piece of the strip and there's a Main Street for a block and a half leading off the arterial, which is just shops and a false second floor. So, it's trying to look like it, but it's not really walking the talk.

After the New Urbanist development Seaside was well along the way, the panhandle of Florida sprouted numerous housing subdivisions in which the houses looked like Seaside houses, but they were not on a street grid, they were not part of a diversely assembled community in the way Seaside is. There was not a variety of unit types; there was not a commercial component; there was not a civic component. It was just houses.

Some of your critics argue that towns and cities are not objects that can be "created," but are the result of a process of cultural, social, political, and religious interactions. They criticize the New Urbanists for seeking to accelerate and simulate this process to make their towns more palatable to their predominantly affluent (and perhaps nostalgic) clientele.

Plater-Zyberk: There's a mixed-up series of issues there. One is the speed with which one desires to produce a community today as opposed to the evolution over time that we assume of the older communities we already know. Second is the effort to make that community look as if it evolved over time, rather than reflecting the real time in which it was built.

First of all, one has to realize that there's a long history of new communities being built all at once from scratch, of utopian settlements, new towns, and garden cities. There's quite an illustrious and dignified history of setting out to make a new settlement and not worrying about evolution over time except for the assumption that the framework or structure that's being put into place is capable of long-term sustenance. And some of those places that we admire tremendously were even built to all look the same, such as Bath, England, or Forest Hills, New York. There are many instances in history of intentional communities built within a short frame of time.

The other issue, making a community look as if it has emerged over a longer period of time, has been articulated by the New Urbanists as one approach, but not a necessary one. More than creating an illusion about time, I think the goals are to show some diversity of effort and some variety of engagement. Most people in the United States think of cookie-cutter subdivisions as something to be avoided. I should say that was probably never an issue before World War II. One thinks of postwar suburban developments, such as Levittown, as having spawned that concern about sameness. This generation's response to that homogeneity is to ask how you can make variety authentic so that it satisfies the need for seeing diversity and it's not being made by one big machine.

Some of our historical communities are made up of buildings that were built one by one with a great deal of diversity. But there are also late-nineteenth-century neighborhoods that are very similar unit by unit. Even colonial Philadelphia, from the 1700s, is cheek-by-jowl repetitive building. So I think we have both traditions in this country. That probably reflects a history of two methods of producing housing: people producing houses for sale and people producing houses for themselves. Speculative real estate development has long been a part of housing. Bath was produced as speculative development.

I'd like to ask you, as a renowned town planner and anti-sprawl activist, how does sprawl challenge the American dream?

Plater-Zyberk: I think it's important to understand that sprawl emerged from the American dream being articulated as homeownership, as the ownership of a single-family house on a lot. Its emergence can be traced back to the first settlers, to our French and English roots, to Andrew Downing Jackson's images in the nineteenth century of the garden city. But I think the continuation of that dream in the second half of the late twentieth century is what we're reacting to. And that has to do with the extensive building of the single-family house on the individual lot in such a way that its role in the city and community was ignored. In other words, for many decades we built residential subdivisions under the illusion that we were not building cities and that we were somehow building autonomous places whose interconnections with other places were not important.

That extensive building, which abnegated the forming of a city and tried to ignore the fact that one *was* building a city at the same time—a different kind of city—has resulted in a series of problems that are well documented. The problems range from the social isolation and economic segregation that result from the price point of houses and therefore the income level of residents to the traffic congestion that comes from the road arrangements that focus traffic that's going a long distance on certain roads. The distance from job to residence and from residence to school, the dependence on the vehicle, the use of non-renewable resources for mobility, the inability to walk—those are the things we're reacting to, not the idea that homeownership is in some way negative. I think many economists would tell you that one of the strengths of the American system and much of our political ascendancy come from precisely that kind of stakeholding in the land.

There's a contemporary belief that a true definition of sustainability is the combination of high-density design and transit service. What does this mean for traditional single-family residential design?

Plater-Zyberk: I think the New Urbanists would give you a larger range for sustainability. I don't know if you've heard of the concept of the "ecological transect." We've developed a framework for understanding and positioning different densities relative to each other, from rural stewardship and farming cultivation to the suburban neighborhood to the small town to the urban core. The range is from low to high density, with the proposal that in fact we need all of them. The higher densities can be served by transit. But there are some environments that are better preserved with lower densities.

I currently have a project at the University of Miami that's working with Jonathan Barnett and a University of Pennsylvania studio. Their students and our students are trying to plan for the whole state of Florida what a large amount of growth could look like with projected modes of transportation, both roads and trains.

One of the things we realized is that nobody has ever said, and maybe it's impossible, what the optimum mix of high density and low density is in any given region relative to transit and relative to impact on open space. And that emerges from an ongoing discussion of urbanists and environmentalists in which one says the lighter footprint on the land is better, and that would imply lower density. And the other says, well, higher density, like Manhattan, is better because you limit the sprawl. And then you look at Manhattan and you say, if we were landing on Manhattan today, you would never allow us to build to that density because you would find all sorts of environmental components that you would like to preserve. I think there's an understanding that the high-density, transit-oriented, extremely compact footprint plays a role as well as a lower-density environment where the natural environment takes precedence. And the key issue that's facing us is how to interrelate them.

Is it possible for you to frame for me the opposing arguments of New Urbanism versus the postwar modernist project?

Plater-Zyberk: We shouldn't be posited in opposition to that. In fact, the New Urbanist charter says style is not an issue, meaning that style should not be an impediment. It is an issue because it's always an important issue for the people living in it, the people who desire that identity through the morphology of a building design. We designed a project called Aqua in Miami Beach that is entirely of a late-modern aesthetic.

I don't know everything about the Case Study houses, but I do know that many of them were placed in locations in which they were virtually autonomous, in which they had views in all directions and nobody could look into your glass walls because nobody was living next door. They were very much of that American dream of the individual in the landscape. And so that indeed may be oppositional to the two points you mentioned under sustainability: high density and access to mass transit. There's a contradiction to that kind of glazed house in the forest already just by dint of density. Nevertheless, I think a lot of the high-rises being built these days are almost like those Case Study houses, but agglomerated into a single building.

The early New Urban projects all conformed to whatever the cultural requirements were for market-based housing, for speculative housing, because they were all being produced by the middle-class development industry. In other words, it wasn't the client as patron but the client as customer. And the customer in the US housing market for decades has expected some reference to the traditional style of their region. But in the last decade we really have seen a new market acceptance of modernism in a residential context, and I dare say you'll be seeing more New Urbanist projects that have the full range of style.

Corner notching from the Daniel Wilkins Log House, Montevideo, Minnesota.
Wilkins was an early settler who built the house in 1865.

DAVID SALMELA

"There's also the reference to the
vernacular of our cultural buildings,
not only longhouses but also chicken
coops and sheds."

"The architecture of David Salmela is a quiet one," says the website of Danish Teak Classics (where David Salmela's furniture design is presented), "in tune with nature and the moments in the day that deserve a quiet reflection."

Salmela's architecture and furniture design combine regional vernacular elements with modernist design. Practicing mostly in his native north woods of Minnesota, Salmela has developed a unique style attuned to a snowy winter climate. Though nearly all his buildings are local, he is internationally renowned. Architects across the globe have admired Salmela's modern homes, which draw upon Minnesota's Scandinavian culture, his own Finnish-American roots, and the region's rugged and varied landscape, with, as Danish Teak Classics suggests, "the distinctly playful Salmela perspective."

David Salmela (b. 1945), FAIA, is the principal architect of his firm Salmela Architect, based in Duluth, Minnesota. He has become one of the most awarded architects in Minnesota with more than thirty state and national design awards, including the Honor Award from the national AIA.

Salmela is self-trained, receiving his license to practice architecture at a time when work experience could substitute for formal education.

David D. Salmela looks at the concept of regional architecture and culture's role in design. In the contrast of modernist and traditional forms, amid the enduring landscape, he asks how architecture can have a social compact with the community it arises in.

If I Google you, I get a description that includes the phrase "critical regionalist." Can you explain what that means to you?

David Salmela: Well, I think that my approach to architecture is very related to the region that I was raised in and still live in. First of all, the Native Americans were here, and then came the immigrants. My father was the first white boy born in Vermilion Lake Township in northern Minnesota, and he was born in a sauna. My grandparents all homesteaded on raw land. So the notion of how you start out to build dwellings to survive the weather is rather interesting. I am of Finnish descent, and when the Finnish immigrants came, the first thing they built was the sauna because it was small, you could live in it, you could bathe in it, you could do all you needed to in that building. Then they would build either a house or a barn. I didn't experience this sort of primitive approach, but my parents experienced it, and it influenced my generation.

A lot of the Finnish immigrants built log buildings. The wind would often pass through the logs, so to make them a little more resistant they'd side them. Being immigrants, I also think they sided them so they would fit in and become Americans; they would have houses that looked like everybody else's in the more established communities in the country.

Aspects of the culture still remain and have been raised to another level of sophistication, like the sauna. In 2005, we won the AIA National Honor Award for the Emerson Sauna, which was designed and built here in Minnesota. It was one of thirteen buildings in the whole country to get an honor award. That's quite a distinction for a primitive type of building that now has become very sophisticated. Yet the goal from a design standpoint is to still have both: to have a primitive quality about it in reference to materials and the feel of being in the building as well as having the latest technology.

Your approach to residential architecture appears rooted in this place. Would your work travel, say, if you received an international commission?

Salmela: I think that my architectural theory—and I don't have a lot of them—is that if you can't understand your culture, how can you understand other cultures if you find the opportunity to design somewhere else? I think that in architecture there is a weakness, a human weakness, that architects want to be designing things all over the world and be welcomed and perceived as a great architect everywhere; we want to be international. The whole notion of the International Style was that one style could be repeated anywhere in the world. It was a great idea, but it also was its own weakness in that it disregarded the regional cultures of the world. I think modernism really needs to be able to take the modern ideas of why we build things, how we build things, and the materials we use, but adapt those ideas to each region. I think that's probably what I am subtly attempting to do. Clients can't always articulate what they want or even know what they want, but when they start to see references or let the design evolve, these old cultural roots come up.

People regard me regionally as a Scandinavian-inspired architect. I don't profess or try to be a Scandinavian-inspired modern architect in Minnesota. I try to be an architect. Many of my clients share these Scandinavian roots, but they don't all drive Volvos and Saabs. Some of them even drive Cadillacs or pickups. But the notion is that when you start to solve problems, you come up and you present options. You have to have options; that's what it's all about, analyzing this versus that. And these old Scandinavian roots—or other cultural influences—emerge, and it's kind of surprising. The roots are deep. Even when people try to deny them, they can't hide their instincts. So how does this relate to working on an international scale? Well, I haven't really done anything international, so I really don't know how it would react, but I would have to approach it in a similar fashion to how I do things here.

Can you talk about how culture and the landscape influence the design of a home?

Salmela: You have to start with the land and the site, and you have to understand the site within the next larger element—the section. If it's in a section, it's in a country, and it's in a cultural region. So you need to understand the land and you have to understand the culture, as well as the vernacular of how things are built within a region. It also has to stand on its own strictly from an artistic standpoint, and artistic means that it's created by emotion and it influences emotion. You have site, you have culture, and you have art. I think those are three key elements that are absolutely necessary in anything that would be regarded as architecture.

Much has been made of the fact that you didn't go to architecture school, as if that freed you to be less academic with your work. You're interested (as you've put it) in experimenting and making things comfortable for ordinary people, though your work is very contemporary and stylistically expressive. That's a hard combination to hold at the same time.

Salmela: It is. I'm not sure how I can explain how it happens, but in a sense that is the whole magic of designing something, of being an architect creating three-dimensional, usable objects. That is really the secret, and whether I went to school or didn't go to school, I have no idea how that has impact on me.

On the back cover of Thomas Fisher's monograph about you, *Salmela Architect* (University of Minnesota Press, 2005), your work is described as "juxtaposing opposites: modernist and traditional forms, open and cellular plans, large and small scales, familiar elements used in unfamiliar ways."

Salmela: It's just like the sauna. We did the interior as well as the exterior of the sauna out of brick. Most saunas are made from wood, but putting the brick in the inside as well as the outside is a logical design solution. When I actually took a sauna there, it exceeded any sauna that I had ever taken in my whole life because there's a radiance that occurs from the masonry holding the heat.

The U-shaped, unenclosed chimney of the outdoor fireplace at the Madeline Island House is the same way. It exceeded my expectation in how much heat actually is radiated toward you. It's a simultaneous thought—the notion of a fire and also creating an archetypal architectural element. It has a primitive sense to it. It's like the remains of a burned building, like the ruins of Rome. Most of the time, little outdoor fireplaces aren't very tall, but the taller it is, the more heat it radiates toward you. It's kind of amazing. In a way, you're symbolizing an ancient thing. If it was in Europe, buildings could have been built around the chimney and then burned down several times over. Here in American culture, we're so conservative that we think we've got to tear anything like that down so it doesn't fall and kill someone. Yet in Rome the ruins have been sitting there for how long? A simple abstraction of a memory is implanted in our minds. "Nostalgic" is probably a bad word for an architect to use—because it's anti-modernist—yet it relates to our memory of seeing things.

I was at a fort in northern Michigan where the officers' log cabins had burned down and all that was left were these big, whitewashed chimneys and fireplaces standing in a row. I think that in my mind I related regionally to that, but if you look at architecture more broadly, the column, the vertical element, is a powerfully pure form. It's a form that is modernist as well as ancient. I think Ludwig Mies van der Rohe would even like it because his architecture was reducing essential things to the very minimum. Now maybe this isn't essential, but it certainly is reduced to the minimum.

You have staked your practice on balancing between vernacular or traditional forms and modern or contemporary forms.

Salmela: We submitted our design for the Jackson Meadow development for a Progressive Architecture Award. The American jurors understood what we were trying to do because Jackson Meadow is a development within the oldest settlement in Minnesota, so it has a historical basis. But a juror from the Middle East who lived in Los Angeles and a juror from London said they would never give a P/A Award for a project that has a gabled roof. It's like the bias where people in our culture would never allow flat roofs. I still say a flat roof that's built correctly is better than a gabled roof.

But culturally, in the Midwest at least, people really need to have gabled roofs just to make them feel comfortable. It's such an inherent thing that a house would have a gabled roof. Even the firm Herzog & de Meuron did a gabled-roof house in Europe that was very traditional looking, but they did it out of concrete. They obviously did it for the purpose of referencing gable-roofed structures. It was a very interesting project.

Being that we're in the middle of the continent, remote from the big cities, I'm trying to address the cultural aspect of our region. And to address the cultural aspect of the region is not to resist the prevalent attitudes but to understand what the attitudes are and then create within those norms, expectations, and preconceptions. They are in a way obsolete and unfounded, yet they exist, and you just can't totally change society. You can try, but they'll tear it down if they don't like it. I'm trying to build these really modern houses that, using an inappropriate term, disguise the modernism with something that is very familiar, while keeping it very pure and geometric. Familiarity has a huge impact on the public accepting something and even keeping something. Some buildings that I did in my early career that were very modernist—very good, powerful buildings—have already been torn down.

The thing is you can't force things on people, and you can't fool people. You have to design and build something that is about them, that they can witness and say, I really like that. Take the Wild Rice restaurant that we built in a little fishing town that has orchards and dairy farms; it looks like a bunch of barns. It's very familiar. The people who live around there probably don't frequent the restaurant because it's a first-class, expensive restaurant, but they might come once a year. And they're still going to be proud of that place. A farmer will go in and say, boy, we could really store a lot of hay in here.

Another example is the Jones farmstead in southern Minnesota, an assembly of very traditional metal-roofed structures on a farmstead. The chimney is at least 8 feet wide, but it's only 2 feet deep and it extends up 34 feet from the first floor. It's like a knife sticking out of the roof. It's far more radical than it appears. The chimney goes all the way down to the foundation and by code it has to stand by itself. So it's a highly reinforced slab of masonry that projects into the sky. Yet I have never had anyone criticize that chimney because the forms are so familiar, and artistically the chimney balances out the forms. Yet the chimney is just ridiculously liberal, on the verge of overstatement. One of my friends, Vince James, who's an outstanding architect, was laughing and saying, "The wind's going to blow it over. It's so thin!" But he would have done it, he would have loved to have done it, I'm sure. The joke is that it's so ridiculously thin. But it's the architectural element that was absolutely necessary in this series of familiar buildings. These are the subtle things that are so base that you wouldn't discuss them with an architect interviewing for a major museum in Los Angeles. But they are about our culture.

The home and studio that you built for the photographer Jim Brandenburg often elicits comparisons to Fallingwater. Were you thinking about Frank Lloyd Wright when you designed it?

Salmela: The thing about Brandenburg is that there are two references; well, there are many references. The first reference was that Brandenburg was half Norwegian, and he really liked the notion of the Scandinavian longhouse, which is far older than the Prairie Style.

There's also the reference to the vernacular of our cultural buildings, not only longhouses but also chicken coops and sheds. Chicken coops especially were narrow and long, and they faced south so the sun would come in through the south elevation. It's easy to make a steep roof on them because if you get too wide and you make a steep roof, a huge volume is wasted. Brandenburg's studio is only 15 feet wide. The reason it's 15 feet wide is the setbacks from the creek and the rock ledge adjacent to it. The fortunate thing is that it was 15 feet wide, and three stories high, because that's what makes it so powerful. So in a sense it has all the attributes of what Wright was talking about—fitting into the landscape—but our reference was about our cultural roots, while Wright was very influenced by Oriental or Japanese architecture.

It also referenced farmsteads like those in the Finnish community where my father was born. These little farmsteads had assemblies of small buildings all over the property. When you look at the photos of Brandenburg, you see all of these small buildings. Four were already there; we added to them and added new buildings. In a way, it's more about our northern Minnesota culture than even the references Wright used in creating the Prairie Style. "Prairie Style" is a great name, and it does look good in the prairies, yet nobody in the prairies is building those things. In a sense, Wright created a myth about something that's very artistic and that expressed his own personal roots rather than the culture's. Not that there is anything wrong with that.

I tend to think that the best buildings that Wright did about our culture are actually the barns at Taliesin East, which are very seldom referenced in the books on Wright. But I think they were the most meaningful. And you see them from the road. When you're looking west, Spring Green is up on the hill and then below that, between the school and the house, are the barns. I'm not trying to put Wright down, but I am trying to point out the deep roots of culture that go all the way back to the Vikings.

Can an architect have a social impact?

Salmela: Yes. What I'm trying to demonstrate with my work is what can be done with the preconceptions of culture; if you have to reference cultural forms, how do you do it?

We're doing three houses right now in Duluth that are in the midst of the city in a blue-collar area that has magnificent views. How do you build modern, affordable houses within that context and do drastic things? These three houses we're doing are black. They're sided with Skatelite, which is a material used to make skateboard parks. They're perfect cubes; the roof is framed flat. We used tapered insulation to create a very subtle 1/8-inch-per-foot slope in all directions, and then we put a rubber membrane right over the whole roof. It looks completely flat, but there's a slight hip that distributes the water evenly so that you don't have an onslaught of water coming down a roof drain. The houses are very quick and economical to build, and they're safe—people aren't sliding down a 12-pitch roof and falling. The materials we're using, you can't refinish them, they're permanent. We're using the best: clear-anodized windows, cladding, and particleboard and melamine—plastic laminate—for cabinets.

Rem Koolhaas is known for innovative designs utilizing unconventional materials. Do you consider his work to be enduring? What about that of other contemporary architects?

Salmela: Koolhaas does some very gutsy things using new materials in new ways. In a sense, I'm trying to do the same thing but within a culture that does not even know who Rem Koolhaas is. So it's essential to forefront the level of comfort in modern thought and in modern buildings. The majority of the buildings I'm doing now aren't 12-pitch roofs with wood siding.

My goal is to be contextual, meaning that you fit into a setting. That isn't the same thing as the New Urbanist idea that to fit in you have to imitate the style. I'm exaggerating, but there is a style rule that you have to follow if you're going to create a New Urbanist community.

I'm saying that there is a more sophisticated way of being contextual. Probably the most refined architect to do that is Rafael Moneo. He builds in a European culture—well, he builds all over the world—but he is able to be contextual in a way that's unexpected. It's not in the style; his solutions are unpredictable, but they're contextual. Another amazing architect is Renzo Piano. I think he's more subtle, more skilled. I think those two are more skillful than, for instance, a lot of the modernist architects, for example, Rem Koolhaas. Koolhaas is contextual in that it's so radical, and sometimes that works. Frank Gehry has a way of creating a contextualism that is about being in the midst of a condensed city. It's like taking the energy of the whole city and putting it in a clump of paper and crushing it. There is a contextual quality to his work, but it seems as if other aspects suffer in comparison to Moneo and Álvaro Siza, who is a regionalist who works in Portugal.

Is there anything else that you'd like to talk about that I didn't bring up?

Salmela: When I used to work for a firm as an employee, we had two offices. One office was very quiet, and the other office was very noisy. I was in the noisy one, and when the bosses from the quiet office would come, they'd always go back and they'd call my immediate boss and say, "Those guys talk way too much. They don't get any work done." My answer was, "Look at how much work we do. We actually do twice as much as the quiet office." Why is it we talk? Because that's how you solve things. You don't solve things with your head and your hands over a table. You solve things by talking about the problems and all of a sudden the solutions come out of the air or they come out of the words that we express. That's why interviews are interesting, because there are things I said and discovered just now in our conversation that I didn't even think about before.

PART 5

Technology, Innovation, Materials

With today's digital and manufacturing technologies, there is practically no limit to what can be built—which can be both a blessing and a challenge to forward-thinking designers. In this final section, we talk to five architects at the forefront of innovation in home design—they discuss the frontier of computer-aided design (CAD), new approaches to preservation, and the potential of high-tech custom-made materials.

The discussion closes with the recognition that, as much as we are giddily taken with the potential marvels of technology, First World desires are not interchangeable with Third World needs. We need to check our presumptions of universality. Truly innovative technology provides local solutions.

TOSHIKO MORI

"There are two properties of structures. One is resisting against the force. That's been the traditional way of looking at structures. You make it thick and fat and strong and resistant. Another formula for resistance is yielding."

Toshiko Mori (b. 1951) is a techno-nerd of material science and, as an avid conservationist, a missionary of material salvation. Her strong, research-based work demonstrates creative opportunities derived from a respect of materials.

She is the principal of Toshiko Mori Architect, which she established in 1981 in New York City. In 2003, Mori was awarded the Cooper Union's inaugural John Q. Hejduk Award. In the fall of 2005, Mori's work was exhibited in *Frank Lloyd Wright: Renewing the Legacy* at the Heinz Architectural Center of the Carnegie Museum of Pittsburgh. A profile of Mori, "Postscripts: Building on Sacred Ground," appeared in the *New York Times* in May 2005.

Mori has edited volumes on material and fabrication research, including *Immaterial/Ultramaterial* (George Braziller, 2002), which investigated revolutionary new materials and methods of fabrication that have profoundly altered the direction of contemporary architecture. She also wrote *Textile/Tectonic: Architecture, Material, and Fabrication* (George Braziller, 2005). In 2008, Monacelli Press published a monograph of her work: *Toshiko Mori Architect*.

Mori, a graduate of Cooper Union in 1971, is the Robert P. Hubbard Professor in the Practice of Architecture and the former chair of the Department of Architecture at Harvard's Graduate School of Design, as well as the first female faculty member to receive tenure there.

Facing: Santana Sanchez House, Acoma Pueblo, New Mexico. The Acoma Pueblo Indians have lived in the area for at least eight hundred years.

Toshiko Mori makes the case for architects as "civilization builders" and looks at the isolation that results from modern-day fears and our basic desire for safety. "I think connectivity in humanity is the biggest goal of the built environment." Mori uniquely explores the importance of new materials in enabling that broad building goal.

A major concern of your work is to, as you've put it, "embrace the possibilities presented by new materials with the hope of reaffirming the role of the architect as deeply involved in civilization building." How have developments in material technology inspired you to see architects as being able to fulfill this higher calling?

Toshiko Mori: When you look at the history of materials, you are witnessing the history of civilizations. Some materials seem to be new to us, like computer chips, but they are merely clay. You can go back to ancient Mesopotamia and you can see the same material used as a vessel. In that time, clay vessels were used to carry water and food, but now clay is used to carry information. When you look at the history of housing and how materials have been used, you will see how much has changed and how much hasn't changed. When you have a holistic vision of what you do with materials, then you start thinking how material is made, whether we're using it most economically and efficiently, and from where we are obtaining it. That brings up issues of economy, sociology, and the sustainability and performance of those materials, which are mostly natural resources; and natural resources are becoming scarce. Those questions come to mind even in an environment like one's home. And I think the most important thing for us to think about as individuals living in the cities or in suburbia is how we connect ourselves to the rest of the world and to the history of civilization. Otherwise, I think we have a very limited future.

How can an architect be a civilization builder?

Mori: Architects are uniquely able to connect the dots between different fields—archaeology, anthropology, material sciences, mechanical engineering, and physics. Physics is the study of phenomena and thermal dynamics, how different materials can absorb heat and also insulate. Physicists will analyze the phenomena, and mechanical engineers will make it work, but architects have to create an environment in which all these mechanics and physics will work together. So our task is taking many aspects of different disciplines and making them come together in an economical solution. Therefore, we have a unique role in what I call *lateral vision*, instead of linear vision or a narrow point of view.

An architect's mission, simply stated, is to improve the quality of life of human beings. To improve the quality of life, it has to appeal to human senses with beauty, comfort, security, and user function. When we think of quality of life, we engage other disciplines and expertise to try to make it happen in our time.

You have strongly expressed your ideas about subtle nuances of design that attend to not just obvious visual things like light but also to things like sound, smell, and the feeling of air. At the same time, you've expressed your concern about the growing emphasis in Western culture on virtual reality and simulation and the danger that we are becoming increasingly desensitized and deprived of real beauty and real experience. What would compel contemporary architecture to reconsider the auditory, the virtual, and the olfactory?

Mori: You can use the human senses, which I think are an untapped resource, as potential materials. Instead of building walls or building rooms, you can create boundary conditions using levels of light, such as from dark spaces to bright spaces, or consider sound as a barrier. For example, our architecture students collaborated with Harvard graduate students in music to create an invisible barrier; when you cross it, it makes a very slight sound. The music students made a sound of breaking glass so slight that you immediately became alert and paid attention. Without putting up any signage or boundaries or walls, we were able to exhibit some very fragile material out in the open. And that way of considering a new boundary uses less energy and less material. Can we use other resources to create the condition of territoriality or privacy?

We also made a small booth that is imbued with the smell of lavender. The smell was contained in a certain space, so there was a sense of privacy. Students loved to go in that particular zone, and they felt private enough that they would make cell phone calls. Although it was in public, in broad view of everybody, it created a sense of intimacy. We have so many other devices, such as tactility, creating different textures in surfaces to make people slow down or stop. It's like the bump in the road that slows traffic down. You can do a similar thing with human beings so that they will travel slowly. So it is manipulating of the senses, and that's a very intelligent way of utilizing human capacity to create alternative boundary conditions.

In your book *Immaterial/Ultramaterial*, you explore the relationship between very low-tech and high-tech materials. For example, the transformation of pure silicon to pottery and from pottery to PowerBooks. You ascribe an ethical dimension to the economic and political implications of the use of specific materials. As we march into the twenty-first century, what in residential design should be subverted or replaced, and how do ethics play a role?

Mori: I think residential architecture will change because of the cost of energy and CO_2 emissions. Bill Beckman from the University of Wisconsin gave a great lecture to us recently. He's been called the pope of solar energy. Everybody is concerned about CO_2 emissions by automobiles, but no one realizes how much CO_2 is emitted into the environment by water heaters in the home. A single-family house emits an equal amount of CO_2 gas as an automobile. Once we start converting all the water-heating elements to solar power, we could cut emissions in half. And it's not a very difficult thing to do. It has a cost involved, but it's not as cost prohibitive as changing automobiles. This is a mobile society. People have to drive to commute. But if architects were to promote solar heaters for every single home, can you imagine? Emissions cut in half immediately. That's ethical.

At the same time, an architect's role is to design homes and institutions that conserve energy using natural resources such as sun and wind, recycle the gray water for plumbing usage, and deal with storm water drainage—recycling, reusing, regenerating. If one is ethically minded and very careful in designing, buildings should also be able to generate energy for other uses, and one can create less dependency on natural resources such as oil and gas. And it's not rocket science; it's really about common sense, like having a proper orientation, using a solar gain maximally for winter, and having proper insulation where it faces cold wind in the wintertime. This is ancient wisdom. Many of our traditional homes have taken that into account and also promote natural ventilation so you use less air conditioning. And there's also wisdom such as using snow. I'm old enough to remember having ice in the icebox, instead of electrically charged refrigerators. Ice and snow still can be used, if you can keep it through the summer months, as a coolant for air conditioning purposes, instead of using chemicals, electricity, or other types of resources. That way of thinking is an absolute necessity and totally ethical.

What are some of the new materials that you are interested in and have worked with?

Mori: I'm interested in materials of regulating light. One is air gel, which is a material that is 2 percent silica and 98 percent air, and also a lot of different materials that contain air. I'm interested in material efficiency. You use very little materials, and they get suspended in air. Air is an amazing resource because it insulates heat but it also creates an acoustical barrier. You could create an environment where you can see through but have acoustical privacy. You can see through, yet it's fireproofed. You can see through, out in the cold and ice, but it's warm. I'm really interested in air plus another material to create differing environmental conditions between spaces.

What has been obsessing you lately?

Mori: I witnessed 9/11. I live in the neighborhood, and from my rooftop I saw the plane hit. All I can think of is if I had made a building that bounced back that plane, lives could have been saved. So it's been my obsession.

There are two properties of structures. One is resisting against the force. That's been the traditional way of looking at structures. You make it thick and fat and strong and resistant. Another formula for resistance is yielding. By being more flexible, the dynamic forces bounce up against it. So the more force you apply, the more bounce you create to force it out, and at the same time it absorbs the forces and spreads out. The formula of a traditional structure is that it doesn't absorb, it resists and breaks. Trees bend to resist the wind; it's the same formula.

We should be thinking differently about issues of resistance. If we can come up with solutions, then we can create a safer environment without having to build huge bunkers. And for that I am looking at textiles. That's another book I've written—*Textile/Tectonic: Architecture, Material, and Fabrication*. Textiles are woven. When you press textiles, the tension spreads across the surface so that you don't need as much thickness of material to resist the same forces. That technology is already used in bulletproof walls. Layers of fiberglass are woven together. It's very thin, not like a two-layer brick wall, but because it spreads sideways on the surface, it keeps dispersing energy, not in the depths but on surfaces. And it disappears faster and easier. This material is already being used behind the walls of bulletproof buildings, in safes, and so forth. Boat builders are using that technique to build highly efficient, faster boats. I just did an exhibition design and have advised on extreme textiles, like Kevlar jackets, bulletproof jackets, and different military structures.

The way we build buildings, we think of forces as something constant, as sitting on the building. We tend to think statically, but wind is a dynamic force. It's not hitting the building all the time. The building is designed as if it's being hit by a hurricane all the time, but it's not designed to take the force and distribute it and work it out in a much more holistic way. Structural engineers in Stuttgart are coming up with a different formula, called *dynamic structure*. This is a new way of thinking of structure in a dynamic diagram. Think of a train moving on the rails. At some point, the rail is not bearing the weight of a train anymore, so that part doesn't have to be as strong as where the rail has a train on it. How can you translate that particular force there so that one uses less material but increases efficiency? In a sense, it's as if you get punched, it just gets absorbed. Where you get punched, you can resist it, but where you're not getting punched, it could be weak. This is a totally new way of thinking about the environment and structure.

> **I'm thinking about safety and what it means to feel safe in one's home today. It seems like there is a different kind of intimacy and emotional safety, and a very different way of thinking about space, than people experienced in the past.**

Mori: Because of concerns with safety, people are becoming more isolated. People in public health talk about the increase of obesity in this country because people are not moving except to go to work. They don't actively socialize and walk around the cities anymore, and there's a disengagement from the environment in general, and disengagement with the family, even among immediate family members. Everybody is doing different things. This disintegration of the social structure is quite disconcerting.

I think a lot of us architects are interested in issues of safety. What would make people feel safer in this world? Can an architect make that happen? There are larger issues, really, and building design may not be able to resolve them. They have to do with issues of urban planning and urban design. I think connectivity in humanity is the biggest goal of the built environment.

GREG LYNN

"Palladian domestic architecture is
important only because Palladio
was the first person to take classical
architecture and bring it to the style
of a house. That was perhaps the
most radical move any architect
has ever made."

Greg Lynn (b. 1964) is an American architect, philosopher, and science fiction
enthusiast. He is a visionary in the field of contemporary architectural practice
and theory and has an international reputation as one of contemporary architecture's most provocative thinkers and teachers. Profiled by *Time* magazine as one
of the innovators of the twenty-first century, Lynn uses computer-aided design
to produce irregular, biomorphic architectural forms. One of the forerunners in
exploring the possibilities of digital fabrication, Lynn's "blob architecture"—a term
he coined based on the software acronym BLOB (Binary Large OBject)—explores
how to bring complex binary forms into architectural design in terms of construc-
tability and economics. In 2005, *Forbes* named him one of the ten most influential
living architects. In his TED talk of the same year, Lynn discussed the mathematical
roots of architecture—how calculus and digital tools allow modern designers to
move beyond the traditional building forms. In 2008, he won the Golden Lion at
the 11th International Venice Biennale of Architecture.

Lynn graduated from Princeton University School of Architecture. Examples of
his work include the Korean Presbyterian Church in Queens, New York; an eco-
minded museum, Ark of the World, in Costa Rica; and a residential community in
Amsterdam. He is a Studio Professor at UCLA's School of Architecture and Urban
Design, where he is currently spearheading an experimental research robotics lab.

Palladian windows along the stairway of the Major General Solomon
Cowles House, Main Street, Farmington, Connecticut

Greg Lynn redresses the misperception of the term "blobism," what it describes, the role of technology in architecture today, whether the computer has liberated him aesthetically, and what the future looks like for young architects today.

When you look at the sweep of the history of residential architecture, what are the things that endure?

Greg Lynn: You're talking to an architect, so the things that are going to stand out for me and that I would treasure are the exceptions rather than the rule. There are a few very important domestic precedents that I always think about. Palladio would be my first touchstone. Palladian domestic architecture is important only because Palladio was the first person to take classical architecture and bring it to the style of a house. That was perhaps the most radical move any architect has ever made. It's also in Palladianism where the institutional vocabulary becomes domestic.

What's interesting is that from that moment forward, you see experiments in residential architecture becoming the standards for institutional architecture, and that's a very important shift. Take somebody like Mies van der Rohe. The Barcelona Pavilion is a public building that wants to be a house. Now you see architects experimenting with houses and then bringing that back to the public sphere.

Frank Lloyd Wright's Prairie Houses were really amazing to me as a kid because they had this balance of radicality and cozy familiarity. I think those houses were pioneering in a soft way, which I'm also really drawn to in terms of domestic architecture.

If you asked me about a great house, I would give you Le Corbusier's Villa Savoye, Villa Stein-de-Monzie at Garches, and any of the Corbusian houses of the 1930s in Paris. Those were radical houses at the time, and they set the bar so all other modern houses had to talk to them. It doesn't mean that suddenly everybody was living in a Corbusian house, but it changed the landscape, and everybody started to think about houses differently because of those canonical ones.

A house is not a product. It's not something disposable. It's not something you have a casual relationship with. So in that sense, the most special houses tend to be the greatest houses.

Tell me about the term that you coined, "blobism." Has it become a straitjacket, or are you comfortable with it? What is it describing?

Lynn: It's funny. I was the person who first used the term "blob" in reference to architecture. It was a software-modeling tool. It stands for "binary large object," which is a constellation of points out of which you generate a service. I use that term to describe a calculus-based model of drawing where instead of having a point as a radius with an infinite number of points, you could have a whole lot of points and generate a service out of it.

To me, architecture has a few fundamental problems, and one of those problems is how you put a whole bunch of pieces of things into a whole. So I thought this idea of a blob, this array of things that makes a whole, was a nice model, rather than, say, a well-proportioned man. Unfortunately, "blob" was so catchy and so visually loaded that it came to mean a big, unarticulated, lumpy surface, and that is a straitjacket. It's very funny that I always approached it as how do you take a variety of pieces with their own identity and make a whole out of them with a kind of array. But instead, everybody assumed I was talking about making these big, unarticulated surfaces.

"Unarticulated," meaning anti-angular?

Lynn: Meaning featureless. The example I use is the Ford Taurus, which was the first computer-model-engineered car. It had no seams or creases in the body, because the modelers didn't know how to make a seam or a crease. Then the software designers and the engineers got more sophisticated. They started making cars with more features and more articulation. The things they used to do with knives and tools to physically shape clay models they could start to do with computer software and CNC routers. The same thing has happened in architecture.

What blobism in architecture meant was a whole field of designers made into rank amateurs with the new software platform. All we could do were these big, lumpy things with no parts and pieces. It's taken ten years, but now architecture is developing the same expertise that automobile design developed a few years ago. Now the designers are pretty adept with the software, and we're starting to do elegant, well-proportioned, articulated, beautiful things with a new medium: the digital medium.

Is software a medium?

Lynn: I think you can approach software as a tool, which is how architects developed it. Really, 3D modeling was invented in architecture, as a tool. It then went out into Hollywood films and all over the place. Now we get it back and we understand that it's a medium. I used to be very fetishistic about Rapidograph pens and Mylar and 9H pencils, and I paid a lot of attention to precision in my medium. Even as a graduate student, I was buying every kind of compass and curve drawing tool I could get my hands on. That was a big part of how I designed.

The computer to me is not a tool in a cold, analytic sense. It's like oil paint versus acrylic. It has its own characteristics, and you have to figure out how to work with it and be creative with it. If you don't acknowledge that it's a design medium, you miss the real power of a computer.

Your work is notably in the vanguard in your use of the computer. That also seems true for other Southern California architects, including Frank Gehry, who, in his early work, seems to legitimize a lot of that, not that he's the progenitor.

Lynn: I think it's because Southern California has a confluence of architecture, aerospace, and entertainment, which is why I moved out here. London has it, there are a few other places that have it. But take somebody like Frank Gehry. He has no interest in the computer at all. Neither does Thom Mayne or Craig Hodgetts. All these people would never have found a computer if it dropped on them. It's just that it facilitated their work and it's the cultural milieu they live in, so they're on the leading edge of computer technology.

How has the computer liberated you aesthetically?

Lynn: I've always been interested in curvature, and the real trick with modeling and curves is how you do something that has some openness, freedom, and continuity. You think of these as being characteristics of a curve, but in fact it's a little bit of a trick because sometimes you end up making cavernous, dark, enclosed spaces. One of the things I really try to do is use curves without making caves. Like in the Bloom House, there's a crispness and angularity mixed with curvaceousness and voluptuousness. You don't end up with a cavernous space because it's a very tight site. My own house, the Slayton House, has strong edges. The curves flow, though, so you don't end up with a cave.

What aspects of contemporary architecture would you most like to subvert?

Lynn: Let me put it in positive terms. What I think is most exciting about what's happening now is that architects, in part because of the computer, are talking to other designers and people in the culture industry. The most important thing that could ever happen to architecture is that it get hooked up with fashion, art, film, and literature, and get connected in a broad cultural way that's understandable and provocative both to itself and outside itself.

I think that architecture is relevant and of interest to the general public more now than it's been for the last fifty years. I think it's like it was in the 1940s and 1950s—people are turning toward design and asking it big questions. And I think it's not too arrogant to say that architecture will lead the way in terms of automobile design, infrastructure, and a lot of big global problems. Right now, the only field that really has the tools to think through those things as design problems is architecture, and I think that's why a lot of people are turning to it. I don't mean to make it sound too practical, because it really isn't that, it's just the interest in buildings and what they symbolize is higher now than it's ever been. Therefore, architects are in discussion with a lot of interesting people with interesting problems. That's much better than when architecture was just providing a home, whether for a corporation, institution, museum, or individual. It's much more exciting to be provoking discussion and defining and solving problems outside yourself.

What does the future look like for young architects starting out today?

Lynn: There are two tracks for architects to take. If you are providing a service, which means filling a known gap, like designing ten thousand tract homes in the San Fernando Valley, you're in big trouble, because big homebuilders no longer need you for that. You can throw certain assumptions about the need for architecture as a service industry right out the window, because there's an investment, development, and design machinery that's dispensed with the friction that an architect would introduce into that system. So, that's depressing if that's what you want to do.

If you think about the design of buildings as a bigger problem than just designing a building and delivering a service, there's probably never been a better time to be an architect. You can completely rethink the institution of a library. You can completely rethink the design of a bridge. You can do all these things that you wouldn't have been able to do a little while ago. Those things are having a bigger impact both in urban planning and building design, as well as other fields. For the people who are tackling the big problems, I think the field of architecture has never been more exciting.

THOM MAYNE

"Of course, Los Angeles is the center
of the world. You are here. It's the
default culture."

Thom Mayne (b. 1944) is the principal of Morphosis, founded in 1972. Deriving its name from metamorphosis, "change in form or transformation," Morphosis is a renowned architectural office located in Santa Monica, California. Mayne's design process and philosophy are concerned with a groundless modern society exemplified by the shifting landscape of Los Angeles. His working method values contradiction, conflict, and change, and he approaches each project as a dynamic entity. Aided by computer technology, Mayne's designs have a layered quality that often includes multiple organizational systems and sculptural forms that appear to arise effortlessly from the landscape. Recent projects include graduate housing at the University of Toronto; the San Francisco Federal Building; the University of Cincinnati Student Recreation Center; the Science Center School, in Los Angeles; Diamond Ranch High School, in Pomona, California; and the Wayne L. Morse United States Courthouse, in Eugene, Oregon.

Educated at the University of Southern California and the Harvard University Graduate School of Design, Mayne helped found the Southern California Institute of Architecture (SCI-Arc) in 1972. Prior to teaching at SCI-Arc, he held teaching posts at Columbia, Harvard, Yale, the Berlage Institute in the Netherlands, and the Bartlett School of Architecture in London. Mayne was a recipient of the Rome Prize from the American Academy of Design in 1987, and he received the Pritzker Prize in March 2005.

Courtyard of the 1926 John Sowden House, 5121 Franklin Avenue, Los Angeles, California. The house was designed by Lloyd Wright, son of Frank Lloyd Wright.

Thom Mayne discusses software as a "medium" and how, in shifting from smaller-scale domestic work to larger-scale public work, his design ideas have gone from "implicit" to "explicit"—transforming the city in a relational way, as part of its connective tissue. But he doesn't like being called experimental: "I don't think I'm so outrageous or avant-garde. I'm just real. Now it's a question of is my reality more relevant than your reality."

You've said, "We will hold to that which is difficult because it is difficult and by its difficulty is worthwhile."

Thom Mayne: First of all, the difficult, the complex, is reality, so this is not an invention. This is James Joyce looking out of the window and writing *Finnegans Wake* and advancing a language, advancing a new framework of a narrative or a meta-narrative or an anti-narrative. Now they call it chaos theory. Like all artists, Joyce sensed things before his time. I'm interested in that tradition. I seem to have been born with this kind of wiring that causes me to ask certain questions.

This way of thinking doesn't have to be located in the arts, but it seems to be a primary necessity in the art world to have some contact with one's internal life. One has to have one's own compass, which has to do with autonomy and independence, and being able to think something out clearly and arrive somewhere is necessary in the arts versus in law or medicine, where you may be following the status of a discipline and you're not asked to challenge it.

You're in your early sixties now. In what ways has your belief in the transformative power of architecture changed since you became "the man," as opposed to challenging "the man"? In other words, does architecture need to be antagonistic toward institutionalized ideas to be effective?

Mayne: I think this is a complicated question. Discussion is not antagonism; it's interrogating and questioning, and that's part of inquiry. I have a certain kind of curiosity that leads me to ask questions. If you're asking certain types of questions consistently, in my experience, it's annoying to a lot of people. They try to ostracize you; they want to put you to the side because you're disturbing things. People like things the way they are. My office teases me that I'm a pit bull. Once I grab on, I don't let go until I'm satisfied that I've received an answer.

I think the antagonistic part is connected to personality, maturity, and a certain type of character. As I've gotten older, I've become more comfortable with myself in social situations. I'm a somewhat private person, but I've learned to be a more public person. In the past, a lot of the interpersonal stuff was masking my own insecurity and social discomfort. I've grown more diplomatic. I see my own frailties, imperfections, and incompleteness in a different way. It makes you a bit more empathetic rather than having the rebellious attitude of an eighteen-year-old. At twenty-five, you can still do it. At thirty to thirty-five, you can still be that antagonistic person. At forty, people are starting to say, "Well, we hear the critique, but what are you doing about it?" At some point, the balance is starting to tip.

And now that you've gotten over the wall, how does that affect how you work?

Mayne: I'm not sure I got over any wall. I don't see myself that differently than I was when I was forty or thirty. I have different opportunities, and I behave in a different way in terms of my relationship to the world I live in.

The elusive thing that I'm after is if you need, as an artist, a challenge to overcome, an obdurate, resistant establishment to inspire you.

Mayne: I'm not aware of a need to overturn or attack the institutionalized nature of the norm. I just behave naturally. I've been in many conversations where people look at me and say, "Oh, you take the cup and turn it upside down or squish it and put it back. There's some normative institutionalized behavior that you're attacking." And I'm really not doing that. I'm not even aware of what I'm doing.

I read the newspaper—I'm an avid world news character—and reality is fucking lunacy. I'm going, "It ain't my reality!" This is the craziest world I've ever lived in. This is the most insane kind of dream. We know that we live in our minds. Our unconscious and conscious lives are sometimes interchangeable. You don't always know if actually you did something and if it's real, or you just thought it was real. I love that part of the world, and it all connects to what I do. When I'm working, I don't have to worry about debunking some institutional idea. I just have to be normal. I have to behave authentically and see what happens.

The architects you're talking to have cultural practices. Today, it's a complicated situation because we understand, in a postmodern framework, what Duchamp articulated in the 1950s: The artist does the first half of the work and the user, the viewer, does the second half.

Elaborate on how that collaboration works in architecture.

Mayne: Architecture is a cultural practice. Whether somebody likes or doesn't like a work of architecture depends on who is looking and what reference point they're looking from. That's an incredibly freeing idea for an artist, because you no longer have to worry about whether the people like it or not. Residential architecture is the most fluid, malleable subject matter for architecture, and that's the reason it's become the most useful experimental tool. It's malleable in cultural terms and within performance terms. And with the architects that you're talking to, their work is usually about *enhancement* versus *status*.

"Enabling" would be another word for it; that's Cedric Price. How does it enable or enhance some aspect of your life, whether it has to do with the understanding of nature, the understanding of ecological processes, space, habitation, functionalities, or social connection and the way it affects social behavior? That's why the house is so incredible. You can dig a hole in the ground. You can put it in a tree. It's so bloody fluid. It's more or less infinite in terms of possibilities. It's a subject matter with enormous range. Looking at it historically, you can look at those cave dwellings in China. They look like bees carving out rooms. Or you can look at the tree houses in Borneo.

Of course, Los Angeles is the center of the world. You are here. It's the default culture. It's the key. San Francisco, they know who they are, they're a predominant culture. Ditto Boston, Philadelphia, and to some degree New York, but in a little different way, more to do with status and capital. The South—Charlotte or Atlanta—forget it. Los Angeles has culture, small culture. It's radically heterogeneous. There are 134 different ethnicities here, over two hundred languages spoken, and 16.5 million people in search of some collective culture. Because of that you end up in this default place. Since the turn of the century, Los Angeles has been a place looking for its future and never finding it. It's Sisyphean. Everybody is still looking for Los Angeles and what it's going to become, because it's this young place that doesn't ever seem to arrive. It makes for an incredible milieu for creativity and for those that are looking to concretize the future.

I see your work as transformative and very interested in social development. You've spoken of architecture as a public discourse, a metaphor that resolves inherent social conflicts. Can you explore this a little, following on what you've been talking about?

Mayne: If there's anything that's changed in the last ten years with my work, as it's gone through the transformation from smaller-scale domestic work to larger-scale public work, it's that the values have gone from implicit to explicit. If you look at my Sixth Street House or Angelle Bergeron's house or the smaller projects, certain critics will say they convey implicit ideas about urbanism and architecture. I see it as a political act. You have to read into it, but it's key. When I did the larger work, we did a building that has no air conditioning. All of a sudden, I became a green architect, and some people found that surprising. I did a whole series of public spaces that are explicitly about transforming the city. They are part of the connective tissue of the city. They belong to the city and are relational—not autonomous objects but connected objects. They're demonstrative of architectural culture as it intersects with social institutions and ideas of congestion and connectivity that are important for city life.

Going back to the earlier question, what's normal to me is living in this heterogeneous polyglot that doesn't have simple, easy alignments. Culture, food, lifestyle, architecture, and a technology that builds that architecture—it's normal to me. I was raised here in Southern California. I was born in 1944, and I was raised in a tough little town near Santa Fe Springs, in a mixed cultural environment. I wasn't even aware of it; it was just my home. It was also fueled by real tensions. I got beat up and was in gang fights. I grew up in that world, so it's not unnatural that I see architecture in some way—this is going to sound very romantic—as being about healing. I see it as therapeutic. My youngest students laugh at me. They find me insanely anachronistic. It ages me.

My formal ideas are very much connected to the generative ideas of biology, to the diversity of the species having to do with organizational ideas. And I'm interested in the kind of work that intentionally puts together non sequiturs or complex information in one single, unifying idea. That became part of the style or the symbol of the work coming out of my office. Again, it comes directly out of living in a complex culture that is quite different from the French countryside or some monolithic place that would allow you to pursue different ideas.

And then, of course, you look at your own history. I've got a grandfather born in London, grandmother born in Copenhagen. I'm a bit German, a bit Irish, a bit Scottish, English, and French. That's who I am. I am a mutt. With that comes a style of work. Early on, I recognized I'm an incomplete person. I need feedback, and I need it at every level. I need it humanly, where I work with people, and I need it in terms of the stuff in my work.

I look at life, and it seems like I'm on a plane. I live around the world, and I raised my kids in the same way. You can take them any place in the world, and they're comfortable. I took my kids to my hometown in Tipton, Indiana, and it was the most foreign place they'd ever been to. I can be in Tokyo, Berlin, Mexico City, London, Paris, or Vienna. Architecture today is totally global. We see the same films, we're educated more or less in the same way, and it has nothing to do with your origin. Geography is less and less important. We live within subcultures, and the connectivity between people is intellectual, psychological, and informational.

As you look at the world politically, you see a complete division between the provinces and the cosmopolitans—the country people and the city people. And the suburbs seem to fall more to the country. It's not just the United States that's suffering this divide. I look at the kinds of questions that are being asked by politicians, and it's insane. We don't have time to be dealing with these nineteenth-century questions that were answered a long time ago. You've got schools that are questioning Darwin. I'm doing an astrophysics lab at Cal Tech, and they're all Nobel laureates. The trouble is, they think it's so absurd that it's not worth talking about. My son, who wants to be a cardiac surgeon, is doing stem cell research. The same people who have had a quadruple bypass are questioning stem cell research. How do they think they got the quadruple bypass? It's not a theory; it's reality. We have these arguments that are totally absurd today. It seems like there are some extremely compelling biological questions at the survival level that we need to be getting on right now. I don't think I'm so outrageous or avant-garde. I'm just real. Now it's a question of is my reality more relevant than your reality. I'm going to be on the side of chemistry, biology, and physics. James Turrell had an outrageous line. He said, "There's no metaphysics, there's only physics."

A bedroom in the Lovell Beach House, 1242 West Ocean Front, Newport Beach, California.
The early-modern house was built in 1926 and designed by Rudolph Schindler.

LORCAN O'HERLIHY

"I think that those modernist houses, such as the Schindler House, were about a program—a political and social agenda. There was an idea about how we were supposed to live, but it was deeply driven by ideology."

Lorcan O'Herlihy (b. 1959) was raised in Dublin, Ireland, and came to Los Angeles at fifteen years of age. He sees Los Angeles as a place for innovation because it's in a constant state of flux. In 1994, he founded Lorcan O'Herlihy Architects [LOHA], whose work is "driven by ruthless optimism, creative pragmatism, and a profound conviction that bold, enlightened design elevates the soul and enriches communities."

In 2004, the Architectural League of New York selected O'Herlihy as one of the eight "emerging voices" in the United States. He is a very popular architect and has a client base that shares his belief in the transformative properties of design to enrich their lives. Interested in the density problem of Los Angeles County, O'Herlihy's single-family hillside houses are complex assemblies of simple rectangular forms. His work draws inspiration from R. M. Schindler and Richard Neutra. Indeed, O'Herlihy won the commission to design the 100-by-200-foot plot adjoining the Schindler House in West Hollywood.

After receiving his Bachelor of Architecture from California Polytechnic State University, San Luis Obispo, O'Herlihy worked for Kevin Roche on an extension to the Metropolitan Museum in New York. He worked at I. M. Pei and Partners on the Grande Louvre Museum in Paris and as an associate at Steven Holl Architects, where he was responsible for several projects, including the Hybrid Building, which received a National Honor Award from the AIA, in Seaside, Florida, the master-planned community designed by Elizabeth Plater-Zyberk and Andrés Duany.

Lorcan O'Herlihy looks at innovation in architecture, how the computer changed the direction of design, and how his work is about "rethinking the conventions of modernism." He discusses the importance of passion and how people's lives are invariably improved by good design—possible only through a passionate engagement.

As one looks back at hundreds of years of design in American residential architecture, certain things endure. What stands out for you?

Lorcan O'Herlihy: Historically, modernism has been a very strong movement since it started around the 1930s. Here we are today, and people still look at the Case Study houses from the mid-twentieth century as being progressive. When you have a movement that has stood the test of time for nearly eighty years, that says a lot for the original ideas that the early modernists came up with.

Do you think of your work as a continuation of modernism?

O'Herlihy: Not specifically my work. You were asking about a movement; I'm not saying I'm part of it. Frankly, I am at a point where my work is rethinking the conventions of modernism. I think a lot of architecture is doing that today.

With modernism, one of the key moments was the advent of concrete, which allowed you to play with form. Today there is generative form architecture that is generated by the computer. Also, with new technologies you can really push the envelope or be inventive with the materials themselves. My work tends to be about inventiveness in the material systems and a more systemic approach, as opposed to a formal one. I'm an artist, and my paintings tend to be very gestural, very form-driven. That's the nature of painting with the stroke of your hand. When you work with systematic processes in architecture, it's about the medium and the tools of that art form.

I've heard similar comments, from Greg Lynn, Toshiko Mori, and Doug Garofalo, about what the computer and new materials offer.

O'Herlihy: My approach tends to be more systematic than Doug's and Greg Lynn's, not so formally driven. Our inventiveness comes from using off-the-shelf materials in new ways, trying to make something ordinary extraordinary. Our work is driven also by volume, light, and space.

The computer is changing the direction of architecture in a way that is similar to how concrete reinvented architecture, which is very exciting. Today, parametrics allow you to generate architecture through the computer and then be able to use that as a way to build it. You can actually jump from architectural drawings to construction without having to go through shop drawings and other strategies. My work is different in the sense that I'm more interested in information. The geometry of the form is less sculptural; the inventiveness is in the material systems and the way we work.

We use a term called "operational layers," meaning the information you get not only from the people you are working with but from your everyday life experience and exposure to things. A lot of people are involved in putting together an important building; it's not only the clients. A number of civic, social, political, and economic issues come into the process. As opposed to ignoring them, all those economic, social, and political forces help inform the building. You take that information, and you develop architecture.

There is another layer that we add to it, which is the idea of researching materials, finding new ways to apply them to buildings of all scales. That's what our work is known for. We are a research-driven firm.

Clearly, your work is invested in innovation. At the same time, would you say that you still hold on to certain traditions?

O'Herlihy: I think that you cannot know the future without knowing the past and present. When I talk about research, I mean that ability to see where architecture comes from so you can use that as a springboard to move forward from a smarter perspective. If you really know history and do your research, you can drive a project forward.

In terms of innovation, we work with materials that are nonstandard and nontraditional. If we work with a wood building, we don't do traditional clapboard; we float the skin off the building. We work with transparency and create dynamically filtered light through layers. We don't work from the standard A-frame with a chimney. Our buildings tend to have flat roofs because roof decks are interesting; you can use that space. We like to activate the spaces. You take a floor, wall, and ceiling, and you say, "What can we do with these? How can we rethink this? How can we make the space more interesting and make it a great place for people to live?" That's what drives our projects.

On a recent project, for example, we're taking an existing structure, stripping it back, and wrapping it in an outer skin, like the skin of a person, or clothing. We're turning the project inside out by putting art on the outside and then creating a container for art on the inside. We're not traditionalists at all.

Our approach never has been to consider the traditional sense of a home. People look at our projects, and they don't initially think of them in terms of being homes. They think of them as architecture that happens to house someone. We do a lot of multifamily residential housing, offices, and all kinds of commercial projects. Each project is driven by the program and the information we get for it.

One of the criticisms of modernism is that, while there's a program for living, such as bringing the inside outside, modern residential architecture often doesn't contain the qualities that were once associated with hominess.

O'Herlihy: When I was at university, I was inspired to try to change architecture. A number of architects take a traditional approach and embrace the idea of what a home is supposed to be. It's just not my nature. I've always wanted to rethink the conventions. I've always wanted to push it further.

It seems to me that there is an O'Herlihy style.

O'Herlihy: I think there is, to be frank with you. Our practice has grown from four people to eighteen people. I tend to be the chief architect and designer, but we have some committed and passionate people here who are doing a great amount of work. It's a collaborative process. I tend to be the one who drives it, but there's an openness in the design. I've always been developing consistently in one direction. People know when my office does a project.

I think also your research-driven ethic is the engine in the center of your practice.

O'Herlihy: The engine in the center, yes. That's why we say we're a research office or why we work with the idea of operational layers. It's the process that drives the architecture, and that's why there's a consistency. We've never been swayed by fashion. I was interested, as a student, in Mies Van der Rohe, when postmodernism was at its strength. I was unique at that time. People didn't understand why I was interested in modernism or the utopian vision of housing the world, which was a principle of modernism.

Your process of design sounds innovative. Do you think that it is unique?

O'Herlihy: It's instinctive, it's intuitive. I think architecture is about the process. Each project is driven by a specific client. In painting, I have to answer only to myself. In architecture, you have to try to achieve the same sense of direction or strength in your work, but you're working with a client, you're working with the city, you're working with layers of information. But instead of negating that, I embrace it and let it be part of the process to develop the architecture. It's the process that I've always worked with, and it leads to each project being unique in its own way. This process is the underlying connective tissue. And my role in the office is to be the author and to facilitate how you take all those layers and assemble them into, hopefully, great architecture.

It's almost antithetical to the classic concept of the Frank Lloyd Wright-type architect.

O'Herlihy: It absolutely is. I'm convinced that this process has been successful for us because we're not the master architects of the Frank Lloyd Wright period. It's not about the artist in the cape and hat, so to speak. It's being an artist, but it's actually using the medium of architecture, the operational layers of information. You have to weave together the political, economical, and social forces; the client's information; and the city's information. All those aspects create an impact, but instead of pushing against them, you let them help define the space. And you'd be surprised; you can get some amazing architecture.

The building isn't driven by style; it's driven by information. It's not traditional; it's not modern; it's not deconstructivist; it's not representative of any of the periods or styles that you speak about. It's strictly information driven, which means the by-product is a building that is unique in its own way.

Looking toward the future, what is the one thing you want to see subverted, supplanted, or removed from the process of architecture?

O'Herlihy: I think you need to be passionate about architecture. It's crucial. People's lives are improved by good design. In the world in which I exist, with all of my colleagues here in this office, there's a great appreciation for great architecture and great space. But that's only 1 percent of the world, if that. Just .05 percent of the world even understands or embraces architecture. For most, architecture is a building; but it's not. Architecture is architecture, and it would be great to be uncompromising or to be able to get more people to think of architecture as making everyone's lives better. My mission would be to educate the 99.99 percent of the people out there who don't understand it.

Shelter cabin along the Chisana Trail in Wrangell-St. Elias
National Park and Preserve, east of Anchorage, Alaska

FRANK ESCHER AND RAVI GUNEWARDENA

"This is a convoluted way of responding to your question, but the basic needs for the dwelling have always been to provide shelter—a place for us as beings, whether we are animals or not, where we are safe, where we feed ourselves, and where we are with our families."

Frank Escher grew up in Switzerland and studied architecture at the Eidgenössische Technische Hochschule (ETH), Zurich. He is the author of the monograph *John Lautner, Architect* (Princeton Architectural Press, 1998), and is on the advisory board of the Los Angeles Forum for Architecture and Urban Design.

Ravi GuneWardena was trained at California State Polytechnic University, Pomona, and spent a year studying art and architectural history in Florence, Italy. He currently serves on the Hollywood Public Art Advisory Panel for the Community Redevelopment Agency.

The work of Escher GuneWardena Architecture, which ranges from residential to commercial, master planning, and institutional projects, has been published and exhibited internationally and has received numerous awards. The firm, which addresses issues of sustainability, affordability, and the dialogue between form and construction, seeks to distill simple formal manifestations of the complexities of each project.

In 2003, Escher GuneWardena was one of six architectural practices included in the National Design Triennial, an overview of current American design. Escher and GuneWardena won the Dwell Home II competition in 2005 and were chosen by the Eames Foundation to develop a 250-year conservation plan for the historic Eames House, designed and built by the late Charles & Ray Eames in 1949 as part of the Case Study House Program.

Frank Escher and Ravi GuneWardena explore architecture in the developing world, where novel but impractical technology must take a backseat to meeting basic human needs. They discuss how politics and economics influence design.

When you look at the sweep of the history of building houses, what are the things that endure?

Frank Escher: This is a very interesting question. We were invited by the Vitra Design Museum to be in an exhibition about the future of housing [*OpenHouse: Architecture and Technology for Intelligent Living*]. They were looking for people to address four issues: sustainability, healthy living, connectivity, and how technology—digital technology in particular—influences the way we conceive of, develop, build, and use houses.

Ravi GuneWardena: They prefaced it by saying that technology is the question of our time.

Escher: The exhibition, at least the way we understand it, was geared toward seeing how these marvelous new ideas can be introduced into the house, like walls that turn into TVs or fridges that turn into stoves. Our response to that was, well, this is interesting to 3 percent of the world population. But to the majority, it's not about a wall that turns into a TV, it's about having a wall or a roof; not about having a fridge that turns into a stove, but about having food. So we were proposing to look into what are the basic needs of housing that have not changed or can't be changed.

GuneWardena: And then finding applications of simple technologies that can be made accessible to the 60-70 percent of the world that doesn't yet have electricity or running water in the house. The technology is out there, even if it's not shared or it comes at a great expense. We would like to propose not making the next smart house or pushing high technology to its limits, which is only accessible to a very small percent of the population, but rather bringing the future to a greater population.

Escher: One of the basic needs is how to prepare food without depleting natural resources, because in large parts of the world deforestation is an enormous problem. People need firewood to be able to prepare food, have access to clean water, or just improve hygienic conditions.

This is a convoluted way of responding to your question, but the basic needs for the dwelling have always been to provide shelter—a place for us as beings, whether we are animals or not, where we are safe, where we feed ourselves, and where we are with our families.

GuneWardena: Some of the issues that endure are having water and sanitation and the conditioned environment that is warm enough or cool enough to be able to live comfortably. Beyond that are also ideas of connection to the outside world and how you frame your view to the outside—what's the relationship between the inside and outside of your dwelling.

Admirably, you introduce the point that if you really want to address the future of design for houses, the questions have to be examined in the context of the majority of the people who have a pressing need to be housed. But isn't there a prevalent Western belief in technology that we're going to come into your world and solve these problems for you?

Escher: That's a very good point. Yes, I think any time you are proposing to improve someone's condition there is an assumption that what you are bringing them is better than what they have. And you have to be enormously careful about that, whether it is in a political context, where we are bringing democracy to somebody, or whether we are bringing electrical energy, or we are going to show people how to live or use their resources. I think it has to be a two-way street. Even before you get there, though, I think there are certain very basic needs that everybody has. That is really what we are trying to get at with the Vitra project.

GuneWardena: And they're not culturally exclusive. In every society, the access to water is a central need; certain sectors of any culture have this assured, but other sectors historically have not. We're trying to look at simple technologies that would give people a way to access things like water and sanitation.

Escher: And means of preparing food, for example, without having to rely on non-renewable energy sources.

This is clearly relevant to the developing world, but are these still challenges in the United States?

GuneWardena: Absolutely. You'd be surprised. Organizations like Habitat for Humanity, for example, have identified a percentage of the population living in rural America that still doesn't have running water in the house, adequate sanitation facilities, or a good way of heating or cooling the house, so they get into a crisis situation every time there is a snowstorm or heat wave.

Escher: If you look at how we live in North America—and it's difficult to generalize because we have huge differences from region to region and from one socioeconomic group to another—the fact is that currently the average American house that is being built, which is controlled by what is available, affordable, and desirable, is in complete contrast to what and how we should be building. New houses continue to deplete our natural resources. They can only function by using an enormous amount of electrical energy to heat or cool. And we are using water in ways that are obscene.

Look at Los Angeles. This last winter we had enormous rainfalls. All of our rainwater water gets flushed into the ocean within one hour. This was the premise when our flood control system was built—to get every drop of rain into the ocean within one hour. At the same time, we're importing, at a great economic and ecological cost, water from the entire western United States. And if we look at our long-term strategies to secure a water supply for North America, it's a very grim future. In twenty years, water is going to be what oil is now. We are going to be fighting over access to water. Many countries will be left out or will have to pay enormous prices to have access to water. The only countries that won't have that problem are probably the Congo and Switzerland, because of the amount of rainfall they receive. This is a problem that we have to address here in the United States. We live in this bubble where we think, because we have vast land resources and we can buy things, nothing is going to change, we're always going to live in this paradise. It's a very dangerous mind-set.

Are you saying that technical innovation can redress this massive stock of already built housing so that we can avoid jumping off the cliff?

GuneWardena: Maybe you won't be able to avoid it, but at least you can start to slow it down. Look, for example, at the thousands of units of housing that are being built daily in suburban America and the kinds of things that people consider amenities that they're willing to pay for, like having a prefab fireplace in three rooms of the house at $5,000 a pop. You can have a fireplace in your ballroom-sized bathroom. Some companies are starting to offer a solar collector on your roof as an added amenity, but nobody wants to pay for that. First of all, they think it looks ugly; they don't want to have these black or blue things on their roof. And they don't want to pay $5,000 or $10,000 more for it, but they are willing to pay that much for three fireplaces or to have Internet access in every room. We need to start looking at things on a larger scale.

Escher: I'm more optimistic. I think that the society can change. It's enormously difficult and requires a lot of education. The biggest problem is that here in America the market controls much more than we do as idealists or educators. It comes down to how much money something costs and what the financial benefit is. I think we can get to a point where the producers of building supplies, for example, see that they can actually make money in this. And there's nothing wrong with making money. I think once we get to that situation, more and more people are going to buy into this because they realize it is a good thing.

At this point, it's a very small sector of the housing market, but it's growing. And I think it's a matter of pulling from one side and pushing from the other to get the elephant to turn and walk the other direction. I think it's doable.

That is very optimistic. You're suggesting that we can convince industry that there's a buck to be made in sustainability or new energy systems.

Escher: I grew up in Switzerland in the seventies, and at the time, Central Europe was having the same kinds of aches and reservations we are having here now. The people in Europe are not naturally more interested in preserving the natural resources. In fact, in the mid-twentieth century, the prevailing attitude was that everything was available, we could use as much oil as we wanted. The change in attitude that followed was painful. It worked because there was a financial aspect to it—gasoline was enormously expensive. So it meant that we had to try to use less gasoline to heat or drive around. People were being taxed on the garbage they were producing, and they had to buy a certain garbage bag, which cost a lot of money. So people tried to produce as little garbage as possible. Recycling and reusing were important, too. Companies realized they could save a lot of money reusing glass bottles. It wasn't so much about it being the moral thing to do or the right thing to do; it was about saving money.

Your hopefulness is based on the presumption of an impending crisis that will generate a right turn.

Escher: Yes, and on having seen this work in Central Europe over thirty years ago, because we were in the same situation there as we are now in here.

We've been talking here about technical solutions, but style has some bearing here, too, doesn't it?

Escher: Style is a canon of forms that are arranged along certain rules of composition. The aesthetic or formal characteristics of these forms change, and the rules of composition also change. To use deconstructivism as an example, what started as an intellectual strategy or a way to understand—a way to read—became only a style. And I say *only* deliberately, because it really came to the point where you knew how to use certain forms and in what manner you could compose them and, voilà, you had a deconstructivist building. And it had absolutely nothing to do with the philosophy or idea that started it. I think that once something becomes an architectural style, it has lost its cultural and intellectual edge and it has become something that you can teach. You can explain how to do it. It becomes these little coloring books or color-by-number paintings. How do you do a deconstructivist building, how do you do a Louis XVI building? Well, you take these forms and arrange them this way.

GuneWardena: I think it's one thing to identify a historical style. For example, a Beaux Arts building can be identified as a style; it has integrity. But when you talk about applying that same style to a twenty-first-century building, it becomes purely decoration and façade-ism. I think one question that we are trying to figure out, and a lot of architects are, is what makes people yearn for these various styles and what defines some kind of individual identity. Why are people more comfortable living in a housing tract where you have an option of five styles, even though those five styles repeat every fifth house? Why do people feel like that's more of an expression of individuality than living in a housing scheme that has no style or is based on technological concerns? That's an interesting question. Why do people need that?

Escher: It's also interesting what we associate with certain architectural styles; much of it has to do with money and political power. To the nineteenth-century Viennese bourgeoisie, for example, architecture was a way to show off their power. It's always interesting to see what style is used to express certain political or economic situations or ideals. In the eighteenth century, Europe rediscovered Greece as the cradle of European civilization and a political ideal of democracy, and they used this to develop an architectural style that we now know as classicism. If you look at France and the late eighteenth century, the style of Louis XVI is a precursor to classicism. This is an architectural style that was talking about democratic ideals at a point when the cultural leadership had shifted from the court of France to this bourgeoisie that had risen to power.

Now, after the postmodernists, we have decided that anything goes. Social groups will use a certain architectural style without asking where it comes from and what it meant in its original context. We have completely divorced ourselves from those questions, and it becomes a matter of yellow versus gray and this is prettier than something else.

GuneWardena: It's almost the things that are considered to be lacking in style, or anachronistic, or that you can't peg down, say from the mid-twentieth century, that end up being timeless.

ACKNOWLEDGMENTS

With deepest gratitude I would like to acknowledge the people without whom this book would not be possible: Peter and Hadley Arnold, two thoughtful architects who, as community leaders and my teachers, awakened me to how architecture, in its essence, is a conversation about how to live; and Les Walker, whose book *American Homes* illuminated how rich our history of American residential architecture is, and whose simple but compelling drawings originally sent me off on this journey.

Several individuals provided invaluable skills: Kristin Landholt painstakingly and carefully transcribed all my original interviews. Elizabeth Pulcinelli worked with me to edit the collection of interviews into a true book manuscript. Susan Davis helped me prepare the packaging of the manuscript to acquaint publishers to its potential. Mary Cullather researched and helped me find my way to the University of Texas Press (as only a daughter of Texas would).

The esteemed photography editors, writers, and publishers Michael Williams and Richard Cahan led me to the Historic American Buildings Survey archive and guided the visual component of the book. Peter Rader's clear thinking and insightful provocations helped me with the introduction and the biographies. It has been my extreme good fortune to work with the University of Texas Press Editor-in-Chief Robert Devens, whose enthusiasm for the project and wise guidance of a publishing newbie have been fundamental to its realization.

Finally, to Lesley Hyatt, my beloved partner in life, whose steadfast force of encouragement kept me at it.

PHOTOGRAPHY CREDITS

Meghan Daum: Amstel House façade in New Castle, Delaware. Photo by Edward M. Rosenfeld. www.loc.gov/pictures/item/de0074.photos.031666p/

Bernard Friedman: Coburn Tyler House fence in Rockport, Maine. Photo by Cervin Robinson. www.loc.gov/pictures/item/me0072.photos.088289p/

Richard Meier: Library in the William Watts Sherman House. Photo by Cervin Robinson. www.loc.gov/pictures/item/ri0036.photos.144937p/

Grant Hildebrand: From the north porch of the Hill-Stead House. Photo by James W. Rosenthal. www.loc.gov/pictures/item/ct0689.photos.222686p/

Witold Rybczynski: The reading room alcove of Evergreen. Photo by James W. Rosenthal. www.loc.gov/pictures/item/md1633.photos.578331p/

Lester Walker: Window at the Peak House. Photo by Earl Kintner. www.loc.gov/pictures/item/ks0163.photos.209656p/

Sarah Susanka: Small house in the Boise National Forest. Photo by J. Ceronie and Marie Neubauer. www.loc.gov/pictures/item/id0073.photos.060264p/

Barbara Winslow and Max Jacobson: Front porch of the Dixon H. Lewis House. Photo by W. N. Manning. www.loc.gov/pictures/item/al0317.photos.003565p/

Hadley Arnold: View from the balcony into a courtyard at the Stoltzfus-Humphries House. Photo by Jack E. Boucher. www.loc.gov/pictures/item/ca1705.photos.036460p/

Robert Venturi and Denise Scott Brown: LaRionda Cottage. Photo by Richard Koch. www.loc.gov/pictures/item/la0040.photos.072806p/

Kenneth Frampton: Pueblo Ribera Court. Photo by Marvin Rand. www.loc.gov/pictures/item/ca0571.photos.015091p/

Lee Mindel: Attic of a Shaker Centre family dwelling. Photo by Walter Smalling Jr. www. loc.gov/pictures/item/ky0033.photos.071826p/

Eric Owen Moss: Frank Lloyd Wright's Fallingwater. Photo by Jack E. Boucher. www.loc. gov/pictures/item/pa1690.photos.134154p/

Robert A. M. Stern: Home at 1225 Martin Avenue. Photo by Jane Lidz. www.loc.gov/pictures/item/ca0969.photos.018655p/

Sam Watters: Walter Luther Dodge House. Photo by Marvin Rand. www.loc.gov/pictures/item/ca0221.photos.012033p/

Douglas Garofalo: A prefabricated Lustron house. Photo by Jack E. Boucher. www.loc. gov/pictures/item/in0372.photos.048710p/

Tracy Kidder: Frame house from the 1800s. Photo by Laurence E. Tilley. www.loc.gov/pictures/item/ri0247.photos.145381p/

Marianne Cusato: Row of shotgun houses. Photo by Jet Lowe. http://hdl.loc.gov/loc.pnp/hhh.la0203/photos.072539p

Andrew Freear: An early stone house. Photo by Cervin Robinson. www.loc.gov/pictures/item/pa0126.photos.141306p/

Cameron Sinclair: Row of houses at 300–306 North Canal Street. Photo by James W. Rosenthal. www.loc.gov/pictures/item/ms0337.photos.361316p/

Robert Ivy: Typical New Orleans home from the 1800s. Photo by Richard Koch. www.loc. gov/pictures/item/la0015.photos.072695p/

Charles Gwathmey: Charles H. Baldwin House. Photo by Cervin Robinson. www.loc.gov/pictures/item/ri0323.photos.144569p/

Paul Goldberger: Monkey Fountain at the J. Paul Getty Museum, Ranch House. Photo by Tavo Olmos. www.loc.gov/pictures/item/ca3096.photos.376245p/

Jeremiah Eck: Elias Olcott House. Photo by Ned Goode. www.loc.gov/pictures/item/vt0060.photos.167226p/

Tom Kundig: Joe Pfeiffer Homestead. Photo by Alan Bucknam. www.loc.gov/pictures/item/wy0096.photos.373371p/

Elizabeth Plater-Zyberk: Techwood Homes. Photo by Jennifer Almand. www.loc.gov/pictures/item/ga0789.photos.332306p/

David Salmela: Corner notching from the Daniel Wilkins Log House. Photo by Charles E. Peterson. www.loc.gov/pictures/item/mn0026.photos.090496p/

Toshiko Mori: Santana Sanchez House. Photo by M. James Slack. www.loc.gov/pictures/item/nm0095.photos.114111p/

Greg Lynn: Palladian windows along the stairway of the Major General Solomon Cowles House. Photo by Stanley P. Mixon. www.loc.gov/pictures/item/ct0124.photos.023072p/

Thom Mayne: Courtyard of the 1926 John Sowden House. Photo by Marvin Rand. www. loc.gov/pictures/item/ca0267.photos.012473p/

Lorcan O'Herlihy: A bedroom in the Lovell Beach House. Photo by Marvin Rand. www. loc.gov/pictures/item/ca0448.photos.014329p/

Frank Escher and Ravi GuneWardena: Shelter cabin along the Chisana Trail. Photo by Jet Lowe. www.loc.gov/pictures/item/ak0038.photos.000895p/

INDEX

Page numbers in *italics* refer to photographs.